A Time for the Humanities

FUTURITY AND THE LIMITS OF AUTONOMY

Edited by

JAMES J. BONO, TIM DEAN, AND
EWA PLONOWSKA ZIAREK

FORDHAM UNIVERSITY PRESS
New York 2008

Copyright © 2008 Fordham University Press

All rights reserved. No part of this publication may be reproduced, stored in a retrieval system, or transmitted in any form or by any means—electronic, mechanical, photocopy, recording, or any other—except for brief quotations in printed reviews, without the prior permission of the publisher.

Fordham University Press has no responsibility for the persistence or accuracy of URLs for external or third-party Internet websites referred to in this publication and does not guarantee that any content on such websites is, or will remain, accurate or appropriate.

Library of Congress Cataloging-in-Publication Data

A time for the humanities : futurity and the limits of autonomy / edited by James J. Bono, Tim Dean, and Ewa Plonowska Ziarek. — 1st ed.
   p. cm.
Includes bibliographical references and index.
  ISBN 978-0-8232-2919-2 (cloth : alk. paper) — ISBN 978-0-8232-2920-8 (pbk. : alk. paper)
  1. Humanities—Philosophy. 2. Humanities—Social aspects. 3. Autonomy. 4. Humanities—Forecasting. 5. Geopolitics—Forecasting. 6. Civilization, Modern—21st century—Forecasting. 7. Social change—Forecasting. I. Bono, James J. (James Joseph) II. Dean, Tim, 1964- III. Ziarek, Ewa Plonowska, 1961-
  AZ103.T56 2008
  001.3—dc22   2008034767

10 09 08   5 4 3 2 1
First edition

CONTENTS

Acknowledgments vii

Introduction: Future, Heteronomy, Invention 1
JAMES J. BONO, TIM DEAN, AND EWA PLONOWSKA ZIAREK

Part I   THE NEW AND ITS RISKS

1. Life and Event: Deleuze on Newness 17
   PAOLA MARRATI
2. A Precursor: Limiting the Future, Affirming Particularity 29
   ANDREW BENJAMIN
3. Visual *Parrhesia*? Foucault and the Truth of the Gaze 45
   MARTIN JAY

Part II   RHETORIC AND THE FUTURE OF THE POLITICAL

4. Articulation and the Limits of Metaphor 61
   ERNESTO LACLAU
5. Answering for Sense 84
   JEAN-LUC NANCY
6. "Human" in the Age of Disposable People: The Ambiguous Import of Kinship and Education in *Blind Shaft* 94
   REY CHOW

Part III   HETERONOMY AND FUTURITY IN PSYCHOANALYSIS

7. The Foreign, the Uncanny, and the Foreigner: Concepts of the Self and the Other in Psychoanalysis and Contemporary Philosophy 109
   RUDI VISKER
8. An Impossible Embrace: Queerness, Futurity, and the Death Drive 122
   TIM DEAN

9.	Luce Irigaray and the Question of Critique ELIZABETH WEED	141

Part IV INVENTIONS

10.	Parapoetics and the Architectural Leap STEVE MCCAFFERY	161
11.	The Future of Literature: Complex Surfaces of Electronic Texts and Print Books N. KATHERINE HAYLES	180
12.	Crisis Means Turning Point: A Manifesto for Art and Accountability DORIS SOMMER	210

Notes	227
Contributors	265
Index	269

ACKNOWLEDGMENTS

We would like to acknowledge the support we have received from individuals as well as institutions. The initial impetus for this collection came from the inaugural conference of the University at Buffalo Humanities Institute, "New Futures: Humanities, Theory, Arts," which was graciously supported by the College of Arts and Sciences. We are especially grateful to our colleague Martha Malamud, founding executive director of the Humanities Institute, for her support and inspiration. Buffalo's new Humanities Institute has provided us with an important opportunity for interdisciplinary exchanges and collaborations, of which this book is one result. We owe a deep debt of gratitude to our friend and colleague Henry Sussman, whose vision and persistence coupled with the critical support of then Dean Uday Sukhatme are together responsible for the very existence of the Humanities Institute at Buffalo. Dean Bruce McCombe has continued this tradition of support for the humanities, providing both moral and material encouragement that has allowed the Humanities Institute to expand its activities and extend its impact both within and beyond the University at Buffalo. We thank assistant director Michele Bewley, whose tireless efforts on behalf of the Institute made our work possible.

Our editor, Helen Tartar, has assisted us with her editorial wisdom and acumen. More important, her brilliant advocacy of the humanities and critical theory has created an indispensable forum for the exchange of books and ideas. The care and critical attention of our copy editor, Edward Batchelder, has made this a better book. We would also like to thank our colleague and friend Gary Nickard for providing inspiration and initial suggestions for the cover image.

We thank our partners and colleagues—Barbara Bono, Ramón Soto-Crespo, and Krzysztof Ziarek—for their companionship, humor, and generosity. Finally, we wish to acknowledge that most of the editorial work for this volume took place at our neighborhood teashop, Tru-Teas, where the host Trudy Stern provided excellent tea, superb ginger scones, and warm hospitality.

James J. Bono
Tim Dean
Ewa Plonowska Ziarek

Buffalo, New York
April 2008

A Time for the Humanities

INTRODUCTION

Future, Heteronomy, Invention

James J. Bono, Tim Dean, and Ewa Plonowska Ziarek

A Time for the Humanities: Futurity and the Limits of Autonomy brings together an interdisciplinary and international group of renowned theorists and scholars to reflect on the future of the humanities. Whereas many recent works have addressed this issue in primarily pragmatic terms, this book seeks to examine its conceptual foundations. What notions of futurity, of the human, and of finitude underlie recurring anxieties about the humanities' future in our current geopolitical situation? How can we think about the unpredictable and unthought dimensions of praxis implicit in the very notion of futurity? What kind of agency is implied by future-oriented praxis? In what sense is such agency linked to heteronomy rather than to the autonomy of the subject?

In popular and academic publications alike, the question of the future is becoming increasingly urgent because of growing anxiety about the status of the humanities. After an extraordinary period of institutional growth from the late 1940s through the mid 1970s, the humanities have confronted two challenges: external pressures exerted by economic difficulties, and an internal crisis over its intellectual self-definition and public mission.[1] In addition to the decline of federal funding, a shrinking job market, and the new pressures of globalization, the most significant internal challenges confronting the humanities have emerged from the hegemony of technoscience, the impact of the "new media" revolution, the rise of expert cultures on the one hand and, on the other, the unprecedented democratic proliferation of new interdisciplinary fields, such as gender, ethnic, disability, and African-American studies, as well as studies of non-European cultures, all of which put the traditional canon and the "common" mission of the humanities into question.[2] More recently, academics have become concerned about whether the humanities—so intertwined with the democratic culture of free inquiry—still has a future in the current, increasingly conservative, political climate.

The necessity of responding to both the economic crisis and the crisis of legitimation is reflected, for instance, in the symptomatic title of a collection of essays on the status of the U.S. research university, *The Research University in a Time of Discontent*, a project organized jointly by the American Academy of Arts and Sciences and Columbia University in 1993. More than ten years later, William Paulson warns readers in his 2005 study, *Literary Culture in a World Transformed: A Future for the Humanities*, that "The field of literary studies is in danger of being left behind in the twenty-first century."[3] In response to such pervasive sentiment, a forthcoming special issue of *SubStance*, a journal of interdisciplinary approaches to literature and literary theory, is devoted to "discouragement." To alleviate these anxieties, intellectuals and journalists alike offer a range of diagnoses of current impasses, as well as propose various concrete recommendations for the transformation of the humanities as a field of knowledge, education, and action. While some of these recommendations focus on particular curricular reforms or more efficient political advocacy, other proposals contest the very autonomy of the humanities and call for its complete restructuring, suggesting that humanistic knowledge should no longer focus primarily on the study of culture, but on its interactions with sciences, technologies, and, increasingly, ecological concerns instead.[4] Still others call for the creation of "public humanities," oriented towards engagement with and accountability to "the diverse and multiple *publics* that constitute our society."[5]

Although such pragmatic proposals are an indispensable part of public debate on the status of the humanities, this collection argues that the urgent concern with the future cannot be limited to critical assessments of our situation or to practical projects for change. We need, first of all, to recognize that the worry about the humanities is not a new phenomenon. Here we encounter an uncanny companion of thought about the future, namely, the recurrent anticipation of death, whether Hegel's death of art, Freud's speculations on the death drive, the dark side of Bloch's hope, Fukuyama's end of history, or, as the emphatic title of Lee Edelman's *No Future: Queer Theory and the Death Drive* suggests, "death" and kinship.[6] We can also add to this list "the end of the book." By taking into account the finitude implicit in such worries about the "end," a critical reflection on the future exceeds any and all pragmatic diagnoses. This necessary implication arises precisely because the very force of the "ought to"—on which the specific content of pragmatic prescriptions depends—opens the unknown and unforeseeable dimensions of temporality. Although always embedded in the historical situation, the relation to the future, whether theoretical or prescriptive, is counterfactual; it exceeds the present possibilities of thought and action. Consequently, the thought of the future places the categorical "ought to" of any prescription or pragmatic program in an unknown—literally utopian—interval between determination and indeterminacy, the known and the unknown, imagination and the radical alterity of the unimaginable. Paradoxically, if the force of prescription—that is, the performative power of what ought to be done—is not to be curtailed, it has to both include and exceed the power of human action, imagination, and thinking.

One of the most important implications of such unforeseeable futurity is to be found in the constitutive tension between human and nonhuman (or impersonal) aspects of agency and praxis. Already our own historical situation presents us daily with innumerable examples of human–nonhuman linkages, among them complex interfaces involving machinic assemblages of biological "wetware" and nonbiological "hardware." According to the numerous theorists working in science, technology, and media studies, we are far from even beginning to grasp the transformative possibilities that the codependencies facilitated by still-emerging technological–biological–cultural environments might make possible in the near future.[7] As Katherine Hayles argues in this collection, the posthuman "agency" of digital technologies actively reshapes not only print culture but also our critical and interpretative practices.

Yet, this fundamental tension between human and nonhuman dimensions of agency and praxis cannot be limited to new technologies, digitality, or autopoietic systems alone; such tension stems from the "agency" of time itself, as well as from the register of unconscious sexuality elaborated by psychoanalysis. One aspect of the nonhuman "agency" of time manifests itself in the orientation of any praxis toward the unforeseeable future. In Fredric Jameson's words, such futural orientation of "the shaping power of human collective agency"—which includes the productive power of new technologies or the new technologies of power—inevitably discloses "an incomprehensible, unimaginable, utopian temporality beyond what thought or action can reach."[8] As Paola Marrati argues in this volume, the temporality of praxis requires a rethinking of "the ontological agency of time itself" vis-à-vis our notions of political agency and progress. In a similar vein, in his defense of the humanities, Christopher Fynsk argues elsewhere that critical and "vital" inquiries should move beyond the "applicable" knowledge already presupposed by established disciplines and modes of practice.[9] In yet another arena, that of Freudian and Lacanian psychoanalysis, we encounter the "inhuman" and the "incomprehensible" primarily in the context of the conflicting agencies and temporalities of the drive and the "letter," or the Real and the Symbolic registers of praxis and subjectivity. It is one of the original contributions of this collection that it insists on the necessity of thinking together all three "inhuman" dimensions of human practice: digital technologies, utopian temporality, and "extimate" sexuality.[10] Only then can we avoid the common reduction of practice and pragmatics to the domain of the narcissistic Ego and the spatial captation characteristic of the structure of such an Ego.

The multiple senses of human and nonhuman agency elaborated in this collection—the agency of citizenship, power, kinship, gaze, time, the death drive, new technologies and media, sexuality, and finally, the agency of rhetoric and politics—imply that praxis and freedom are based on the heteronomy rather than the autonomy of the subject. The confrontation with such an ineluctable heteronomy is perhaps a cause of even greater anxieties than the known dangers of the present situation. Unlike related terms in contemporary theory—such as heterogeneity, otherness, or difference—the notion of heteronomy, in addition to maintaining the reference to differentiation and to the multiplicity of heterogeneous principles, more specifically links "otherness" to the questioning of subjective autonomy and agency as the principle of freedom. Indeed, the anxiety raised by the prospect of heteronomy largely resides in its challenge to the autonomy of the free, self-legislating subject of the Enlightenment, as well as to the self-legislation of different spheres of activities of such a subject: knowledge, art, politics. Although it has frequently been questioned in abstract terms, the premise of autonomy as the basis of freedom remains unexamined at the heart of the myriad prescriptions advanced in the face of an uncertain future and efficacy of the humanities. Such proposals and prescriptions represent the programmatic response of "autonomous" individuals, groups, and, more typically, institutions to the future and to temporality that this collection challenges and reconfigures. Confronted with an as-yet-unimagined alterity of the future, such autonomous collectivities seek to recuperate the new and unforeseeable within strategies that confirm rather than challenge their capacities for self-legislation and self-production. At its most extreme, such instrumentality treats the future as a matter of engineering: of deploying ever proliferating social, genetic, and other yet-to-be-discovered techniques to devise solutions to new problems. In this respect, institutional or academic responses to the threatening novelty of the future unsurprisingly find their dialectical counter-image in those tamed and domesticated tropes of heterogeneity found in the banal utopian projections and formulaic visions of pulp, and even "serious," science fiction.

By contrast, this collection calls for an entirely different approach to heteronomy, treating it as an enabling rather than a threatening condition of agency. By opening unknown and unforeseeable dimensions of temporality, it challenges the autonomy of the self-legislating subject as the premise of freedom and social action. Yet, rather than being a threatening prospect of subjection (as it has been postulated in moral philosophy at least since Kant's *Critique of Practical Reason*), this ineluctable heteronomy that haunts our experience of temporality enables transformation, which exceeds subjective and collective capacities of legislation, prediction, and self-production. Thus, heteronomy implies a shift from recuperable difference (the fitting object of pragmatic changes imagined by autonomous institutions and agents) to unimaginable, not-yet-encountered potentialities. Consequently, by revisiting the problem of heteronomy specifically in the context of the future of the humanities, the essays in this collection confront two intimately intertwined tasks: First, they work out the effects of such temporality for different kinds of practices in the humanities, ranging from criticism and the production of knowledge to the arts and politics. Second, they reconceptualize the heteronomy of the future beyond the threat of subjugation that the term *heteronomy* still implies, approaching it instead as a source of transformation and creativity in the broadest possible sense of the word.

Examining different aspects of the future from diverse disciplinary perspectives, the essays in this collection explore the constitutive tension between human agency and its incomprehensible "beyond," and regard this tension as a source of new possibilities for the fundamental practices in the humanities. The essays in Part I, "The New and Its Risks," assess the implications of the transformative "agency" of time for the concepts of history, invention, and becoming. Part I also opens two crucial questions that are developed throughout this book: The first question pertains to the relation between heteronomy and progressive politics; the second one addresses the manner in which transformative temporality enables us to revise the notion of the visual beyond the spatial captation of the imaginary Ego and beyond what Rey Chow calls the closure of the global world picture. Building on the critique of the coherent human agent secured by historical chronology initiated in the first part, Part II, "Rhetoric and the Future of the Political," focuses primarily on the heteronomy and the future of politics. Addressed by Jean-Luc Nancy in the context of writing, the problematic of heteronomy is then developed in the context of numerous tensions: between kinship and homelessness; between political affiliations and disposable populations; between global capital and democratic politics. Inflected by interpretations of sexuality, jouissance, the death drive, and aggressivity, Part III, "Heteronomy and Futurity in Psychoanalysis," examines heteronomies of the subject and the effects of such heteronomy for the politics of cosmopolitanism and queer becomings, on the one hand, and for the fundamental interpretative practices in the humanities, on the other. And finally, Part IV, "Inventions," raises complex questions about the transformative possibilities of heteronomy for the future of diverse artistic practices, ranging from architecture and poetry to performative activism and digital textualities. At stake here is an aesthetic disclosure of liberating possibilities in participatory public culture.

Although we have divided this collection into discrete parts in order to underscore its main themes, there are numerous connections and conversations among the essays that go beyond such heuristic divisions. For instance, the question of the relation of the political to artistic practices runs across the entire collection, beginning with Paola Marrati's reflection on the political possibilities of Deleuze's work on cinema and ending with Sommer's support for interactive art in the public sphere. Similarly, there are strong resonances among a number of essays concerning the rethinking of visual space apart from the controlling gaze: the challenge of homelessness to the geopolitical space of globalization in Rey Chow's analysis of Chinese cinema; the discussion of the architectural space of poetry in Steve McCaffery's essay; and the city as the space of performative citizenship in Sommer's. Another ongoing preoccupation in several essays is the multiple types of agency and their limits, beginning with the more familiar notion of political agency and power, and ending with the more paradoxical "agency" of the death drive, digital technologies, and diverse media.

Part I: The New and Its Risks

Paola Marrati's, Andrew Benjamin's, and Martin Jay's essays underscore what is at stake in this collection as a whole: the claim that the affirmation of the heteronomous temporality of the future contests the spatial closure of action and thought. According to Jameson, such closure manifests itself not merely as an intellectual impasse but as the political "colonization of reality by spatial forms, which is at one and the same time a commodification of that same intensively colonized reality on a world-wide scale." Intertwined with the closing down of frontiers and the decline of old-fashioned imperialist expansion, "these spatial dilemmas" characteristic of the age of globalization are "what immobilize our imaginative picture of global space today."[11] Rey Chow's contribution draws out the contemporary geopolitical dangers of such immobilization of the political. Consequently, in order to resist the spatial blockage of thought and action, it is important to release time itself from its traditional association with the interiority and the mastery of the subject. Yet, as the immobilization of the "global picture" of the world suggests, such a rethinking of heteronomous futurity is closely intertwined with an attempt to invent alternative visual practices that would resist the colonization of space by scopic regimes.

The first essay in this section, Paola Marrati's "Life and Event: Deleuze on Newness," contests the closure of spatial forms by developing "the ontological agency of time" in Gilles Deleuze's work on philosophy and film. In contrast to human agency, the new and creative effects of time cannot be known in advance since they emerge from a process of differentiation conforming to no pre-existing pattern. Consequently, she distinguishes what Deleuze means by the new from both history and futurity, explaining that newness concerns neither progress nor any movement of teleology. In place of a philosophy of history, then, Deleuze offers a philosophy of the new, which knots together differentiation, event, and life. By extending Deleuze's work on cinema, Marrati explores the implications of such a heteronomous agency of time for emancipatory politics. Contending that emancipatory politics tend to remain inseparable from a belief in progress, she elaborates how "the 'politics of history'" entered an irreversible crisis around the middle of the twentieth century. Intriguingly, she maps this crisis of political action by tracing its manifestation in cinematic technique. Marrati's essay concludes by sketching the Deleuzean response to this crisis. As cause for neither pessimism nor hope, the differentiating process that characterizes modernity calls instead for a political belief in this world. This is a belief not in what transcends the material world or attains eternal existence, but in the "becoming" of the virtual through the creative action of time.

The unpredictable effects of temporality and irresolution are also at stake in Andrew Benjamin's formulation of the type of criticism that would respond adequately to the singularity of art. His essay, "A Precursor: Limiting the Future, Affirming Particularity," complicates the modernist concept of the new as the break from the past by investigating the enabling logic of the precursor. Although he shifts the discussion from the ontological register of "life" to aesthetics and criticism, Benjamin, like Marrati, interprets the new not as a break but as a creative effect of repetition and differentiation. "What is the new once it can no longer be identified with novelty?" he asks. Warning against the naturalization of the new by subjective invention, or worse, by fashion, he investigates the new in relation to the precursor, who limits and opens the future of the work of art, allowing for affirmation of its particularity. Since the affirmation of the particular is an act of irresolution, it is linked to both the new and the process of repetition: The particularity of the work of art demands to be affirmed again and again, each time in a new way.

By switching the focus from the temporal to the visual, Martin Jay's essay, "Visual *Parrhesia?* Foucault and the Truth of the Gaze," examines the genealogy of scopic domination that begins with the shift from the premodern ascetic regimes of truth to the practices of modern science, based on visual evidence. In light of this shift, he asks how it is possible to conceive the future of the visual beyond the global "world picture" and its dominating gaze. In an answer to this question, Jay examines the relationship between truth and the visual in the work of Michel Foucault, who is often taken to exemplify French criticisms of the "ocularcentric" bias of Western thought. By critically revisiting his own claims in *Downcast Eyes: The Denigration of Vision in Twentieth-Century French Thought,* Jay offers a fresh assessment of the argument that Foucault's critiques of scopic regimes—such as the panopticon and the medical gaze—do not extend to all visual practices.[12] Consequently, his essay speculates on the possibility of alternative visual practices that would resist the "power of the eye to dominate what it viewed" and thereby dislodge the notion of truth as evidence or representation, embodying instead the risk of "truth-telling." Foucault's preoccupation with the Greek notion of *parrhesia*—"frankness in speaking the truth" that involves the individual's willingness "to take a risk ... to speak truth to power, no matter the consequences"—is exemplary of the alternative "practice of truth-telling." Jay asks whether there might be a visual equivalent of *parrhesia*—visual practices that exemplify unpredictability and risk-taking rather than the power of visual domination. Through its inquiry into the possibilities of resistance within the register of the visible, Jay's essay provides an important extension of Marrati's and Benjamin's rethinking of heteronomous and creative temporalities.

Part II: Rhetoric and the Future of the Political

The essays in this section focus more explicitly on the future of emancipatory politics by contesting humanistic ideologies of kinship, agency, and nationality, and by examining instead heteronomies of responsibility, rhetoric, and human plurality. Interrogating the future of political praxis from various theoretical and cultural perspectives, all three essays not only propose heteronomous models of collectivity beyond the "human," but also perform such heteronomy by engaging those dimensions of culture—whether writing, cinema, ontology, or rhetoric—that traditionally have been conceived as "other" to political autonomy.

In "Articulation and the Limits of Metaphor," Ernesto Laclau develops his well-known theory of hegemony in the rhetorical terms of metaphor and metonymy. As he shows in his comparison of Sorel's and Lenin's political theories, politics consists in the articulation of heterogeneous elements, and such articulations are structured tropologically. Building on Gérard Genette's analysis of metaphor and metonymy in Proust, as well as on Roman Jakobson's famous analysis of aphasia, Laclau demonstrates both the mutual implication of metaphor and metonymy, and the inseparability of these tropes from any signification and praxis. In the Marxist vision of history, Laclau argues, different stages of diachronic unfolding are conceived as teleological fulfillments; that is, they are conceived metaphorically in terms of essential analogies. Laclau's insistence on the inseparability of metaphor from metonymy recasts this vision of history and futurity by pointing to the ineluctably contingent elements that undermine any telos.

As if in response to a Marxist vision of the literary, Jean-Luc Nancy develops the consequences of his well-known political critique of community in *The Inoperative Community* in the context of writing.[13] He declares that "all writing is 'committed'"—though what he means by this notion of commitment exceeds the programmatic sense of "committed writing" that knows in advance how the future should look. In his rich philosophical meditation on the senses of responsibility entailed by writing, Nancy argues that to write is always to respond to—and therefore to listen for—the voice of an other. This involves an ethical commitment prior to any particular political commitment, just as it involves a consciousness of the non-human agency that resonates through any writing. Revealing how there is no original voice that is not already a response to some prior response, Nancy discredits the notion of creative autonomy; he thereby brings out the ineluctable heteronomy of all writing and voicing, even as he enlarges our sense of what "writing" is. Finally, he too—like Laclau—indicates the role of contingency in this understanding of the responsiveness and responsibility entailed by writing: "In order to come from the outside, to respond to this outside and to answer for it, the incision [of writing] must owe something to chance, to surprise and to *kairos*, the favorable moment whose favor consists in offering itself to the one who exposes himself to the outside, and who consequently *no longer wills-to-mean*." Here, writing gives itself over to the heteronomy of an uncertain future.

The intertwined questions of heteronomy and the future of emancipatory politics are pursued further by Rey Chow in her essay, "'Human' in the Age of Disposable People: The Ambiguous Import of Kinship and Education in *Blind Shaft*." Situating her analysis of the political in the context of contemporary China, with a special focus on the controversial, award-winning Chinese film *Blind Shaft* (dir. Li Yang, 2003), Chow proceeds to diagnose the ways that global biopolitical warfare disrupts the very notion of the "human" by producing "disposable populations" on an unprecedented scale. In the homelessness of the miners represented in the film, she reads both a biting indictment of "the bankruptcy of Chinese socialism at the turn of the twenty-first century" and a broader comment on the ontological homelessness produced by modern world politics. Resonating with Nancy's tacitly Heideggerian meditation in the preceding essay, Chow develops the Heideggerian implications of homelessness for cultural politics. Responding to the ruptures she has diagnosed so acutely, Chow claims that the possibilities for survival and emancipatory politics depend not on reclaiming outmoded "human" ideologies of kinship or nationality, but rather on an ethico-political confrontation with "our contemporary global condition of homelessness." Within the cinematic microcosm of *Blind Shaft*, she discerns a "sentimentalizing of kinship" that betokens not only fidelity to Chinese cultural tradition but also a particular conception of the future—one that imagines futurity exclusively through the survival of the next generation of kin. What makes the film so fascinating is how, in its violent disruption of this kinship-oriented future, *Blind Shaft* points to the possibility of a different conception of futurity—and thus to the queerer futures imagined in the next section of the volume.

Part III: Heteronomy and Futurity in Psychoanalysis

By taking into account the more intimate, unconscious heteronomy of the subject, the essays in this section develop the most risky aspects of the heteronomy of the political—namely, the tension between destruction and invention, between the agency of the death drive and collectivities, and between the impersonal and the foreigner. On the basis of psychoanalytical accounts of the hostility between the ego and its internal alienating otherness, Rudi Visker examines the effects of such uncanny heteronomy for the politics of cosmopolitanism. In "The Foreign, the Uncanny, and the Foreigner: Concepts of the Self and the Other in Psychoanalysis and Contemporary Philosophy," he takes issue with the common assumption that recognizing foreignness inside the self leads to improved relations among different races and ethnicities. According to Visker, the cosmopolitan ideal of mutual respect between self and foreigner misconstrues the constitutive hostility between the self and its own internal foreignness. In response to this dilemma, he proposes a psychoanalytic politics that would acknowledge the necessity of "framing" or "'stage-ing'" the self's relation to its own foreignness as a means of containing that destructiveness. Anticipating the arguments of contributors to the book's final section, Visker suggests that such "stage-ing" may occur through art.

The problematic of destructiveness raised by Visker is pursued by Tim Dean in his engagement with Lee Edelman's critique of futurity as ineluctably heteronormative. In *No Future: Queer Theory and the Death Drive*, Edelman argues that the political response to what he calls "reproductive futurism" should be an embrace by queers of the radical negativity of the death drive. Developing Lacan's reconceptualization of Freudian drive theory, Dean argues contrariwise that the death drive, rather than a mere will to destruction, can also be a force of invention and creation. Showing how, as one of the drive's "vicissitudes," sublimation implies that the death drive is not always simply destructive, Dean's critique—like Visker's—anticipates the arguments in Part IV of this collection. In elaborating a psychoanalytic theory of drives by way of Deleuze's critique of the normalizing effects of Oedipus, Dean's essay also makes use of Marrati's discussion of Deleuze and the new. Finally, his emphasis on the creative yet impersonal agency of the drive contests the ideological alignment of the future with heteronormative kinship structures or reproductive politics, and thus resonates with Chow's critique of group formation based on kinship.

Following Visker's and Dean's critical interrogations of the relation of psychoanalysis to politics, Elizabeth Weed's concluding essay in this section brings psychoanalysis together with feminism to examine the possibilities of critique as such. In "Luce Irigaray and the Question of Critique," Weed takes some recurring hermeneutical questions posed by Irigaray's discursive practice as an occasion to reflect upon the unforeseeable effects of heteronomy, sexual difference, and jouissance for the fundamental interpretative practices in the humanities. She argues that the function of critique cannot be limited to the production of knowledge, but must leave room for the unknown and for the erotic dimension of any encounter with a text. What Weed diagnoses as the waning of critique is bound up with the critical impulse to make sense, to retrieve meaning, and to convert the unknown into the known. In this endeavor, the unthought of sexual difference is too easily left behind or translated into more readily assimilable formulations. Although never completely severed from the production of meaning, a critique (in Weed's sense of the term) keeps open the gap between the known and the unknown, between the possibilities and impossibilities of sense.

Part IV: Inventions

Building on numerous references to different art forms in the preceding essays, the final section of this collection is explicitly devoted to the aesthetic disclosure of more liberating possibilities of thought, creativity, and action. Resisting the closure of thought and action implicit in prescriptive visions of the arts and humanities, the essays in this section insist upon the futural orientation of artistic practices, while exploring the transformative possibilities of heterogeneous genres, media, and spatial configurations. Steve McCaffery turns to the architectural as a space of experimentation and renewal for poetics, a turn that is at once a turn away from figurations of "endings," "ruptures," and the "death of poetics" and, alternatively, a turn toward Deleuzean "becomings." N. Katherine Hayles analyzes how dynamic media ecologies—both print and digital—create their own possibilities for thought and action that transform the spatial experiences of textuality and reading, thereby challenging the "interiorized subjectivity" of autonomous readers and creating in its place a new form of cognitive engagement marked by the processing of "multiple data flows": "hyperattention." For her part, Doris Sommer paints a compelling picture of a future for the arts and interpretive humanities as reinventing participatory democratic public culture, communal ethos, and agency, starting with the transformation of public spaces into sites of progressive sociopolitical performativity and cultural *poiesis*.

Steve McCaffery's essay, "Parapoetics and the Architectural Leap," proposes a leap—a tropic turn—to the architectural. The leap into architecture is far from arbitrary, since language itself continues to be figured architecturally, while the human—*dasein*—dwells no less in language than in architectural habitations. McCaffery thus explores the linkages among language, architecture, and the human from the biblical myth of Babel to Derrida's grammatological explorations of writing, space, and architecture. In turning to the architectural, McCaffery seeks to "activate" the parapoetic—to evoke its transgressive, viral capacity to disturb the stability and unity of the proper. Thus, McCaffery's essay draws on architectural configurations and notions of "site," seeking to "rethink the concept of a poetic movement" and community. Yet it is as practices, rather than simply as metaphoric resources, that he seeks to place architecture and poetics in dialogue with one another. Here, McCaffery points to those architectural practices that disavow traditional desires for stability and permanence—for "place" as "ground"—in favor of the making of place as, in Solà-Morales's words, the "production of an event." Diagrams—the diagrammatic dimension of not simply writing but architectural practice as well—become tactics for opening up possibilities, rather than occasions for exercising mastery and control and for the production of stability. Returning to Deleuze and the Deleuzean fold, McCaffery looks to the production of heterogeneous multiplicities and to the city as "the most fruitful target for parapoetic attention." In short, parapoetics seeks in architectural practices a "becoming" and thus an opening to the future.

N. Katherine Hayles dares to imagine an emerging future of literature by exploring how print media are being transformed through their interaction with electronic media. Given the ubiquity of electronic modes of production, Hayles insists that the "dynamic media ecology" within which writing's engagement with digitality occurs is transformative. Comparing the "interiorized subjectivity" of traditional narrative fiction to the immersive experience of electronic literature, she argues that "multiple data flows" stimulate a new mode of cognitive engagement that she terms "hyperattention." Hayles's claim is that such hyperattention has begun to transform the experience and possibilities of print. Her essay thus conjures visions of a heteronomous future, one that raises questions of human and nonhuman agency and praxis yet also presents possibilities for transformation, for a creative *poiesis* working to shape a future for the novel.

For Doris Sommer the crisis of public support faced by the humanities presents an opportunity for reasserting the significance of practices nurtured by humanistic inquiry. Like McCaffery, Sommer urges a reorientation toward the city—toward the very ways in which we inhabit public space. Her chapter is, in fact, a manifesto for the transformative power of humanistic inquiry and of art—of artists and critics—to effect change and thus improve social systems through creative action. She argues that we must find ways of developing "best cultural practices," enabling the humanities and humanists to engage with and activate the public sphere, and thus move beyond the insight afforded by critical practices that, too often, offer critique while leading to inaction. Sommer draws on a number of concrete examples: Antanas Mockus, artist and mayor of Bogotá, and Augusto Boal, founder of "Theater of the Oppressed" and "Forum Theater" and twice councilman of Rio de Janeiro. Mockus sought to revive a city devastated by violence, corruption, and a dysfunctional economy by utilizing art to promote accountability and awaken a "democratizing desire for civility." Facing an unimaginable future, Mockus hired pantomime artists, replaced corrupt traffic police, and deployed similarly concrete artistic stratagems to transform chaotic public spaces into a "stage for daily merriment." Envisioning thus a "humanities in action," Sommer challenges humanists to provide ordinary citizens with tools for acting, by showing how art can "build society," how the very act of making—*poiesis*—involves bridging differences, confronting resistances in one's subjects and one's materials, overcoming constraint not as "nemesis" or as intractable heterogeneity, but rather as "a condition of creativity."

Taken as a whole, this collection makes a strong argument that what is missing in too many debates over the future of the humanities is, surprisingly, an analysis of the future itself.[14] By addressing this crucial omission, the essays gathered here aim to approach the necessarily futural orientation of the humanities in terms of the tension between yet-to-be-imagined human capacities and unimaginable posthuman agency. Rather than increasing anxieties about the future, the unpredictable and unthought dimensions of praxis emphasize the role of becoming, heteronomy, and invention—or what Deleuze calls "the new in the making"—in art, politics, and intellectual inquiry. These closely intertwined dimensions of cultural *poiesis* allow us to question existing assumptions and to invent alternative possibilities for a whole range of practices in the humanities, from art and intellectual inquiry to emancipatory politics and ethics.

PART I

The New and Its Risks

CHAPTER I

Life and Event: Deleuze on Newness

Paola Marrati

Whether cinema, as Deleuze claims, is Bergsonian, remains an open question; that Deleuze himself was a Bergsonian, however, is beyond doubt. Still, we should ask ourselves: What, exactly, does the Bergsonian inspiration to be found across Deleuze's *oeuvre* consist of? There are, to be sure, several ways to take on this question, but there is one that, to my mind, is decisive: the problem of the new. In *Cinema 1: The Movement-Image*, Deleuze writes, "Bergson transformed philosophy by asking the question of the new in the making instead of the question of eternity."[1]

This claim, for all its clarity, is no less enigmatic. What transformation of philosophy are we dealing with, according to Deleuze? Or, which amounts to the same, what does "asking the question of the new in the making" mean? What is the problem of the new, of newness, or novelty? Not only did Deleuze intimately know the history of philosophy and thus knew very well that the questions of time, of becoming, of history did not wait for Bergson to be asked—and that therefore it would appear paradoxical to speak of philosophy as having to wait for Bergson to stop asking the question of eternity—Deleuze was also fully aware of what was going on around him when he published these lines in 1983, that is to say, at a moment when, in France and elsewhere, philosophical—and political—debates were centered around the concept of postmodernity. (Jean-François Lyotard had published his famous book *The Postmodern Condition* in 1979.) This was not a time, therefore, in which the question of the new was "hot" in any possible sense; on the contrary, speaking about newness seemed to evoke an optimism, a confidence in progress and a happy tomorrow, that one had rather forgo, shelve next to the memories of a *belle époque* definitely gone by.

But if all of this is true, what could be the sense, and the implications, of Deleuze's claim? In what follows I would like to develop a hypothesis about what Deleuze understands by "new" and about the significance of such a concept for our contemporary politics and ethics.

I

Let me remark, first of all, that the question of the new in the making is situated at the intersection of three major themes in Bergson's philosophy, all of which are crucial for Deleuze's own thought: the themes of difference, of time (duration), and of life.

In Deleuze's interpretation, Bergson's thought is a philosophy of difference because it is not content with a description of differences between things as they are once they have been produced; rather, it aims at capturing the constitutive difference, which Deleuze calls "internal" difference, that distinguishes a thing in itself, that makes a thing what it is in its own singular being. Such a difference is a process of production, of creation, of invention *of the new*. That is why, in Bergson, as read by Deleuze, difference and time, duration, necessarily coincide. Let me quote from the very first essay published by Deleuze on Bergson in 1956, "Bergson, 1859–1941," though analogous passages can be found in many later texts, and namely in *Cinema 1* and *2*:

> Bergson tells us, moreover, that his work consisted of reflecting on the fact that all is not given. But what does such a reality signify? Simultaneously that the given presupposes a movement that invents it or creates it, and that this movement must not be conceived in the image of the given. What Bergson critiques in the idea of the *possible* is that it presents us a simple copy of the product, projected or rather retrojected onto the movement of production, onto invention. But the virtual is not the same thing as the possible: the reality of time is finally the affirmation of a virtuality that is actualized, and for which to be actualized is to invent.[2]

Indeed, the opposition between the possible and the virtual, which Deleuze was to systematize in *Difference and Repetition*, is decisive if we want to understand the reality of time and its more than intimate link with a productive difference.

According to Bergson, assuming that the possibility of a thing precedes its existence is a way of denying the reality of time, a denial that is all the more powerful for its not being explicit. In this regard, it is of little importance whether one thinks the possible, with Kant, as the set of transcendental conditions of experience; with Leibniz, as the worlds that God contemplates; or, with the Wittgenstein of the *Tractatus*, as a logical space—to give but a few examples. In all these cases, time is reduced to an exterior frame within which events take place, but this frame has no bearing on the events themselves since their possibility, be it logical or transcendental, precedes them. To put it into Bergson's terms: When we deny time a true power of invention, we take away all of its ontological reality, *we name it without thinking it*, and thereby assume that "all is given"—once and for all.

But in order not to fall prey to yet another form of the illusion of the possible, more is needed than just affirming an ontological agency of time. It is necessary to think the creative power of time as a process of *differentiation*. The possible and the real are made one in the image of the other; no conceptual difference separates them—for the simple reason, according to Bergson, that the possible is "a mirage of the present in the past"; it is constituted retrospectively by an act of the mind that projects backwards in time the possibility of an event that has already taken place. The power of time, however, its reality, what Deleuze calls the *virtual*, deploys itself in a completely different way. The actualization of a virtuality does not entail any resemblance whatsoever: On the contrary, it implies the creation of lines of differentiation that neither existed—in a logical or transcendental form—nor could be foreseen in advance.

It is at this point that the third of Bergson's themes comes in: the theme of life or, more precisely, the concept of the *élan vital*. The conjunction of time and difference, of the creative power of time and processes of differentiation, is made possible by the concept of life. In *Creative Evolution*, Bergson, after a series of analyses too long to be recalled here, defines the "essence" of life, the unity of its *élan*, as a tendency towards change and differentiation. What makes life what it is would then be nothing but this tendency towards movement, change, the creation of new and unforeseeable forms of life. It is for this reason that Deleuze can write, in "Bergson's Conception of Difference": "When virtuality realizes itself, which is to say differentiates itself, it is through life and in a vital form; in this sense it is true that difference *is* vital," and, at the end of the same text, "Bergsonism is a philosophy of difference, and of difference's realization; there we find difference in itself, and it realizes itself as novelty."³ What time *does* is create, bring about novelty and newness. This can be done only by processes of differentiation, the paradigm of which is the evolution of life. The notions of time, difference, and life cannot be separated. Deleuze's Bergsonian inspiration lies in this conceptual frame. One could speak of "vitalism," but we have to keep in mind that this is a vitalism of time and difference, and that "life" is both organic and inorganic.⁴

We can now understand why Bergson, according to Deleuze, so profoundly transformed philosophy. Only when we begin with the question of the new in the making can we think the reality of time, since a universe in which nothing new comes about is a universe in which "all is given"—which is what, implicitly or explicitly, all sorts of otherwise very different philosophies as well as certain scientistic dreams assume.

But even if we now better understand the importance of the transformation of philosophy brought about by Bergson, the most pressing question remains: What, exactly, is the new? And why is it decisive to ask this question today? And why is it relevant for ethics and politics?

2

To try to understand why we are still concerned with the problem of the new, we must first emphasize that the new, for Bergson as much as for Deleuze, does not in any way coincide with the future. If that were the case, we would be dealing not with a transformation of philosophy but with some version of the idea of progress, be it in an Enlightenment manner or in the manner of a philosophy of history (and it would matter very little, in this regard, whether it would be of the Hegelian type, or the Marxist, or the phenomenological, as in the late Husserl). Now, while it is certain that the new in Bergson and Deleuze always has a positive connotation—I will return to this point—it is just as certain that, for the one as for the other, not everything that will happen in a near or faraway future will be new. The future and the new do not necessarily overlap, and this for essential reasons.

The idea of progress or, for that matter, any version of a teleology of history, dialectic or not, is not only an illusion, but it is, to say it once more, an illusion whose function it is to make us believe that "all is given." To think that history follows laws that govern its course or, at least, that its movement despite halts and detours is oriented by a sense or towards an end, comes down to assuming that the time of human events does nothing but realize a possibility, an idea, a plan that preceded it. In a text that is entirely dedicated to the critique of the category of the possible, Bergson writes:

> How can we fail to see that if the event can always be explained afterward by an arbitrary choice of antecedent events, a completely different event could have been equally well explained in the same circumstances by another choice of antecedent—nay, by the same antecedents otherwise cut out, otherwise distributed, otherwise perceived by our retrospective attention?[5]

And in the most political of his books, *The Two Sources of Morality and Religion*, he maintains that if one would like, one may call "progress" the moments of history in which something new opens up, and one may believe that these moments all go in the same direction.[6] But that would be just another retrospective illusion of the possible since, in reality, there is no direction established in advance. It would also mean that there is no need for creating and producing moral and political renewals given that they preexist in some ideal form anyway, that they are always already given as possibilities that just wait for the right moment to come into being.

The new, on the contrary, anticipates neither the happy unfolding of history nor, for that matter, the certainty of a future apocalypse. Optimism and pessimism, in this regard, are equally inappropriate, since the new functions as a criterion of evaluation, not of foresight. It is not surprising to see Deleuze bring in, next to Bergson, another major reference of his *oeuvre*: Nietzsche. Let me quote from *Difference and Repetition*:

> Nietzsche's distinction between the creation of new values and the recognition of established values should not be understood in a historically relative manner, as though the established values were new in their time and the new values simply needed time to be established. In fact it concerns a difference which is both formal and in kind. The new, with its power of beginning and beginning again, remains forever new, just as the established was always established from the outset, even if a certain amount of empirical time was necessary for this to be recognized.[7]

What needs to be stressed in this quote is that the power of the new as the power of time is radically distinct from history. In other words, be it in his reading of Bergson or of Nietzsche, the *question of the new, for Deleuze, takes the place of the question of history. The new, to be sure, is a category of time, but precisely not of history. To say the same thing otherwise, time takes the place of history.* This does not imply, however, that Deleuze subscribes to any discourse on the "end of history" whatsoever: He never did, and for good reasons. Any discourse about the end—of history, of modernity, of metaphysics, of philosophy, etc.—

for him implies a teleology or a dialectics that is unable to think the reality of time (or the reality of the virtual, if you prefer a properly "Deleuzian" idiom).

This in turn, however, implies that the task of philosophy, as well as of ethics and politics, is to grasp the new in the making, the constitutive difference that makes something come into being, the singularity of any event, on the one hand, and, on the other, to discern the "old" and the "new" in what is given. And such a task is precisely what the philosophies of history, according to Deleuze, are incapable of achieving.

3

To maintain that the problem of the new comes up in the place of the problem of history is not a self-evident claim (not even for readers of Deleuze) and needs to be backed up. Let us begin by trying to understand its implications in the field of the political. Revolutionary or emancipatory politics, so often associated with the very idea of modernity, are inseparable from the belief in progress (let us think of American Revolution, or French Revolution, of Rousseau or Marx). The denunciation of injustice and the very form of any political action to be taken in order to put an end to injustice are predicated on a confidence in the future of humanity. Yet the politics of progress not only falls prey to the retrospective illusion of the possible, as we have seen, it also introduces a form of transcendence that, to Deleuze's mind, is unacceptable. The future of the revolution or of a radical democracy as the horizon of political action and as a belief assumes the function of a doubling of the world. The present conditions of life may be intolerable, but the judgment of history, like the judgment of God, justifies them in the promise of a redemption to come. The future, taken in this sense, makes acceptable that which is not acceptable in the name of another world that, though not present, surely won't fail to come. When Deleuze repeats—as he does so often—that the question is not one of "the future of the revolution," or of the taking over of power, but one of becoming-revolutionary, he does not merely respond to the easy and widespread discourses that condemn any revolution in principle on the basis that revolutions always "go wrong"; it is also, and more profoundly, to stress that the ethical or political value of what is or what makes itself, in politics and elsewhere, is immanent to it.

But there is yet another aspect of the question that is, to my mind at least, even more decisive: It concerns the model of action, of human agency, political or otherwise. The forms of political action sustained, explicitly or implicitly, by a thinking of history, by a belief in history, bring into play specific conceptions of the subject, community, human agency, and their relation to the natural and historical world. This model—in all its strengths and in its crisis, a crisis that, according to Deleuze, is irreversible—is described with precision in *Cinema 1* and *Cinema 2*. This is why these books, dedicated entirely to cinema, also contain an essential part of Deleuze's political philosophy—much like, if not more so than, the more explicitly political books such as *Anti-Oedipus* or *A Thousand Plateaus*.

The "politics of history" (if you will grant me the expression) correspond exactly to what Deleuze analyzes as the cinematographic model of the action-image that dominated cinema before the First World War, whose exemplary figures are Griffith and Eisenstein. But what does Deleuze mean by "action-image"? Without being able to enter into the details of Deleuze's analyses, let me recall that it is a film-form in which the composition of images is thought of as the composition of an organic unity. The greatness of Griffith is to have been the first to provide a powerful and coherent conception of editing, in which the parts of an organism, while differentiating themselves, stand in relation with one another. (This, according to Deleuze, is the function of parallel editing where shots of the different elements of the organism—whites and blacks, men and women, rich and poor, city and countryside, etc.—alternate according to a certain rhythm.) This is the first aspect. The second aspect concerns the life of the organism, the laws that govern the relation between its elements. In Griffith, the actions that get started always take the form of a duel that opposes the villain to the good man, good to evil, since the unity of the organism is always threatened and its equilibrium must constantly be re-established. Confronted by danger, the other parts of the whole unite to bring aid to the good, the actions converge towards the place of the duel in order to reverse its result, to restore the compromised harmony. This aspect of the organism's life is brought out by convergent and accelerated editing. (The insertion of close-ups, in turn, shows the relation between a part and the whole, as is the case, for example, in the famous close-ups of soldiers that alternate with the shots of the battle in *Birth of a Nation*.) This conception of the composition of images constitutes, in Deleuze's words, "a powerful organic representation" and would become the paradigm for Hollywood movies:

> The American cinema draws from it its most solid form; from the general situation to the re-established or transformed situation through the intermediary of a duel, of a convergence of actions. American montage is organico-active.[8]

But organic editing is just as important for the Soviet school, and notably for Eisenstein. In his films as well as in his theoretical writings, Eisenstein places himself within Griffith's heritage; what he puts into question is not the organic conception of editing, but the idea Griffith has of an organism. The unity of an organism is constituted by a juxtaposition of parts that are external one to another; rather, it is a unity of production. An organism produces its parts according to laws of genesis and growth, and the oppositions that threaten the organism are not due to chance or individual passions. Conflicts are the result of the internal force of the organism that breaks the unity in order to reproduce it at a higher level. Eisenstein subscribes to a conception of montage that leads from a situation to its modification through a series of actions, but the organism is a dialectical unity, and the composition and deployment of the images must therefore follow very different rules. (Opposition and attraction editing therefore take the place of parallel editing.)

Hollywood and Soviet cinema before World War II thus share the essential: an organic conception of montage whose power we should be careful not to underestimate. It is this power of representation that brought about the "universal triumph" of American cinema before the war for reasons, and this needs to be stressed, that are not simply the result of economic or commercial superiority.[9] Organic montage brings about a conception of individual and collective action from which it derives its power. The milieu and its forces act on the characters by creating a situation in which they are taken up and to which they must react. They must respond to the challenge of the situation and this response produces a different, modified situation. Milieu and character are like the two terms of a relation that is at the same time one of reciprocal dependency and of antagonism. The action, in the strict sense of the term, has the form of a duel, or of a series of duels: with the milieu, with others, or with oneself. Deleuze suggests a formula to describe the structure of the action-image: "S—A—S," from the situation at the beginning to the situation transformed by the intermediary intervention of the action.[10]

Deleuze calls this cinematographic form "realism." However, he gives to the term a very peculiar meaning. As defined by Deleuze, realism by no means excludes the extraordinary, the fantastic, dreams; even less does it exclude melodrama, which is, on the contrary, one of its essential forms. It only requires that the space-times be determined geographically, historically, and socially, and that the emotions or drives of the characters be embodied in their behavior.[11]

A last thing to be noted is that, in Deleuze's analyses, the question of community and of the people is always present in the cinema of the action-image. Even when the action is centered on a hero figure, the hero can only become heroic, that is to say, be up to the situation and capable of responding to the challenge of the milieu, to the extent to which he or she represents the collectivity. It is only through the mediation of the community that an individual can become a leader and accomplish a great deed.[12] This allows Deleuze to write:

> Finally, the American cinema constantly shoots and reshoots a single fundamental film, which is the birth of a nation-civilization, whose first version was provided by Griffith. It has in common with the Soviet cinema the belief in a finality of universal history; here the blossoming of the American nation, there the advent of the proletariat.[13]

There would be many things to say about the insistent parallel that Deleuze establishes between the American dream and the communist dream—in the context of this essay, I will limit myself to the following remark. In the century of the cinema, more precisely, of the "classic" cinema before the war, the American dream and the communist dream are—at least seen from Europe—the only two great political projects of universal emancipation and freedom, grounded in a thinking of history and of individual and collective action. The organic conception of editing expresses the belief in a finality of history and in a common becoming of humanity, where the belief in a transformation of the world by humans and the belief in the discovery of an internal spiritual world are intimately related.[14]

4

Yet, despite the success of the films that continue to be made according to this model, the action-form, for Deleuze, has entered into an irreversible crisis. "The soul of cinema" is no longer there, as he writes.[15] New forms of editing, new ways of composing images come about in the postwar period that Deleuze analyzes under the title of "time-image." Italian Neo-realism provides the first great example of this kind of cinema.

While I cannot analyze here the question of a cinema of time in itself, let me stress that these new forms of editing put into play a thinking of the relation between actions and situations that is nonorganic and nonrealistic (in the specific sense that Deleuze gives to these terms) as well as a conception of time that is nonchronological and nonteleological. Stated more clearly: For Deleuze, the crisis of classic cinema coincides exactly with the fact that we no longer believe in the coherence that the thinking of history gave to human agency. We no longer believe that individual or collective actions have any bearing on a situation taken as a whole, that they could modify it or reveal its meaning, that the success or defeat—in this regard it doesn't matter—of our actions are up to the situation we are confronted with. We no longer believe that our affects are embodied in behaviors that express them in a coherent manner. In short, what we are lacking now is the "realistic" assurance that an action has a bearing on the situation, the "vital illusion" of the health of a community that always reinvents itself anew. To say it with Stanley Cavell:

> We no longer grant, or take it for granted, that men doing the work of the world together are working for the world's good, or if they are working for the world's harm they can be stopped. These beliefs flowered last in our films about the imminence and experience of the Second World War, then began withering in its aftermath—in the knowledge, and refusal of knowledge, that while we had rescued our European allies, we could not preserve them; that our enemies have prospered; that we are obsessed with the ally who prospered and prepared to enter any pact so long as it is against him; that the stain of the atomic blood will not wash and that its fallout is nauseating us beyond medicine, aging us very rapidly. It is the knowledge, and refusal to know, that we are ceding Stalin and Hitler the permanent victories of the war (if one of them lost the old world battle, he shares the spoils of the present war of the worlds), letting them dictate what shall be meant by communism and socialism and totalitarianism, in particular that they are to be equated.[16]

This analysis of "our present"—whose pertinence is of course debatable—describes exactly the modern condition. If there is a modern fact, for Deleuze, this fact is not some kind of death of God, according to a certain Nietzschean or Heideggerian doxa, nor is it a "return of the religious"; the "modern fact" is that we no longer believe in the links that bind us to the world. What is lost is the world, not in itself or as an object of knowledge, but for us. "We no longer even believe in what happens to us, in love or death."[17]

Certainly, modernity thus understood has no easily assignable and unique date of birth, the postwar period, for instance. But that is not the question, since, for Deleuze as for Bergson, what defines the essence of a thing or an event is always a tendency towards differentiation, a movement, a process or a becoming and never a fixed state. Modernity, like everything else, is a tendency one can only hope to grasp—taking the risk of failing—in its becoming.

5

While we should not regret the loss of the transcendence of the future and of the teleology of history that revolutionary politics—in the widest sense of the term—put to work, we can certainly not be content with the mere acknowledgment of a broken link to the world, of the fact that the world is lost (to us). Disenchanted cynicism was never an option for Deleuze. If the modern problem is the one I have just described, it interpellates us, it calls for a response. Deleuze did not avoid the task. As far as possible new forms of political agency—of an immanent politics, if you like—are concerned, the major text remains *A Thousand Plateaus* with its analysis of the concepts of majority, segmentarity, becoming-minoritarian, etc. In turn, it is *Cinema 2* and *What is Philosophy?* that sketch a response to the problem of the world. What could take the place of the old "realism" with its "vital illusion," and the revolutionary hope for a better future? Yet another belief, another hope, but a belief that has changed objects:

> The link between man and the world is broken. Henceforth, this link must become an object of belief: it is the impossible which can only be restored within a faith. Belief is no longer addressed to a different or transformed world. Man is in the world as if in a pure optical and sound situation. The reaction of which man has been dispossessed can be replaced only by belief. Only belief in the world can reconnect man to what he sees and hears. The cinema must film, not the world, but belief in this world, our only link. The nature of the cinematographic illusion has often been considered. *Restoring our belief in the world—this is the power of modern cinema (when it stops being bad).* Whether we are Christians or atheists, in our universal schizophrenia, we need reasons to believe in this world. It is a whole transformation of belief. It was already a great turning-point in philosophy, from Pascal to Nietzsche: to replace the model of knowledge with belief. But belief replaces knowledge only when it becomes belief in this world, as it is. . . . We need an ethic or a faith, which makes fools laugh; it is not a need to believe in something else, but a need to believe in this world, of which fools are a part.[18]

This power, or this necessity, concerns not only the cinema, and *What is Philosophy?* dedicates to the theme of an immanent conversion of faith important passages that take up and continue the analyses of *The Image-Time*:

> It is possible that the problem now concerns the one who believes in the world, and not even in the existence of the world but in its possibilities of movements and intensities, so as once again to give birth to new modes of

existence, closer to animals and rocks. It may be that believing in this world, in this life, becomes our most difficult task, or the task of a mode of existence still to be discovered on our plane of immanence today.[19]

The transformation that Bergson had philosophy undergo by asking the question of the new in the making thus acquires yet another facet. Perhaps time, in its essence, is the invention of the new and, certainly, "all is not given." But precisely because not everything is given, nothing guarantees the new forms of life, nothing assures us that other modes of political and social organization will come to "liberate life wherever it is oppressed."[20] As Bergson writes in *The Two Sources*, in human societies as elsewhere, the new is always an invention, a creation.[21] But in order to discover other forms of existence, we must first believe in them. We must believe in life and in this world, we must believe in the new of which life is the power, or the secret, and in this world in which the new may trace itself.

Nobody will deny that the task is, in fact, difficult. But is there another? Whether we agree with the outcome of Deleuze's analyses of what constitutes "the modern fact" or not, we must grant that he asked a question, an ethical and political one, which it would be illusory to try to avoid.

CHAPTER 2

A Precursor:
Limiting the Future, Affirming Particularity

Andrew Benjamin

The possibility of the future, linked though perhaps too often to the unacknowledged positing of the new, endures as a continuing refrain.[1] Hence, there is the inevitable repetition of the problem posed by the need to begin again and anew. Starting with what could have been an epigram—a note taken and recorded during a voyage—allows for an opening to be staged. "The smallest circumstances awaken in the depths of the heart childhood emotions, though always with a new attraction." (*Les plus petites circonstances réveillent au fond du coeur les emotions du premier age, et toujours avec un attrait nouveau.*)[2]

The choice of these lines is far from arbitrary. What they indicate is that here in Chateaubriand, the "new" will have been other than mere novelty. (As such, his formulation would seem to gesture towards the acknowledged truth that accompanies any sustained encounter with the state of affairs opened up by the new's evocation.) This initial articulation finds the new positioned within a form of repetition. As such a different question arises, and it should be noted that the question is not adduced, it emerges from the formulation itself. The question is straightforward: What is the new once it can no longer be identified with novelty? If a conclusion can be drawn from the possibility of posing this question, then it involves the need to return, continually, to the question of the new. A return occasioned by the impossibility of conflating a concern with the new with mere invention. Allowing for the continuity of the return to the new as a question is already to link a questioning of the new to the ineliminability of a form of repetition. Indeed, the question of the new may have arisen from a structure of repetition. Moreover, it has to be understood as that structure's enactment.

This is the setting in which the central concerns of this paper—namely the relationship between the future and the new—will be taken up. As always, it is vital to begin with questions. The opening ones are straightforward: *And the future, what if it weren't new? And the new, what if it were simply part of the past?* Not that there would not be anything new but that *newness, past, future*, etc., would all then be terms demanding forms of thinking that might resist the description "new" or "futural." If any thought of the new had to be incorporated into a framework that has, at the very least, a history, then in terms of a mode of philosophical inquiry there would not have been anything other than a structure in which the new as gesture demanded to be thought. Once it can be positioned in this way—a positioning that undoes the hold of the naturalization of chronological time over the new—then the new would have reemerged subsequently as a question.

What must be allowed—allowing, as a taking place without automatic delimitation—is the pursuit of the new as a question. This will be an undertaking that, by definition, cannot naturalize its object. Consequently, holding that object, the "new," though in the end also the "past" and the "future," apart from their absorption into natural time, also occasions the temporality of all of these terms to be the site of investigation; perhaps, continual investigation. Though it will only remerge in the guise of a conclusion, the interplay of continuity and the place of a transformed, if not transfigured sense of the new within it, hence the continual interplay of continuity and discontinuity needs to be understood as a description of criticism. At this stage, however, what matters is the new. Taking up the new as a possibility within philosophical and literary thinking will occur, in this context, in relation to the precursor.

Opening

If the predicament of poetry—poetry in the modern period and once it is poetry then there is the real possibility that such a concern might extend to writing—has a precursor, a body of work that grounds the current predicament, then the question to be addressed is, what would identify that precursor? Would its presence have been effective? The possibility of this sense of a precursor informs Nathalie Sarraute's 1965 engagement with "le roman moderne."³ Raising, thereby, the question of whether there is a logic of the precursor. While the answer to the question of the precursor bears, for Sarraute, a proper name, in this instance the name in question is not central. The name is of course Flaubert. What matters, however, is the use of this "Flaubert."⁴ What form of argumentation stems from its evocation?

Sarraute uses one of Flaubert's own observations. As always with his most acute reflections, it is advanced in a letter to Louise Colet. While by no means dominating their correspondence, he often wrote to her of writing; the latter—writing—is to be understood as an act, as a strategy and more emphatically as literature. The passage cited by Sarraute circulates around the "nothing." Flaubert proposes, "What seems to me good, what I would like to do, is a book on nothing, a book without attachments to the exterior." (*Ce qui me semble beau, ce que je voudrais faire, c'est un livre sur rien, un livre sans attaché extérieure.*)⁵

While the passage from the letter is well-known, for Sarraute the "nothing" marks the abstract to which the modern novel tends. The important element in this presentation does not concern the abandoning of character or plot but their incorporation into a form of abstraction and thus with the way they would then comprise part of the "nothing." They are integral to "a book on nothing" (*un livre sur rien*), to its presence and thus to its style. Even though Sarraute only quotes the lines cited above, the letter itself goes on to link the "nothing" to "style." The latter is not mere ornamentation. Rather, style in Flaubert's sense dissolves the distinction between surface and depth and thus demands to be understood as the work's internal economy and thus as that which holds its work—as a work—in play.

Sarraute wrote "Flaubert le precursor" in 1965. Dates, of course, mark time. The nature of the mark and the conception of time at work within the dates—the time dated—may be the subject of contestation if not discovery. Indeed, precisely because a date has a form of singularity, the date's reiteration, a movement in which the initial singularity is revealed as itself the mark of an ineliminable plurality, forms an integral part of the founding date. With any date, time as a complex is automatically involved. Precisely because 1965 is not the "now"—where the now is no more than a conception of the now that identifies it (the now) with the date of the time of writing, thus 1965 is explicitly not now—a series of questions emerge. This "nothing" is after all both a temporal as well as an ontological term. Perhaps, therefore, the opening question needs to take the following form: What, now, of this "nothing?" If part of the answer involved a separation occurring presently of the link between the modern and this nothing, what then, now, of the nothing and what moreover of the modern? Again, if this possible separation were maintained, will a concern with the nothing, with Flaubert's possible "book on nothing" (*livre sur rien*) have been overcome and, as a consequence, Flaubert would then not be a precursor, except perhaps only for a past. A past recognized as such though only because nothing would no longer be part of the modern: nothing would no longer be new, even though it had been once. A state of affairs within which designations such as "past," "now," and "modern" derived what meaning they have from the slide between the present (now) and its immediate dating.

While the problems posed by the precursor mean having to consider concerns central to a philosophical understanding of historical time, it remains the case that fundamental to developing a sense of the precursor, though more aptly described as a logic of the precursor, is the interplay of the reworked presence of nothing and abstraction. The latter—abstraction—when won from its initial context, a winning in which the marks of that original setting remain, is then present in terms of its generative capacity and not its having been withdrawn and thus only ever present as an aftereffect. In the end, this sense of abstraction and nothing are knitted together. Separating them, therefore, would involve failing to see the complexity that they stage. To be clear, for Sarraute, Flaubert is a precursor. In other words, the modernity that is associated with Joyce amongst others does not pertain, or at least not fully, in this instance. Moreover, Flaubert can be read as though all that is offered is a literary presentation of manners—one that does no more than provide insight into a specific historical period. And yet, what is opened up on the level of style—style in the sense that is broader than the conception of it found in Flaubert—allows a way through that reduction. The way in question involves a reorientation of approach in which the nothing, rather than a simple counter-position either to form or to presence, becomes a concern in itself. Indeed, if there is a way of opening up this nothing—perhaps, even, for it to become more than a precursor, though it will be important to return, as was noted above, to the precursor—then the possibilities that it opens up have to be pursued.

Nothing, as a trope if not as an organizing principle within philosophical and literary concerns, already figures. Nothing, however, in order that it come into consideration, thus continue to hold itself in place, needs to be opened up beyond a Hegelian concern with negation, i.e., beyond a sense of negation linked either to completion or finality. In the end, what this will open up is an important connection between the impossible of a completing negation and repetition. Examples here are essential since they delimit the scope of inquiry. An important instance of this move, one in which what occurs is the positioned centrality of the negative, can be found in Blanchot's attempt to rescue Mallarmé from Mallarmé's own Hegelianism.[6] The significance of this type of rescue lies in the way Blanchot develops a conception of the nothing (*rien*) that retains its insistent quality, insisting without the possibility of its own negation (where the latter is understood as the negation that completes). Blanchot, in this move, reiterates that which is central to Bataille's emphatic response to Kojève on the question of Hegel.[7] A response in which a conception of a productive negativity, one that is not subject to its own negation, becomes the operative element within philosophical thinking. Again, what is at work is negation as an insistent presence.[8] Returning to this sense of insistence will be important. Insistence as both a literary and philosophical possibility once coupled to the work of a productive negativity will reemerge as a form of affirmation. (Affirmation and criticism are in the end bound together, precisely because affirmation needs to be understood as the ascription of identity.) Moving towards that relation involves staying, not so much with the presence of a precursor, as with the recognition of having to engage with what the precursor will always have brought into play. Engagement, therefore, as the need to retain relationality, marks the complex presence of the logic of the precursor.

While any attempt to take up affirmation demands such an approach, the ineliminable presence of the logic of the precursor means that caution is necessary. Within that logic are the very terms whose clarification defines the project at hand. In other words, the logic of the precursor will bring to the fore a mode of thinking that is surrounded by terms such as the "new." A term whose simplistic evocation, as has been suggested, can only ever obfuscate, at the best, or at worst let thinking slip into the temporality of fashion. In sum, while the logic concerns time, the complex defining the conception(s) of time at work within it has a different exigency. What is needed is an oblique approach, perhaps this time, uniquely, one with its own precursors.

If Not Beauty

Gathered together under the title *L'usage de la parole* are a series of texts written by Sarraute that resist the classification novel (*roman*) or even essay (*essai*); perhaps they are only ever pieces. The question of their status—perhaps more accurately, their status existing as a question—allows their classification to be a concern. What is classified, the terms and concepts of classification, bring time into play. The importance of having to note an already present link between temporality (understood as an inherently plural determination) and forms of classification is that it provides the context in which it is possible to locate the effective presence of the logic of the precursor. On one level, at work in this formulation of the question of the precursor is an array of conceptual possibilities. Holding them in play does not involve providing their detail, as though identifying discreet elements would sustain that play. Indeed, definitions may have the opposite effect. What has to be considered is how a matrix of concerns—a locus of continually produced relations—is to be understood. Pure conceptual identity is, it will be argued, as impossible and as untenable as the apparent relativism that emerges with the undoing of purity. Working through the logic of the precursor, allowing the complexity of its detail to unfold, is the way into this matrix. In sum, the weave set up by a concern with time comprises the interplay of nothing (initially Flaubert's *rien*) as literature's possible topos, then Sarraute's repositioning this nothing as that which tends towards abstraction, and lastly their connection to the nothing as insistent and productive and therefore as bound up with affirmation.

Staged by any concern with nothing and the weave of concerns within which it forms an essential component, especially that approach that begins to define those elements in terms that reach beyond their traditional determinations, is the need to situate those concerns in relation to a specific structure of thought. Beginning with nothing—nothing as an opening—demands a point of departure, perhaps beginning anew.

> The gaze of the other scrutinizes the one who, with a tantalizing, guilty smile, placed sideways on his/her face, miserably tries . . . but what is the good? . . . the word "aesthetic," one can try to turn it round, yet it is identical on all its sides . . . what is the good of dissimulating one of them by plating it with it the word "beauty."
>
> [*Le regard de l'autre scrute celui qui, un sourire fautif, aguicheur, posé de travers sur son visage, piteusement s'efforce . . . mais à quoi bon? . . . le mot "esthétique," on a beau le retourner, il est identique sur toutes ses faces . . . à quoi bon de dissimuler l'une d'elles en plaquant sur elle le mot "beauté."*]

Sarraute wrote these lines within a short text whose title is "Aesthetic" (*Esthétique*).[9] A text within which forms of traversal and the complex determinations that movement brings to the question of identity are central both as a thematic presence, as well as in terms of an operational logic. The question within them concerns what would be at work in the effacing of a plurality of forms of presentation if over them were to be placed "the word 'beauty'." What needs to be distanced therefore is the enforcing hold of beauty. And yet, as always, a preliminary form of questioning is necessary. What conception or conceptions of beauty are envisaged? There are, after all, many ways to refuse beauty. In addition, this also means that the question of what is being refused will also need to be taken into consideration. In sum, what is the beauty whose hold is not be countenanced and whose presence is not to be encountered? In this context, there are two specific senses of beauty that need to be countered in order that the force of what Sarraute has termed *esthétique* can emerge. These two forms of beauty can be productively described as beauty as the recovery of loss, in the first instance, and beauty as the overcoming of discord in the second. Countering them will introduce the temporal and ontological elements that allow for a sustained encounter with the logic of the precursor.

While it is necessary to identify the two forms of beauty that should be distanced, a distancing occurring in the name of the aesthetic, it needs to be noted that precisely because they are defined in terms of the interplay of absence and presence, they overlap at certain crucial moments. The two possibilities reside in the oscillation between loss—a loss that defines the present—and forms of eventual plenitude. In the first instance there is loss. Either beauty is not at hand and has to be recovered—a clear example of which is the philosophical strategy of Plato's *Symposium*—or beauty is simply lost and thus the absence of this guarantor occasions longing and thus differing forms of melancholia.[10] Indeed, such would be basis for beginning to interpret Dürer's *Melancholia*.[11] In the second there is the possibility of plenitude, understood in philosophical terms as the recovery of beauty (beauty within the Platonic configuration; that is, beauty that has an essential quality [an *ousia*], the search for which defines the nature of the philosophical). This set-up has its corollary within a conception of historical time in which the present as a site of loss opens itself up to the possibility of an eventual reconciliation, if not self-reconciliation. In this instance reconciliation is the overcoming of the dissensus marking and defining the present. Arguments for a form of plenitude that need to be defined in relation to the future will, as a consequence, have to be understood in terms of a projected reconciliation or completion to come. The "to come" identified in the present and that defines the present grounds such a definition of the future on a conception of an incomplete present that is to be completed. A completion that, in its occurring, structures the now of this future. The to come, this now, and thus this future are defined, in differing ways, by a disjunction between their realization and the condition of the present. For example, within this set-up the future is not a condition of the present; rather, the future occurs—it is to come—in overcoming the present as a site of loss.[12]

The differing conceptions of beauty that are structured by this complex of concerns are themselves marked by a form of impossibility. Beauty's impossibility involves the question of its presence. Beauty is either longed for or given as a projected outcome. Impossibility should either become a possibility (as is made clear by the structure of progress outlined in Diotima's speech) or it is only ever held as a determining absence—held, for example, in the stern gaze of *Melancholia*. Beauty is therefore present in terms of the impossibility of its presence. What this opens up, however, is another question, perhaps even another track through the continuity of the encounter with the question of beauty. Plato's question, the question that will always seek the universal in its radical differentiation from particulars and thus the one that comes to dominate any sustained thinking of the relationship between universals and particulars and that in turn informs conceptions of historical time, starts from the necessarily disjunctive relationship between universal and particular. The disjunction is such that one approach, as has already been indicated, is to maintain the disjunction's presence. Such an approach would concede the disjunction's inevitability. Hence, it is a position dominated by the aporetic, within which loss is present as the melancholic concession to presence's impossibility. The other possibility, which in the end has the same point of origination, namely, the movement between loss and plenitude, is the literary critical or philosophical project that works with the assumption of beauty's actual or eventual presence. Within such a project, completion is an ever-present possibility. The recovery of presence is, after all, the implicit intention within the Socratic response to the Platonic question.

Within the lines cited above from Sarraute, however, there is the suggestion of another way through. A way that emerges once neither of these possibilities is to pertain. What this would mean is that the reality of presentation—the presence of particulars—would have been repositioned. Hence, what will have opened up is a setting that demands a different mode of thinking. A mode of thought no longer dominated by an oscillation between the discordant and the reconciled, nor articulated in terms of either loss or mourning or, moreover, by the failure of plenitude. Distanced at the same time would be the use of the language of impossibility or the aporetic to describe the positioning of what is given. At this point, a return to Sarraute's text becomes necessary, a return deferring the new (by providing it with another location). As has already been noted, the passage from Sarraute contains the following line: "the word 'aesthetic,' one can try to turn it round, yet it is identical on all its sides." The question to be pursued here is the nature of the identity in question. Returning therefore to the aesthetic—a return guided not by any form of necessity since beauty will always remain a possibility, but because it is opportune and thus a return to be encouraged—demands not just that the identity of the aesthetic be taken up as a concern, but also that the identity in question be disassociated from the way the identity of the beautiful would be understood. The disassociation in question is from a conception of identity that is conceived uniquely in terms of the relationship between universal and particular. Equally, therefore, identity is disassociated from its location within a relationship defined by the interplay of impossibility and possibility.

Whatever force beauty has—understood as Sarraute indicates that, if only as a beginning, "beauty" is a "word"—it inheres in the ontological and temporal determinations that the word brings with it. Beauty, in this precise sense, would work to dissipate the hold of an original sense of plurality. What would have vanished, therefore, is the possibility of working with a sense of particularity that held itself apart from an explication in terms of either the pragmatic or the empirical. Though equally it is held apart from a conception of the particular in which particularity is defined in relation to a transcendent universal. What is still reattained, however—and the retention occurs precisely because of the distancing, thus refusal, of these possibilities—is another way into the question of the identity of particulars. While the term *ésthetique* would usually refer to the experiential, here in its counter-positioning to "the word 'beauty,'" it needs to be understood as announcing the demand of particularity. Thus, it should be noted that what is needed is a sense of opposition that would be significantly different to one given by a simple counter-positioning of the experiential and the conceptual. Moreover, aesthetics would, as a consequence of this difference, then be defined as the response to the demand of particularity. That demand is the latter's insistence. Once there is a concern with beauty, to the exclusion of the aesthetic, then the specificity of any one particular would begin to lose its capacity to insist. Individuality, and thus the identity of the particular, would, as a consequence, no longer exert any hold. Differing versions of subsumption would begin to delimit the particular's particularity. Beauty, in the sense in which it has been presented here, the sense given by the way beauty and the aesthetic are positioned by Sarraute, demands either the excision of the particular's own insistent presence, or, what would amount to the same thing, namely the incorporation of particularity within the identity determining relation between universal and particular.[13] Countering beauty therefore allows not just for particularity. More exactly, what is occasioned is the particular's self-presentation.

Posed in these terms, the demand of the particular remains evident. To take up the formulation of the passage, what is identical in every instance cannot be equated, however, with simple appearance. That would be a position that was still trapped within an opposition between universal and particular. Rather, what is always the same is the particular's insistence. What that means is that attention should be given to each and every particular, and it is on this level, a level positioned beyond a simple reduction of presence to literal appearance, that all particulars are "identical." However, the addition and thus defining position is that in every instance what follows from this identity is the actual appearance, thus, also the reality, of differences. Moreover, it is only by turning from the work attributed to beauty and which results in the leveling and dissipation of particularity, that there can be the identification of the particular. With that identification a new avenue of approach will have been pursued. The use of the term "new" here is of course deliberate. What it marks out, however, is of course a question that needs to be addressed. Particularity—in this context *l'ésthetique*—is not just present. At every moment that presence is under threat. Of immediate concern is the threat of a vanishing caused by the imposition of a concern with "beauty" (with the "word"). As a consequence, what matters is the affirmation of the particular. Not its mere presence but its presence as a particular. A presence that eschews the threat of having been subsumed by "beauty."

The immediate question, therefore, concerns what it means to affirm particularity. The problem of the given returns. A return signaled by the reiteration of the problem of the pragmatic or the empirical. Since it could be that affirming particularity, the particular as given, would be no more than a form of pragmatism. Or, as significantly, it would be the result of the identification of particularity with literal presence. This is the equivalent, within interpretation, to a form of empiricism. If either of these possibilities—pragmatism or empiricism—held sway, then affirmation would amount to no more than a type of description. Presentation, therefore, would be a description articulated with, and as, representation.

To work through these possibilities necessitates a return to the negative. The negative arises because particularity is bound up with what can be described as the necessity for "irresolution." This term does not designate a failure, that is, the impossibility of the particular to have resolved itself and thus to be the enacted adoption of a determinant and final form.

Rather, irresolution points to another quality of particularity, one, as will be noted, that is explicable in terms of a return to negativity. A quality that allows for an opening—a sense of a holding apart—such that what is then given is the presence of the particular as that which comes to the fore through the act of affirmation. The object of affirmation is the particular. And, even though it involves a reiteration of the tautological formulation already used, it remains the case that, as a beginning, what is affirmed is the presence of the particular's particularity: a state of affairs in which particularity, as has been suggested, cannot be reduced to either the pragmatic instance or to the content of a literal description. In other words, once irresolution is taken as defining an approach allowing for that set-up in which what is—"is" in the sense of a-being-present—can never be resolved in any absolute sense (and here resolution means having acquired a singular determination that could as a consequence be represented absolutely), then this entails that emphasis needs to be given to particularity precisely because the demand of the particular falls outside that which can be more generally described as the identity-determining relation between universal and particular. Irresolution becomes a conception of negativity that is inherently generative.

Precision is essential here. The claim that a particular remains without resolution, a claim in which particularity as irresolution can be equated with finitude, concerns the ontological status of the particular. Moreover, it is that ontological status that underpins the necessary impossibility of any form of coextensivity between the particular and its identification. In addition, to the extent that it can be argued that that relation does not establish the identity of a particular, nor equally by the act of description, then the question of how that identity is established or secured emerges as a genuine concern. What this means is that if the opposition between universal and particular is no longer operative, then the question of identity, as has been argued, endures as that which is to be established. The process in question takes the form of the always-to-be-established. The ineliminability of this form, one arising because of the disassociation from the conventions of universal/particular relations, indicates the presence of a dynamic quality: a quality that must acknowledge that what determines particularity is potentiality, with determination understood in the sense of that which identifies the mode of being proper to particularity, specifically to its insistent presence. Understanding the force of potentiality involves noting the inherent connection between irresolution as in part descriptive of the active nature of work—work as an activity rather that as an already-illustrative object—and the demand of the particular.

Identity on the level of particulars, which is a state of affairs allowed for under the rubric of the aesthetic, though only in its counter-positioning to beauty, is therefore necessarily present once necessity is equated with a potentiality for presence. That presence is, however, circumscribed by what was identified above as the always-to-be-established. The significance of this formulation is that it attests to the original relation between potentiality and the particular, a relation in which their inherent disjunction functions as the particular's condition of possibility. This weave of concerns provides the setting in which it becomes possible to continue with particularity.

As a prelude to continuing, some of the threads introduced thus far can be brought together. The particular's insistence is an ontological claim. The rearticulation of that position in terms of negativity is as much implicated in the relationship between the finite particular and what was identified earlier as irresolution. The complex nature of these relations—a complexity that will in the end only be accounted for adequately by the introduction of the notion of "heterology"—is that potentiality figures in terms of an account of the particular. This is an account that formally can never exhaust the particular's potentiality. Such is the limit of finitude. In addition, the response to particularity, the one in which the presence and the content of the particular's finitude, a state of affairs that is the affirmation of particularity, is equally marked by irresolution. However, the irresolution in question, precisely because it is present in terms of the negative, in the sense that what cannot be effaced is completion's impossibility, is also the ground of responsibility.

Being Particular

Emerging from the way in which Sarraute positions the aesthetic is, in the first instance, the structuring distinction between a generalizable concern with insistence and the inscription of particularity within an ontology in which potentiality plays not just an essential role but a determining one.[14] As such, and in lieu of both stasis and the essential, itself a state of affairs in which particulars appear within and as representations, becoming and potentiality have centrality. The correlate of which is that appearance (thus particularity) can no longer be circumscribed either by the structure of representation or, as has already been noted, by the structuring opposition between universal and particular. Related to this complex of concerns is the other element arising from what has been identified, following Sarraute, as the aesthetic. That element is the question of appearance. Appearance is a question precisely because the particular and its appearance are no longer effects of the universal. What this means is that the particular is finite, and therefore particularity is a version of finitude. Once no longer circumscribed by the universal/particular relation, then, finitude, understood as the ontological status of the particular, is that which comes to presence within a process in which its identity is established. Process in this instance defines a practice. Moreover, as shall be suggested, it is a process that can be named. (In addition, it is a process that names.) This preliminary definition of naming particularity as a process allows two specific themes to be drawn together. The attribution of identity to a particular, an attribution that will have entailed responding to the particular's insistence, is the process in which the identity of a particular, its particularity, is affirmed. The next question is then the relationship between this affirmation and appearance.

The particular's insistence delimits an essential quality of all particulars. This quality emerges in the move from beauty to the aesthetic, accepting the sense (historic and semantic) in which the two words have been used thus far. However, there has to be the move from insistence to the ascription of a specific identity to a given particular, recognizing from the start that such a move will always be an act of irresolution. An instance of what that entails is not found, for example, in the identification of a work of art as a work of art, but in the more significant move in which its—the particular's—presence as art is identified. The latter aspect is concerned with how the work of art is a work of art. As a point of departure, attention would then move to detail and technique and thus to the particular's appearance. The move from the fact of existence, the given-ness of a poem functions as a clear example, to the explication of the poem's work as a poem. This is a move that accepts the insistence of particularity as the point of origination. What is accepted, in other words, is an ontological configuration defined by the continuity of the object's becoming and thus its potentiality—continuity and potentiality are interrupted by finitude. The finite as appearance. There is an allowing, what could also be described, as the opening of a space, in which there is the appearance of the particular as the particular. No longer would there be a possible identification of appearance with the given, an appearance would have been repositioned. Henceforth, it is the affirmation of the particular's particularity. The affirmation is grounded in the interplay of finitude and irresolution. This accounts for why, ontologically, finitude is not identical with its appearance.

Taking these aspects of the particular into consideration means that the particular's presence is not a delimited and closed domain. The particular, to continue with one of the examples already used, is only ever poetry's individuated presence. The essentialist position would have necessitated recourse to the question—what is poetry? As though this question harbored the approach to poetry. The task delimited by that question would, as a consequence, only concern the particular to the extent that it opened up or made present the specific philosophical project the question demands. The move from beauty to the aesthetic necessitates working within a domain opened by the abeyance of this mode of questioning (and its enjoined task). The move means that the project at hand is importantly different. The difference exists both on the level of the object—that is, as it concerns the quality of particularity—and in regards to the task demanded by a different form of questioning. Drawing on the formulation within the example already noted, the question would be—how is the poem a poem? This question allows for the process of individuation to be registered within and as part of the particular's particularity. It is as though the individuated, thus the particular's presence, is from the start folded into a field that individuates. That field, or network of concerns, while formal, is the construct through which dominant and counter traditions are articulated. In other words, the field is not merely context, but the interplay of forces that work through and as such are always implicated in the particular. Adumbrating the field's operative quality is to sketch vital elements within the logic of the precursor. In the sense that taken together the activity of place—an activity, which is in part already being made evident through the process of allowing—is interarticulated with the operation of time. The latter—time—has both an interpretive dimension as well as a historical one.

The field, however, is neither smooth nor continuous, and rather than a site of variety it is the locus of the heterological. Particularity, while part of a field, introduces the heterological on two interrelated levels. The heterological forms an integral part of the logic's operation without being identical with it. In the first instance the field is present as a set of infinite possibilities such that finitude and with it particularity, as has been intimated, is only ever positioned disjunctively in relation to its conditions of possibility. The second is that accounting for a particular's presence as a particular is of necessity situated within the "always-to-be-established," where the latter is understood as a process of continual irresolution. The locus of heterology therefore is a site that will have already incorporated the quality that it situates.

Conceived as only ever occurring within a site of individuation, not only positions particulars within a set of relations such that any particular will already have, if only as an ineliminable potentiality, lines of relations drawn through them, it is also the case that these lines bring a complex array of temporal possibilities into play. The logic of the precursor, while undoing conceptions of time that are determined as the run of chronology in which precedent and influence mark the naturalization of chronology, also refuses to allow the new—as a form of alterity—any position within such a set-up. The new, however, rather than being abandoned, is repositioned within a relationship between a field of concerns, understood as the locus of individuation, and the logic of the precursor—a logic in which sequence cedes its place to forms of repetition. It is not just that the question of the new continues to return, more significantly it is that the insistent presence of the particulars—an insistence in which finitude and irresolution are at work together—brings the particular within the ambit of repetition. To argue that the affirmation of particularity, a situation that is always more than a description of the particular's appearance while, at the same time, arguing that the particular is delimited by finitude and irresolution, entails that the particular's potential is to be repeated. (It remains within irresolution.) Iterability is therefore an ontological consideration even if its consequence concerns meaning. This repetition becomes a future affirmation—the future made possible by the ontological formulation of particularity. In other words, it is made possible by what can be described as "being particular."

What occurs with particularity—with "being particular"—is the move from that being to its affirmation. Affirmation becomes the ascription of a specific identity to the particular. That affirmation is delimited as much by finitude and irresolution as it is by the identification of the particular with a universal. The identification, however, does not entail that the particular derives its identity from its relation to the universal. The contrary is the case, since it is the particular that discloses a form of universality by allowing for its (the universal's) repetition without the entailed presence either of an essence or a philosophical or interpretive task whose project is the recovery of the essential. If the argument concerns the way in which a particular poem works as a poem, then while this involves a repetition of poetry, that repetition falls beyond the hold of the essential. In addition, precisely because a response to the question, in what way is a given poem a poem, is itself delimited by the relationship between finitude and irresolution, what can never be precluded are future repetitions. Again, it must be noted that this not an argument involving semantic overdetermination. The continuity of repetition, one that founds discontinuities and which is itself dependent upon the heterological set-up defining the relationship between finitude and potentiality, is ontological.

The logic of the precursor brings the complex of time into a productive connection with a form of negativity. That connection, which is to be understood as a site of activity, and thus the setting for individuation, provides the location (and possibility) for affirmation. It should be remembered that affirmation is not linked directly to value. Rather, what is affirmed is the particular's particularity. The move from the given to affirmation is a move in which attention is given to the recognition of the particular as individuated within a weave or network of concerns. The role of the negative within this domain precludes absolute finality. Thus, what this situation involves is twofold. In the first instance it is the continuity of an activity that establishes the particular's presence (present as the particular). In the second, it is that an intrinsic part of this setting is the ineliminability of conflict. Irresolution's necessity demands it. Nonetheless, what the activity in question does is name. It names the particular by accounting for its presence. Within the realm comprised of artwork and works of literature, the process that names is criticism. The project of criticism is the appearance of particularity, noting that the particular is folded within a field or network within which it comes to be individuated. The field, thus the lines drawn in and through the particular, is established, in part (though only ever in part) by a form of universality and a conception of temporality that has to take repetition as fundamental.

If there is a conclusion that can be drawn, an end that is already an allowing, then it is simply that the logic of the precursor is no longer situated within, or as, a simple positing of the new. The logic has an operative quality and even though the detail will always need to be spelt out, it remains the case that in every instance criticism identifies another—as opposed to the Same—particular. Criticism is inextricably bound up with the process of repetition. That identification therefore—the emergence of singularity—is the life of work. Equally, of course, it is the afterlife of a work.

CHAPTER 3

Visual *Parrhesia*?: Foucault and the Truth of the Gaze

Martin Jay

The task of telling the truth is an endless labor: to respect it in all its complexity is an obligation which no power can do without—except by imposing the silence of slavery.[1]

MICHEL FOUCAULT

Cezanne's famous assertion in a letter to a friend in 1905, "I owe you the truth in painting and I will tell it to you," was first brought into prominence by the French art historian Hubert Damisch in his 1978 *Huit thèses pour (ou contre?) une sémiologie de la peinture* and then made into the occasion for a widely discussed book by Jacques Derrida, *La verité en peinture* later the same year.[2] In that work, Derrida challenged the distinction between work and frame, *ergon* and *parergon*, that had allowed philosophers like Kant to establish an autonomous, disinterested realm for art, distinct from all surrounding discourses and institutions. Instead, Derrida insisted, the frame was always permeable, allowing the external world to invade the artwork. Apparent ornamental excrescences like columns in front of buildings or clothing on a statue cannot be fully detached from the object itself. In fact, the founding notions of artistic value—beauty or sublimity or form—came themselves, as it were, from the outside. So the truth of a painting could never be established by looking within the painting itself.

Similarly, the debate over the actual model for Vincent Van Gogh's *Old Shoes with Laces* between Meyer Schapiro and Martin Heidegger, a debate that saw the American critic accuse Heidegger of projecting his own philosophical investments onto the work by calling them a pair of peasant shoes rather than those of the artist himself, could not be easily decided one way

45

or another. Derrida sought to undermine Schapiro's claim to having corrected Heidegger's attribution by showing that his own argument was not disinterested, that it was impossible to know for sure what the painting depicted. In other words, the truth of painting could not be established outside it either. A third example Derrida explored concerned the status of writing in the paintings of Valerio Adami, which incorporated literal examples of writing in his canvases, signatures, letters, even texts from Derrida's own book *Glas*, but which were hard to read exclusively in formal, semiotic, or mimetic terms. Here the implication was that Cezanne's promise of telling the truth was very hard to keep because radical undecidability undermined any clear-cut search for veracity in painting either inside or outside the frame.

There is no reason to go further into Derrida's complicated argument now. I have introduced it only as a prolegomenon to the question I want to address in this paper, which concerns the relationship between truth and not merely painting, but visual experience itself, in the work of Michel Foucault. Was there in Foucault as well as Derrida a deep suspicion of the ability of the eye to verify truth claims or produce warranted assertions about the truth? What was his tacit response to Cezanne's assertion of the painter's obligation to tell the truth on his canvas? What would it mean for visual truth to be "told?"

There has, of course, been a long-standing, often vexed, relationship between visuality and veracity. In juridical settings, eyewitness testimony often prevails over mere hearsay, and the very word "evidence," as has often been noted, is derived from the Latin "videre," to see. Whether metaphorically or literally, many philosophies, idealist as well as empiricist, have privileged illumination, enlightenment, transparency, clarity, and distinctness in their search for truth. Theory, rooted in the Greek word *theoria*, has often been related to the visual experience of looking at a theatrical performance. Of all the senses, vision has seemed the most disinterested because most distanced from what it perceives.

And yet, as we know, the hegemony of the eye has become a topic of persistent suspicion in many different discursive contexts. In a book published a dozen years ago called *Downcast Eyes: The Denigration of Vision in Twentieth-Century French Thought*,[3] I attempted to trace a variety of criticisms of what can be called the ocularcentric bias of much of Western thought. In that narrative, Michel Foucault played a central role, paired in a chapter with Guy Debord on the contrasting modalities of social control called the spectacle and surveillance. The book was by and large generously received and the larger point about the French interrogation of visual primacy widely accepted. But if there was any part of my argument that aroused significant resistance, it was my treatment of Foucault as an exemplar of its main thesis. In fact, even before the book had appeared, an earlier version of the claim had been questioned by John Rajchman, in an essay whose arguments I tried to address in the book itself.[4] After its appearance, its inclusion of Foucault in the larger pattern I traced was challenged, in a nuanced way, by David Michael Levin and Thomas Flynn, and more vigorously by Gary Shapiro in a long book devoted entirely to the dialectic of seeing and saying in Nietzsche and Foucault.[5] Flynn summarizes their common objections by claiming that, "if Foucault has joined many of his French contemporaries in combating an ocular epistemology that extends from Descartes to the phenomenologists, he does so with the aid of a method that looks suspiciously ocular itself."[6] Shapiro marshals the arguments of Foucault's friend Gilles Deleuze against my reading and argues that Foucault

> must be understood as having substituted a binary of visibility and discursivity for the nineteenth century's transcendental aesthetic of space and time.... Neither the visible nor the articulable (in contrast to a Kantian transcendental aesthetic) would be an eternal given; each mode would be susceptible of a historical, or speaking more precisely for Foucault, an archaeological analysis, that would disclose its specific character in varying contexts. Vision would not be generally suspect or denigrated; rather, every situation would be open to visual analysis.[7]

In all of these instances, the claim is made that rather than being consistently suspicious of the hegemony of the eye in all its manifestations, Foucault discriminated among scopic regimes or at least visual practices, finding some more benign than others. Thus, the implication that his analysis of the medical gaze or evocation of Bentham's Panopticon as typical of the modern disciplinary order of surveillance could be extended to visuality in general is wrong. While acknowledging that Foucault did read the Panopticon as "the analysis of an 'evil eye' transformed into architecture," Shapiro contends that Foucault has "no arguments that vision is generally dangerous; he is an archaeologist of the visual, alert to the differential character of various visual regimes. And within the space of a certain epoch or culture, he is alert to disparate and possibly conflicting visual practices."[8] He finds in a wide variety of painters—Shapiro lists Manet, Kandinsky, Klee, Magritte, Warhol, Michals, and Fromanger—alternatives to the sinister scopic regime based on surveillance and the Panopticon. Foucault, Shapiro claims, took great pleasure in painting, whose materiality caused him to love it even more than literature. Like Nietzsche and Lyotard, he understood the vital role of images in the unconscious, which, *pace* Lacan, was not structured entirely like a language.

Whether or not Shapiro's characterization of my position is perfectly accurate is not something I want to dwell on now, although I should point out that I did cite and acknowledge Rajchman's argument that, for Foucault, seeing was "an art of trying to see what is unthought in our seeing, and to open as yet unseen ways of seeing."[9] I would agree that despite his lament about being trapped in the "empire of the gaze," Foucault did understand its powers to be limited. In all of his treatments of power, including the power of the eye to dominate what it viewed, Foucault did, after all, acknowledge the inevitability of resistance. But it was never resistance that could entirely topple the hegemonic power that prevailed, only prevent its full realization. In the case of the modern scopic regime, alternative visual practices did exist and might be nurtured, but they could not restore the full innocence of the eye.

My real question in this chapter concerns how Foucault understood the relationship between those alternative practices, which Shapiro and others have found benign or even emancipatory, and the issue of truth. The "will to truth" and its relation to the "will to power" was, of course, one of Foucault's perennial concerns, and he is often understood as following Nietzsche in providing us a powerful critique of the truth-claims of traditional philosophy. In his 1970 Collège de France course on "History of Systems of Thought," he spelled out the importance of the visual dimension of those traditional truth-claims, in for example the *Metaphysics* of Aristotle:

> Visual perception, defined as the sensation of multiple objects given simultaneously at a distance and as a sensation that has no immediate connection to the needs of the body, reveals the link between knowledge, pleasure, and truth in the satisfaction it generates through its proper action. At the other extreme, this same relationship is transposed in the pleasure of theoretical contemplation.[10]

Nietzsche, in contrast, had understood that selfish interest comes before knowledge and corporeal needs preceded truth claims based on visual perception.

Even earlier, in his 1963 appreciation of Bataille, "Preface to Transgression," Foucault had linked the tradition of speculative philosophy, or as he called it "the philosophy of reflection," with the subject created by the privileging of vision:

> Lying behind each eye that sees, there exists a more tenuous one, an eye so discreet and yet so agile that its all-powerful glance can be said to eat away

at the flesh of its white globe; behind this particular eye, there exists another and, then, still others, each progressively more subtle until we arrive at an eye whose entire substance is nothing but the transparency of its vision. This inner movement is finally resolved in a nonmaterial center where the intangible forms of truth are created and combined, in this heart of things which is the sovereign subject.[11]

It was Bataille's great achievement, Foucault insisted, to undermine the speculative philosophical grounding of truth in a subject produced by the fantasy of pure, immaterial vision, putting in its place a violently enucleated eye, an upturned eye that can no longer see at all. The result was to disentangle philosophy from its dependence on visual metaphors of clarity, transparency, and distinctness. According to Foucault's gloss on Bataille, "We do not experience the end of philosophy, but a philosophy which regains its speech and finds itself again only in the marginal region which borders its limits: that is, which finds itself either in a purified metalanguage or in the thickness of words enclosed by their darkness, by their blind truth."[12]

Because truth was blind, however, it could not claim to reflect a world of external realities that it adequately represented. In fact, the issue of truthfulness to the outside world had to be discarded as irrelevant. As Foucault put it in his 1977 interview "Truth and Power," "the problem does not consist in drawing the line between that in a discourse which falls under the category of scientificity or truth, and that which comes under some other category, but in seeing historically how effects of truth are produced within discourses which in themselves are neither true nor false."[13] That is, Foucault was interested less in establishing transcendental verification procedures than in examining the specific historical discursive systems that were the sources of the procedures themselves. Bracketing the obvious metaquestion of how he meant his own account of those historical shifts to be taken—as useful fictions or as accurate depictions of real changes—we can say that he always insisted that any truth claim must be contextualized in the discourse out of which it emerged. Or to put it in a somewhat different vocabulary, the issue was the priority of validity claims, how we establish intersubjective consensus, over reality claims, whether or not the consensus judgment corresponds to the state of the world.

In relation to the issue of visuality and veracity, two large questions can be asked. The first is, did Foucault understand certain discursive regimes to single out visually ascertained knowledge—the evidence of the eyes or of their prosthetic extensions—as a privileged source of valid knowledge? And if so, how did he evaluate them? Were they always to be contested rather than affirmed? And the second is, did Foucault himself ever argue that visuality could somehow do an end run around discursivity and provide a basis for a truth that was not merely an effect of a specific discursive regime. And if so, did it also escape the gravitational pull of the field of power in which it was immersed?

Answers to the first cluster of questions are not difficult to discern, for Foucault understood the transition to the modern world precisely in terms of an epochal shift from truth as a function of the right way to live—moral, self-controlling, even ascetic—to truth as the evidence of the external world on the senses, most notably sight. As he argued in his 1983 afterword to Hubert Dreyfus and Paul Rabinow's *Michel Foucault: Beyond Structuralism and Hermeneutics*, the assumption of a link between access to the truth and the ascetic life, which went back all the way to the Greeks, lasted only until the scientific revolution of the early modern period. It was Descartes who

> broke with this when he said "To accede to truth, it suffices that I be *any* subject which can see what is evident." Evidence is substituted for ascesis at the point where the relationship to the self intersects the relationship to others and the world. The relationship to the self no longer needs to be ascetic to get into relation to the truth. It suffices that the relationship to the self reveals to me the obvious truth of what I see for me to apprehend that truth definitively. Thus, I can be immoral and know the truth. . . . This change makes possible the institutionalization of modern science.[14]

That institutionalization was embodied in the creation of the Royal Society of London in 1660 (its official charter came two years later), whose motto was "nullius in verba"—in the words of no one.[15]

Significantly, at the same time as he was writing these remarks, Foucault was delivering the lectures at Berkeley that became known as *Fearless Speech*, in which he developed an analysis of the Greek notion of *parrhesia* or "frankness in speaking the truth."[16] Although not given a final vetting by Foucault himself before his death, the texts of these lectures reveal a great deal about his attitudes towards the issues at hand. The *parrhesiastes* is one who speaks the truth, or more precisely, he "says everything he has in mind: he does not hide anything, but opens his heart and mind completely to other people through his discourse."[17] Because the speaker is willing to expose his sincere beliefs no matter the social cost, the *parrhesiastes* is someone willing to take a risk, willing to speak truth to power, no matter the consequences. Foucault, in fact, goes so far as to say that there is always a power differential between the one who speaks his mind and the one who is the listener, perhaps even the object of the speaker's criticism. He summarizes his argument as follows:

> *Parrhesia* is a kind of verbal activity where the speaker has a specific relation to truth through frankness, a certain relationship to his own life through danger, a certain type of relation to himself or other people through criticism (self-criticism or criticism of other people), and a specific relation to moral law through freedom and duty. More precisely, *parrhesia* is a verbal activity in which a speaker expresses his personal relationship to truth, and risks his life because he recognizes truth-telling as a duty to improve or help other people (as well as himself).[18]

The rest of Foucault's lectures trace the fortunes of this concept in Greek politics, literature, and philosophy. His main point is that it migrated from a public concept as a guide to good citizenship in Athenian democracy into a more personal quality, a way to fashion a good life. Involving ascetic exercises—ascetic in the broad, pre-Christian sense of any kind of practical training—the latter version leads to what Foucault called an "aesthetics of the self." Working out its implications occupied him in his last works in his series on *The History of Sexuality*, *The Use of Pleasure* and *The Care of the Self*.[19] Concerning the issue of truth, it allowed him to make a crucial distinction between what he called the tradition in Western philosophy of an "analytics of truth" and a "critical" tradition.[20] Whereas the former was concerned with veridical statements about the world, the latter focused on the practice of truth-telling, of "veridiction."

Throughout his work, it was Foucault's hope to write a genealogy of truth-telling, validity claims, rather than the analytics of truth, veridical statements about reality. As he put it in one of his last interviews, "while historians of science in France were interested essentially in the problem of how a scientific object is constituted, the question I asked myself was this: How is it that the human subject took itself as the object of possible knowledge? Through what forms of rationality and historical conditions? And finally, *at what price?* This is my question: At what price can subjects speak the truth about themselves?"[21] The stakes of all this were clearly personal for Foucault himself as a political and cultural activist. As Didier Eribon, one of his most insightful biographers, has noted, Foucault came to understand that, "if one wants to be credible and effective, one must first know, and above all *speak*, the truth. Speaking-the-truth, *véridiction*, has to be the founding principle of any journalism of intervention."[22]

In *Fearless Speech*, Foucault once again made the distinction I cited earlier from his afterword to Dreyfus and Rabinow's book between Cartesian notions of truth based on clear and distinct ideas of an external world and the *parrhesiast* tradition of claiming validity via personal qualities: "Since Descartes, the coincidence between belief and truth is obtained in a certain (mental) evidential experience. For the Greeks, however, the coincidence between belief and truth does not take place in a (mental) experience, but in a *verbal activity*, namely, *parrhesia*. It appears that *parrhesia*, in this Greek sense, can no longer occur in our modern epistemological framework."[23] The implication of all this, I would submit, is that there is a radical rupture between a regime of truth based on the allegedly disinterested evidence of the eyes and one grounded in the sincerity of the speaker. In the modern scientific era, Foucault claimed with unconcealed dislike, "the breadth of the experiment seems to be identified with the domain of the careful gaze, and of an empirical vigilance receptive only to the evidence of visible contents. The eye becomes the depositary and source of clarity; it has the power to bring a truth to light that it receives only to the extent that it has brought it to light; as it opens, the eye first opens the truth."[24]

Recent research—I am thinking in particular of the work of the sociologist of science Steven Shapin in *A Social History of Truth*[25]—has shown that this idea of a complete rupture between the premodern and modern scientific regimes of truth is in fact exaggerated. Examining the discursive regime supporting the scientific community in seventeenth-century Britain epitomized by the chemist Robert Boyle, Shapin shows that it relied heavily on trusting in the truth-telling virtues of certain types of people, in particular Christian gentlemen whose word was taken to be honest and disinterested. Although the ideology of the new science was to question authority and distrust textual in favor of direct sensual testimony, in practice it also respected the civil conversation of those with the cultural capital to engage in the language game of science. In other words, the earlier reliance on *parrhesia* survived well into the era when Foucault thought it had been replaced by a disembodied and disinterested knowledge based on the unimpeachable testimony of the senses and instruments alone. "Nullius in verba" was an ideal never fully realized.

Be that as it may, it is clear that Foucault had little sympathy with the latter ideology, especially when it privileged visual evidence, which is of a piece with the types of suspicion of panoptical surveillance and the scientific gaze he developed in other contexts in his writing. As we have noted, he eschewed pursuing a history of the "analytics of truth" for a critical examination of the legitimating underpinnings of truth-telling. That there is a political dimension to all of this is evident in his oft-cited remark in *The Birth of the Clinic* on the French Revolution: "The ideological theme that guides all structural reforms from 1789 to Thermidor Year II is that of the sovereign liberty of truth; the majestic violence of light, which is itself supreme, brings to an end the bounded, dark kingdom of privileged knowledge and establishes the unimpeded empire of the gaze."[26]

Lest there be any doubt that he linked the hegemony of the eye with violence, even in nonpolitical contexts, he added that "the clinician's gaze becomes the functional equivalent of fire in chemical combustion; it is through it that the essential purity of phenomena can emerge; it is the separating agent of truth. . . . The clinical gaze is a gaze that burns things to their furthest truth."[27]

We can now answer our first set of questions—did Foucault understand certain discursive regimes to single out visually ascertained knowledge, the evidence of the eyes or of their prosthetic extensions, as a privileged source of valid knowledge? And if so, how did he evaluate them?—in the following manner. Yes, he did identify certain discursive regimes as privileging visuality as the source of truth, those, for instance, exemplified by Aristotle and Descartes. The modern scientific episteme was based on a belief in the testimony of the senses, most notably vision, rather than the veracity of witnesses. Whether or not he was entirely right in that identification, after we acknowledge the lessons of Shapin's *A Social History of Truth*, is another question, but that he held it cannot be doubted. And when it came to evaluate the modern scientific episteme, he had no hesitation in seeing it as deeply problematic, both epistemologically and politically. These judgments may, to be sure, not be equivalent to denigrating vision as such, but rather only its mobilization in a specific discursive regime. Even if that regime were dominant for most of Western history, it would be wrong to conclude that Foucault thought no other alternative was possible.

This raises our second main question: Did Foucault himself ever argue that visuality could somehow do an end run around discursivity and provide a basis for a truth that was not merely an effect of a specific discursive regime. And if so, did it also escape the gravitational pull of the field of power in which it was immersed? Here we would have to examine the candidates for alternative modes of visual experience and see if they can be said to abet a kind of truth-telling—call it visual *parrhesia*—or perhaps better put, truth-showing.

In his insightful study of Foucault, Gilles Deleuze noted that his friend's hostility to phenomenology meant that he understood the primacy of discursive systems over different modes of visuality or perception. But he added that for Foucault, "the primacy of statements will never impede the historical irreducibility of the visible—quite the contrary. The statement has primacy only because the visible has its own laws, an autonomy that links it to the dominant, the heautonomy of the statement."[28] Whereas the statement is characterized by "spontaneity," which implies human action and will, the visible is determined by "receptivity," which suggests a certain measure of passivity.

In his gloss on this claim, Gary Shapiro argues that "Deleuze suggests a rather Kantian reading of their relations, in which statements play the role of concepts and the visible plays the role of intuition."[29] But to the extent that intuition implies something that is immediate and prior to cultural construction, this interpretation seems to me questionable. As Deleuze notes, "if no original, free and savage experience lies beneath knowledge, as phenomenology would have it, it is because Seeing and Speaking are always already completely caught up within power relations which they presuppose and actualize."[30] That is, we live in a world of "Light and Language, two vast environments of exteriority where visibilities and statements are respectively deposited."[31] Because they are external to our biological perceptual apparatus, they always mediate any pure visual experience, precluding a recovery of an "innocent eye."

These environments, to be sure, are never reconcilable into one unified system, one totalitarian episteme without any internal tension. As a result, discursive regimes can be tacitly challenged and even explicitly resisted by their visual counterparts and vice versa. In much of the literature on Foucault stressing his suspicion of visuality, including my own account, the directionality of this mutual contestation is skewed in favor of language disrupting visuality. Thus, for example, Michel de Certeau in his important essay "Micro-techniques and Panoptic Discourse: A Quid Pro Quo" contended that in *Discipline and Punish*, Foucault had foregrounded three dominant optical figures—representational tableaux, analytical tableaux and figurative tableaux—in his attempt to show how the machinery of modern normalization and discipline functioned. Although apparently clear, transparent, and self-evident, these optical figures were in fact subverted by the way in which Foucault presented them: "The optical space is the frame of an internal transformation due to its rhetorical reemployment. It becomes a façade, the theoretical ruse of a narrative. While the book analyzes the transformation of Enlightenment ideologies by a panoptical machinery, its writing is a subversion of our contemporary panoptical conceptions by the rhetorical techniques of narrative."[32] That is, narrative somehow works to challenge the power of the hegemonic power of the regime of surveillance symbolized by Bentham's infernal machine. Or to put it in another way, truth-telling via story-telling trumps the deceptive and manipulative power of the gaze.

Shapiro rightly draws our attention to the ways in which Foucault could also mobilize subversive scopic practices to destabilize hegemonic regimes of either discourse or visibility, although he has to do so largely by juxtaposing different texts in Foucault's *oeuvre*. He contrasts, for example, Foucault's unfinished work on the painter Manet, abandoned in 1968, with the influential description of the Panopticon in *Discipline and Punish*, written around the same time. In a section of his book entitled "Shutters and Mirrors: Manet Closes the Panopticon Window," Shapiro writes: "In the Panopticon the gaze is mobilized and fixed on each individual; it is a floating or functional gaze that need not appear as the look of anyone in particular. In Manet looks meet no object, no person, even though we see their source. What we see, then, is an eye disconnected from a content of vision."[33]

By stressing the flat canvas against the ideal of an open window on the world, Manet disrupts the traditional perspectivalist visual regime of Western painting. Borrowing explicitly from Derrida's analysis in *The Truth in Painting*, to which we have alluded earlier, Shapiro characterizes Foucault's conclusion in the following way: "Manet, then, has brought the frame into the work; the *parergon* has become the *ergon*. And the frame's function is not to make an interior visible, as in the Panopticon, but to produce an uncanny space in which figures hover between life and death."[34]

But if Manet disconnects the eye from the content of vision and introduces the undecidability of the *ergon* and *parergon* into the uncanny space of the modernist canvas, can we claim that he is offering us a variety of visual *parrhesia*, of truth-showing rather than truth-telling? Clearly, Foucault intended his analysis of Manet, and here I would agree with Shapiro, to disrupt the problematic and perhaps even ideological—if we can apply the vocabulary of ideology critique about which Foucault had his doubts—scopic regime of what I have called elsewhere "Cartesian perspectivalism."[35] But is it disruption of a false system in the service of defending a truer one, either in terms of truth as epistemological adequation to a real world or truth as a function of the legitimate truth-teller? Are Manet's canvases able to provide what Cezanne promised his friend, the truth in painting?

Foucault's examination of René Magritte's *This Is Not a Pipe* provides us with more evidence to address this question. In that remarkable and much discussed little book, Foucault calls Magritte's painting an "unraveled calligram," thwarting the time-honored desire of the calligram to combine words and images in a single, isotropic meaning. But even though in tension, the image and text in this painting are not, strictly speaking, in contradiction because contradictions are only between two statements in language. Moreover, the image of the pipe above the words "ceci n'est pas une pipe" cannot contradict the words because what the canvas shows is not a real pipe, but only a drawing of one. "What misleads us," Foucault concludes, "is the inevitability of connecting the text to the drawing (as the demonstrative pronoun, the meaning of the word *pipe*, and the likeness of the image all invites us to do here)—and the impossibility of defining a perspective that would let us say that the assertion is true, false, or contradictory."[36]

We are no longer in the realm of painting based on resemblance to the world of external objects seen through a window-like canvas—Foucault says "we are farthest from trompe-l'oeil"[37]—and therefore we have left behind the visually privileged episteme associated with Cartesian perspectivalism. This is clearly not a painting based on mimetic representation of an object realm on the other side of the window. But we have not entered an alternative scopic regime that can be understood as the visual equivalent of *parrhesia*, for Magritte has given us a series of similitudes without any objective correlative. "Resemblance predicated itself upon a model it must return to and reveal; similitude circulates the simulacrum as an indefinite and reversible relation of the similar to the similar."[38] What we get in a Magritte painting is the infinite play of transferences and metamorphoses that represent nothing outside of themselves, that reveal a decomposed calligram with no hope of bringing discourse and figure together into a meaningful whole.

What Manet and Magritte—as well as other artists admired by Foucault like Warhol or Gerard Fromanger—do is undermine the pretension to tell the truth in the hegemonic tradition of Western painting based on mimesis, resemblance, and representation. As Foucault puts it in the passage from *This Is Not a Pipe* cited above, they demonstrate "the impossibility of defining a perspective that would let us *say* that the assertion is true, false, or contradictory." But what they do not do, I would argue in conclusion, is replace truth-telling with an alternative way of *truth-showing* that corresponds to the *parrhesia* Foucault admired in the Greeks and sought to emulate in his own activity as a public intellectual.

Gary Shapiro may be right when he argues that "Foucault's iconophilia is part of a general project of finding ways for the enjoyment of 'bodies and pleasures,' despite the disciplinary regimes to which they have been subjected, even the disciplinary regimes of socially established taste and criticism."[39] But merely enjoying bodily pleasure is not the same as practicing the ascesis—in Foucault's broad definition of it as aesthetic self-fashioning—which underlies the *parrhesiastes*' courageous willingness to say truth to power. Shapiro himself inadvertently acknowledges this difference when he defends Foucault against critics who charge he misunderstood Velazquez's *Las Meninas* in *The Order of Things*, by claiming it was a mistake to assume that "he intended to 'get it right,' to deliver the truth about the painting to us in words."[40] Instead, Foucault's effort is directed at denying the possibility of our ever saying precisely the equivalent of what we are seeing.

There are ways, I would agree, in which resistance to power may take visual forms, but these are understood by Foucault in largely negative terms, as disturbances in the hegemonic visuality of an era, like Manet's challenge to traditional perspectivalist painting. They rarely, if ever, translate into positive expressions of another visual order that comes closer to a truth grounded in a form of life, a critical practice whose effects Foucault came to value, both theoretically and in his own life as a deeply engaged intellectual. This restriction of the visual to disrupting hegemonic visualities may not be equivalent to the denigration of all visual experience, but it is a far cry from the positing of a fully healthy alternative, for there is no veridiction of the eye, no intuitive apprehension of the world through sense immediacy. In short, there is no visual *parrhesia* for Michel Foucault, who, like Derrida, would have warned Cezanne that his obligation to tell his friend the truth about painting would be a debt left perpetually unpaid.

PART II

Rhetoric and the Future of the Political

CHAPTER 4

Articulation and the Limits of Metaphor
Ernesto Laclau

I

In a well-known essay, Gérard Genette discusses the question of the interdependence between metaphor and metonymy in the structuration of Proust's narrative.[1] Following the pathbreaking work of Stephen Ullmann,[2] he shows how, on top of the central role traditionally granted to metaphor in Proust's work, there are other semantic movements of a typical metonymic nature whose presence is, however, necessary for metaphor to succeed in its figural effects. A hypallage such as *"sécheresse brune des cheveux"* [the brown dryness of hair[3]]—instead of *"sécheresse des cheveux bruns"* [the dryness of brown hair]—would be a typical example of such metonymical displacements. Genette, however, insists from the very beginning that it is not a simple question of recognizing the coexistence of both metaphor and metonymy in the Proustian text, but of showing how they require each other: how without the one shading into the other, neither of them could play the specific role that is expected from them in the constitution of a narrative economy. In his words, "far from being antagonistic and incompatible, metaphor and metonymy sustain and interpenetrate each other, and to give its proper place to the second will not consist in drawing a concurrent list opposed to that of metaphors, but rather in showing the relations of 'coexistence' within the relation of analogy itself: the role of metonymy within metaphor."[4]

Genette gives several examples of such interconnection. Thus, he refers to the numerous cases in which "bell tower" (*clocher*) is metaphorically (analogically) related to "ear [of wheat or corn]" (*épis*), or to "fish," depending on the environment of the church—rural in the first case, and maritime in the second. This means that the spatial relation of contiguity is the source of metaphoric analogical effects: "Ear–bell tower" (*meule–église* [literally: haystack–church]) in the middle of the fields, "fish–bell tower" near the sea, "purple–bell tower" over the vineyards, "*brioche*–bell tower" at the time of the sweets, "pillow–bell tower" at the beginning of the night—there is clearly in Proust a recurrent, almost stereotyped stylistic scheme, which one could call chameleon–bell tower (*caméléon–clocher*). Thus, there is a sort of resemblance by contagion. The metaphor finds its support in a metonymy. Quoting Jean Ricardou, Genette enounces the principle, "qui se ressemble s'assemble (et réciproquement)."[5]

Many more examples of this essential solidarity between contiguity and analogy are given: that between autochthonous dishes and *vin de pays*; between paintings and their geographical framework; between the desire for pheasants and their rural milieu; between relatives; between images succeeding each other in diegetic metaphors; between landscapes and their reflection in the windows of a library, etc. In all these cases we see that, without the mutual implication between metaphor and metonymy, it would be impossible to ensure the unity of a discursive space. Proust himself was only partially aware of this mutual implication and tended to privilege its metaphorical side. As Genette says,

> The indestructible solidarity of writing, whose magic formula Proust seems to be looking for ("only metaphor can give a sort of *eternity* to style," he will say in his article on Flaubert) cannot only result from the horizontal link established by the metonymical trajectory; but one cannot see how could it result from just the vertical link of the metaphoric relation either. Only the crossing of one by the other can subtract the object of the description, and the description itself from "time's contingencies," that is, from all contingency; only the mutual crossing of a metonymic net and a metaphoric chain ensures the coherence, the necessary cohesion of *text*.[6]

Let us see how this crossing takes place. Central to it is the structure of "involuntary memory." Apparently we have, in the mechanism of reminiscence, the case of a pure metaphor, devoid of any metonymic contamination (the taste of the Madeleine, the position of the foot on the uneven pavement, etc.). But the punctual character of that analogical memory is immediately overflown. As Genette shows, it is only retroactively that the analysis finds that reminiscence starts from an analogy that it would isolate as its "cause." "In fact, the real experience begins, not by grasping an identity of sensation, but by a feeling of 'pleasure' of 'happiness,' which first appears without the notion of its cause."[7] Although the examples in *Du Côté de chez Swann* and in *Le Temps Rétrouvé* differ in their unfolding, the essential point is, in both cases, that the chain of reminiscences goes, in a metonymic way, far beyond the original analogy (in *Swann*, the cup leads to the reminiscence of the room, from the room to the house, then to the village and from there to the whole region). "The essential here is to note that this first explosion [the analogic detonator] is always accompanied also and necessarily, by a kind of chain reaction which proceeds, not by analogy but by contiguity, and which is very precisely the moment in which the metonymic contagion (or, to use Proust's term, the *irradiation*) substitutes the metaphoric evocation."[8]

For Genette, it is this crossing between metaphor and metonymy that ensures that there is a narrative. If we had only had the metaphoric dimension, *A la recherché du temps perdu* would not have been a novel but a succession of lyrical moments without any temporal chaining. So he concludes, "Without metaphor Proust (approximately) says, there are no true memories; we add for him (and for everybody): without metonymy, there is no chaining of memories, no *history*, no novel. For it is metaphor that retrieves lost Time, but it is metonymy which reanimates it, that puts it back in movement, which returns it to itself and to its true 'essence,' which is its own escape and its own Search. So here, only here—through metaphor but *within* metonymy—it is here that the Narrative (*Récit*) begins."[9]

A few remarks before taking leave of Genette. He has illuminated very well the relation of mutual implication between metaphor and metonymy that alone creates the unity of the text. That mutual implication has, thus, *totalizing* effects. He quotes, for example, the following passage from Proust:

> Je me jetais sur mon lit; et, comme si j'avais été sur la chouchette d'un de ces bateaux que je voyais assez près de moi et que la nuit on s'étonnerer de voir se déplacer lentement dans l'obscurité, comme des cygnes assombris et silentieux mais qui ne dorment pas, j'étais entouré de tous côtés des images de la mer.[10]
>
> [I threw myself on my bed and, as if I were on the bunk of one of those boats that I used to see quite near to me, and that in the night one is surprised to see drift slowly into darkness, like the somber and silent swans who do not sleep, I was surrounded on all sides by images of the sea.[11]]

And Genette comments, "One remarks here the explicit concurrence of the metaphoric relation (*comme si* [as if]) and of the metonymic one (*près de moi* [next to]); and the second metaphor is also itself metonymic, grafted into the first (*navires* = *cygnes* [ship = swan])."[12]

The question that remains to be posed, however, is that concerning the kind of unity that the articulation metaphor/metonymy manages to constitute. Granting—as I think it should be—that such a unity is vital to the coherence of a text, there are several possibilities as to how to conceive the interaction between these two dimensions. Genette does not, certainly, suggest that such an interaction should be conceived as the adjustment of the pieces of a clockwork mechanism, and the very terms that he uses (*recoupement, croisée* [crossed]) suggest that he has something considerably more complex in mind. He does not, however, advance very much in determining the specific nature of that *recoupement*, largely, I think, because his main concern is to show the *presence* of both tropes in the Proustian text. Discussing Jakobson's distinction between metonymy as the prosaic dimension of discourse and metaphor as the poetic one, he asserts that "one should consider Proustian writing as the most extreme tentative step towards this mixed stage, fully assuming and activating the two axes of language, which it would certainly be laughable to call 'poem in prose' or 'poetic prose,' and which constitute, absolutely and in the full sense of the term, the Text."[13] For the issues that we are going to discuss in this essay, it is crucial to determine precisely the logics involved in the articulation of the axes of that "mixed stage."

2

Genette is clearly conscious that his use of the categories "metaphor" and "metonymy" is somewhat idiosyncratic, for it goes beyond what canonical rhetoric would have ascribed to them. There is in Proust, for instance, a marked preference for "continuous metaphors" (*metaphores suivies*). "There are very rare in his work those fulgurant rapprochements suggested by a single word, the only ones for which classical rhetoric reserved the name metaphor."[14] In many cases the analogical comparisons take place in a continuous way, occupying several pages of the text. But also, it could seem abusive to call metonymy a contiguity of memories that does not involve any relation of substitution. However, as Genette points out,

> it is the nature of the semantic relation that is at stake, and not the form of the figure.... Proust himself has given an example of such an abuse by calling metaphor a figure that, in his work, is most frequently a comparison explicit

and without substitution, so that the effects of contagion to which we have referred are nearly the equivalent, on the axis of contiguity, of what Proustian metaphors are in the axis of analogy—and are, in relation to metonymy *stricto sensu*, what Proustian metaphors are vis-à-vis classical metaphors.... The signal-sensation becomes very quickly in Proust a sort of *equivalent* of the context to which it is associated, as the "*petite phrase*" of the Vinteuil has become, for Swann and Odette, "as the national air of their love": that is, its emblem.[15]

This passage is crucial. Genette speaks, on the one hand, of an "abusive" use of rhetorical categories, but, on the other, he describes such an abuse as a transgression involving a movement from the *form* of the figure to a *semantic* relation that, while implicit in that form, goes clearly beyond those formed limits. So the following questions arise:

1. If the semantic relations underlying both metaphor and metonymy transcend their rhetorical form, are not those relations anchored in signification as such, beyond classical rhetorical limits, or, alternatively, could not signification be seen as a generalized rhetoric—i.e., that "rhetoricity" could be seen not as an abuse but as constitutive (in the transcendental sense) of signification?

2. In that case, is it enough to conceive of that "beyond the rhetorical form" as simply "semantic"—or that would necessarily attach it to the level of the signified? Would not the relationship signifier/signified involve a dialectic that takes us beyond semantics, to a materiality of the signifier that inscribes rhetorical displacements in the very structure of the sign? (Let us think in Freud's "verbal bridges.")

3. Why are those displacements rhetorical in nature—i.e., dominated by the basic opposition metaphor/metonymy?

4. How to conceive of that opposition? Does it involve a relation of complementarity or, rather, a mutual limitation of their effects, so that metonymy establishes the limits of metaphor and vice versa?

One way of dealing with these questions would be to turn our attention to a theoretical approach that explicitly tries to link rhetorical categories to the structural dimensions of signification as such. I am referring to the famous essay by Roman Jakobson, "Two Aspects of Language and Two Types of Aphasic Disturbances."[16] Jakobson's starting point is that aphasia, being a disturbance in language use, "must begin with the question of what aspects of language are impaired in the various species of such a disorder"; such interrogation could not be answered "without the participation of professional linguists familiar with the patterning and functioning of language."[17]

As Jakobson points out, any linguistic sign presupposes its arrangement through two different operations: *combination and contexture*, by which the sign gets its location, in accordance with syntactic rules, in an orderly succession with other signs; and *selection and substitution*, by which a sign can be replaced by others in any given structural location. This distinction corresponds to the two axes of language identified by Saussure: the syntagmatic and the paradigmatic (which he called associative). Combination and substitution were, for Saussure, the only two kinds of operation regulating the relations between signs. Starting from these two dimensions, Jakobson identifies two aphasic disturbances. The first, *similarity disorder*, is related to the impossibility of substituting terms, while the ability of combining them remains unimpaired; in the second—*contiguity disorder*—that ability to combine words is what is affected. Quite apart from aphasic disorders there is, according to Jakobson, a propensity in each language user to primordially rely on one or the other pole of language.

> In a well known psychological test, children are confronted with some noun and told to utter the first verbal response that comes into their heads. In this experiment two opposite linguistic predilections are invariably exhibited: the response is intended either as a substitute for, or as a complement to, the stimulus. . . . To the stimulus *hut* one response was *burnt out*; another, *is a poor little house*. Both reactions are predicative; but the first creates a purely narrative context, while in the second there is a double connection with the subject *hut*: on the one hand, a positional (namely, syntactic) contiguity, and on the other a semantic similarity.[18]

From these two axes of language—the paradigmatic and the syntagmatic, substitution and combination—Jakobson moves to the rhetorical field: Metonymy would correspond to combination and metaphor to substitution. And this alternative is not purely regional, but regulates human behavior as a whole: "In manipulating these two kinds of connection (similarity and contiguity) in both their aspects (positional and semantic)—selecting, combining and ranking them—an individual exhibits his personal style, his verbal predilections and preferences."[19] "The bipolar structure of language (or other semiotic systems) and, in aphasia, the fixation of one of these two poles to the exclusion of the other, require systematic comparative study. The retention of either of these alternatives in the two types of aphasia must be confronted with the predominance of the same pole in certain styles, personal habits, current fashions, etc."[20] This argument is, for Jakobson at the basis of a wider cultural interpretation. In verbal art, we have that in poetry: Lyric privileges the metaphorical axis, as in romanticism and symbolism. In realist art, whose epitome is the novel, metonymic displacements prevail. We have here again, in different terms, the argument that we had already found in Genette: Proust's major work is a novel and not a paratactic succession of lyrical moments because metaphors are grounded in metonymic connections. For Jakobson, this alternative applies equally to non-verbal art: In cubism, the succession of synecdoches is essentially metonymic, while in surrealism the quasi-allegorical images lean towards metaphor. And, in film, the plurality of angles and close-ups in Griffith's production is metonymic in nature, while in Charlie Chaplin and Eisenstein a metaphoric substitution of images structures the narrative. Indeed, any semiotic system can, for Jakobson, be understood in terms of the metaphoric/metonymic alternative.

The great merit of Jakobson's analysis is to have brought rhetorical categories to their specific location within linguistic structure, that is, to have shown that it is the latter that is at the root of all figural movements. Metaphor and metonymy, in that sense, are not just some figures among many, but the two fundamental matrices around which all other figures and tropes should be ordered. So the classification of rhetorical figures ceases to be a heteroclite enumeration of forms and presents a clear structure anchored in the figures' dependence on the fundamental dimensions of language. The transition from these dimensions to their specific rhetorical investment requires, however, some further considerations that I will summarize in the next few pages.

1. There is, in the first place, the question of the transition from the axis of combination—the syntagmatic dimension—to metonymy. Because, although a tropological movement along that dimension can only be conceived in metonymical terms, there is nothing in combination, considered in isolation, requiring that such a movement should take place. One can perfectly imagine a combination of terms following syntactic rules that would not involve any metonymic displacement. There is a zero-degree of the tropological as far as combination is concerned. I can perfectly say "*sécheresse des cheveux bruns*" instead of "*sécheresse brune des cheveux.*" If so, the figural would be something added to signification from outside, not an integral part of signification, and we would be back to the classical vision of the rhetorical as an adornment of language. So, if we want to establish a more intimate connection between tropes and signification, we have to find a way of undermining the very possibility of a rhetorically neutral zero-degree.

2. This way is quickly found once we move from "combination" to the second axis: "substitution/selection." For here, on the difference with the

axis of combination, there is no zero-degree: Substitution (again, considered in isolation) is not submitted to any a priori syntactic rule. Saussure himself says it, "While a syntagm immediately calls the idea of an order of succession and of a determinate number of elements, the terms of an associative family do not present themselves in either a definite number or in a determinate order."[21] So the axis of substitution, *which is also constitutive of language*, subverts the very principle of structural locations on which the syntagmatic succession is grounded. Saussure's diagram of the ensemble of possibilities opened by substitution (see Figure 4-1) is most revealing.

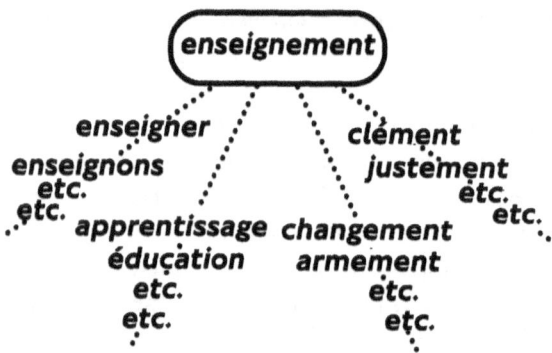

Figure 4-1

One of these possibilities is particularly important for our argument: the impossibility of confining substitution (and, as a result, tropological transgression) to the order of the signified. Saussure asserts, "There is either double community of sense and form, or community of only either sense or form. Any word can evoke anything susceptible of being associated with it one way or another."[22] This is why we asserted before that the "beyond the rhetorical form" cannot be confined to *semantic* associations. One possibility is that rhetorical movements do not only take place at the level of the signified but also at that of the signifier. (In Freud's "rat man," there is displacement from "rat" to *Spielratten*; gambling, and thus the father, a gambler, is incorporated into the "rat complex.")

3. Where do these considerations leave us as far as the relationship metaphor/metonymy is concerned? The main conclusion is that the notions of "analogy" and "contiguity" that are, respectively, the defining grounds of the two tropes, far from being entirely different in nature,

tend, on the contrary, to shade one into the other. Why so? Because both of them are transgressions of the same principle, which is the differential logic associated with the syntagmatic axis of the signifying system. The only distinction that is possible to establish between both figures is that, in the case of metonymy, the transgression of the structural locations that define the relations of combination is fully visible, while in metaphor, analogy entirely ignores those structural differentiations—associations, as Saussure shows, can move in the most different directions. In one sense it can be said that metaphor is the *telos* of metonymy, the moment in which transgression of the rules of combination has reached its point of no return: a new entity has come into existence that makes us forget the transgressive practices on which it is grounded. But without those transgressive practices that are essentially metonymic, the new metaphoric entity could not have emerged. As Genette shows in the case of Proust, analogy is always grounded in an originary contiguity.

We can draw here a conclusion that will be important for our political analysis: Contiguity and analogy are not essentially different from each other, but are two poles of a continuum. Let us give an example, which I have discussed elsewhere.[23] Let us suppose that there is a neighborhood where there is racist violence and the only force capable of confronting it in that area is the trade unions. We would think that, normally, opposing racism is not the natural task of trade unions, and that if it is taken up by them in that place, it is by a contingent constellation of social forces. That is, that such a "taking up" derives from a relation of contiguity—i.e., that its nature is metonymic. Let us, however, think that this "taking up" continues for a long period of time—in that case, people would get accustomed to it and would tend to think that it is a normal part of trade union practices. So what was a case of contingent articulation becomes a part of the central meaning of the term "trade union"—"contiguity" shades into "analogy," "metonymy" into "metaphor." Anticipating what we will discuss presently, we can say that this is inherent to the central political operation that we call "hegemony": the movement from metonymy to metaphor, from *contingent* articulation to *essential* belonging. The name—of a social movement, of an ideology, of a political institution—is always the metaphorical crystallization of contents whose analogical links result from concealing the contingent contiguity of their metonymical origins. Conversely, the dissolution of a hegemonic formation involves the reactivation of that contingency: the return from a "sublime" metaphoric fixation to a humble metonymic association.

4. With this conclusion, however, we have only established: a) that the metaphoric/metonymic distinction has a matricial priority over other tropes—which it is possible, one way or the other, to reduce to that matrix; and b) that such a matricial distinction does not simply refer to opposites but to the two poles of a continuum. But to assert that rhetoricity is inherent to signification requires one more step: to show that without a tropological displacement signification could not find its own ground. I have tried to prove this point elsewhere and I will not repeat it here.[24] Let us just say that this proof requires showing that signification, to be possible, requires its own closure, and that such a closure, because it involves the representation of an object that is both impossible and necessary, leads to the discursive production of empty signifiers. An empty signifier, as I have tried to show, is not just a signifier without a signified—which, as such, would be outside signification—but one signifying the blind spot inherent to signification, the point where signification finds its own limits and which, however, if it is going to be possible at all, has to be represented as the meaningless precondition of meaning. In psychoanalytic terms, it would be the moment of the Real—the moment of distortion of the Symbolic, which is the precondition for the symbolic to constitute itself as totality. Now, if the representation of something irrepresentable is the very condition of representation as such, this means that the (distorted) representation of this condition involves a *substitution*, that is, it can only be tropological in nature. And it is not a substitution to be conceived as a replacement of positive terms: It will involve giving a name to something that is essentially "nameless," to an empty place. That is what gives its centrality to *catachresis*. And as any figural movement involves saying something more than what can be said through a literal term, catachresis is inherent to the figural as such; it becomes the trademark of "rhetoricity" as such.

5. Let us go back, at this point, to the question of the ground of the metaphoric/metonymic continuum. Such a ground is given, as we have indicated, by the opposition of *any* tropological movement to the differential logic of combination inherent in the syntagmatic pole of signification. The difference between analogy and contiguity is that although both, through their substitutions, subvert such a differential logic, the visibility of what is subverted is very much present in the case of metonymy, while it tends to disappear in the case of metaphor. But if this subversion of combinatorial locations is inherent to rhetoricity, and rhetoricity is one of the dimensions of signification, this means that the latter can only be conceived as an endless process of successive institutions and subversions of different locations. That is why structuralism of

strict observance has always tended to emphasize the syntagmatic pole of language at the expense of the paradigmatic one. But the ambiguity created by the operation of the two opposed logics of combination and substitution did not go entirely unnoticed, even in the work of Saussure. As Joan Copjec has pointed out,

> Emphasizing the "synchronic perspective" of the linguist and his community, Saussure eventually decided to give priority to the contemporaneous system of signifiers operating at some (hypothetical) frozen moment: the present. Forgetting for his own purposes his important stipulation that meaning must be determined retroactively, that is, forgetting the diachronic nature of meaning, he ultimately founded the science of linguistics on the systematic totality of language. Thus, the structuralist argument ceased to be that the final signifier S_2 determines that which has come before S_1, and becomes instead: S_2 determines S_1 *and* S_1 determines S_2; that is, reciprocal oppositions stabilize meanings between coexistent terms and differential relations no longer threaten the transvaluation of all preceding signifiers.[25]

If we incorporate, however, the diachronic perspective that Saussure himself enounced but forgot about, the consequence is clear: S_2 can be the ground of the system only as far as it does not have a precise, particular location within it. The same argument can be presented in terms of set theory: What names the set cannot be part of it. What the rhetorical turn would add to this argument is that the term naming the set would be one of the particular elements of that set that splits its own identity between its own particularity and its role of signifying the totality. It is this double role that is at the root of all tropological displacement.

6. Rhetoricity, as a dimension of signification, has no limits in its field of operation. It is co-terminous with the very structure of objectivity. This is, first of all, connected with the notion of "discourse" that we have used in our work, which is not exclusively or primarily linked to speech or writing, but to any signifying practice. This entails that it is equivalent to the social production of meaning, that is, to the very fabric of social life. There is no possibility of any strict separation between signification and action. Even the most purely constative of assertions has a performative dimension, and, conversely, there is no action that is not embedded in signification. For the same reason, there cannot be any stark separation between signification and affect, given that the latter is only constituted through differentially cathecting the various components of a signifying chain. As in Wittgenstein's "language games," words and actions (to which we should add affects), are part of an interdependent network.

This means that linguistic categories such as the signifier/signified and syntagm/paradigm distinctions—if properly theorized—cease to belong to a regional discipline and come to define relations operating in the very terrain of a general ontology.

But, secondly, if signification could close itself in syntagmatic terms—i.e., if paradigmatic relations of substitution could themselves be reabsorbed by combinatorial rules—the role of rhetoric could not be ontologically constitutive. The structuralist closure of the relation of mutual determination between S_1 and S_2 could be achieved without any tropological device being brought into the picture, and so rhetoric would be relegated to its traditional role as adornment of language. But it is here that our remarks concerning the impossibility of achieving any closure of a signifying system without representing the irrepresentable become relevant. Once the centrality of catachresis is fully accepted, rhetoricity becomes a condition of signification and, as a result, of objectivity.

Thirdly, once the status of rhetoric has been recognized in its true ontological generality, relations that in this essay we have approached within a strictly tropological terminology are likely to be reproduced at different levels of analysis of human reality, even when the rhetorical nature of the distinction introduced is not perceived or recognized. In psychoanalysis, to give the most obvious example, the rhetorical character of the workings of the unconscious has been explicitly recognized a long time ago. Condensation has been assimilated to metaphor and displacement to metonymy. The logic of the object *a* involves precisely an investment by which an ordinary object becomes a substitute for the unreachable Thing. In Lacan's terms, sublimation is to elevate an object to the dignity of the Thing. This operation of investment is catachrestical through and through. And Copjec, in her film studies, has shown how the close-ups are not a part within the whole, but a part that functions as the very condition of the whole, as its name, leading to that contamination between particularity and totality that, as we have seen, is at the heart of all tropological movement.

In the rest of this essay, I will try to show the operation of those distinctions that we have been discussing within the political field. I will argue that those tensions that we have detected along the continuum metaphor/metonymy, can be seen as fully operating in the structuration of political spaces. I will discuss two cases. In the first, we will see an almost complete unilateralization of the metaphoric operation; in the second, a systematic blockage of the transition from metonymy to metaphor—i.e., the prevention that contiguity shades into analogy. The first possibility I will illustrate with the logic of the general strike in Sorel; the second, with the political strategy of Leninism.

3

We have to give some precise theoretical status to the operation in which we engage ourselves when trying to see the way rhetorical categories are (implicitly) present in those logics governing the distinctions that structure areas different from those in which rhetoric was originally thought to be operative. We should basically avoid two temptations. The first is to make of rhetorical categories the locus of a hard transcendentality, that is, of a level in which all pertinent theoretical distinctions would be formulated and which would reduce the terrains of their "application" to the empiricity of "case studies." But we should also avoid the other extreme, consisting of seeing the two levels as fully enclosed universes, whose mutual relations could only be conceived in terms of purely external homologies. The question of the comparison itself between regions and levels should be conceived in tropological terms: No level has a transcendental priority over the other, so that their very interaction should be seen as an area of displacements blurring the frontiers between the empirical and the transcendental. Each should theoretically enrich the understanding of the other in an intertextuality that has no ultimate anchoring point.

If we try to think those organizing categories of the political field that make possible a comparison without rhetorical analysis, we could advance the following thesis: Politics is the articulation of heterogeneous elements, and such an articulation is essentially tropological, for it presupposes the duality between institution and subversion of differential positions that we found as defining a rhetorical intervention. Social organization is not, however, exclusively political; to a large extent it consists of differential positions that are not challenged by any confrontation between groups. It is only through this confrontation that the specifically political moment emerges, for it shows the contingent nature of articulations. Using a Husserlian distinction, we could say that the social is equivalent to a *sedimented* order, while the political would involve the moment of *reactivation*. Contemporary forms of technocratism would express this dissolution of the political and the reduction of the management of the community to a mere question of expertise. It is the replacement of politics by knowledge, whose earliest formulation we find in Plato.

We have here the basis for a comparison between this duality politics/administration and the two axes of signification—that of combinations and that of substitutions. The more social order is stable and unchallenged, the more institutional forms will prevail and will organize themselves in a syntagmatic system of differential positions. The more the confrontations between groups defines the social scene, the more society will be divided into two camps: At the limit, there will be a total dichotomization of the social space around only two syntagmatic positions: "us" and "them." All social elements would have to locate their identities around either of these two poles, whose internal components would be in a mere relation of equivalence. While in an institutionalist political discourse there is a multiplication of differential positions in a relation of combination with each other, in an antagonistic discourse of rupture the number of syntagmatic differential positions is radically restricted, and all identities establish paradigmatic relations of substitution with all the others in each of the two poles. In my work I have called these two opposed political logics the logic of difference and of equivalence, respectively. Given that the equivalence chain establishes a paratactic succession between its component links, none of them can have a position of centrality founded in a combinatorial logic of a hypotactic nature. So, if the unity of the equivalence chain is going to be organized around a privileged signifier, such a privilege cannot be derived from a differential structural position, but from a cathectic investment of a radical kind. The symbols of Solidarnosc in Poland got their success not from any structural centrality of the Lenin shipyards in the country, but from the fact that they expressed radical anti-status quo feelings at the moment in which many other social demands were frustrated for not finding institutional channels of expression within the existing political system. This process by which identities cease to be purely immanent to a system and require an identification with a point transcendent to that system—which is the same as saying: when a particularity becomes the name of an absent universality—is what we call *hegemony*. Its logic is identical with the logic of the object a, which we have already referred to, and, for the reasons that we have given, it is essentially catachrestical (= rhetorical).

One last point requires our consideration. A hegemonic operation is essentially tropological, but requires very particular strategic moves to be performed within the metaphoric/metonymic continuum. Other moves, however, are equally possible, given that the continuum does not prescribe a priori either the direction that the interventions in it should take, or the different forms of articulation between its two extreme poles. Genette presents the decision by Proust that made possible the existence of a narrative as precisely that: a decision. But he himself points out that other decisions would have been equally possible, in which case we would not have had a novel but, for instance, a succession of lyrical moments. In the same way, the emergence of a hegemonic logic in Gramsci's political thought takes place against the background of various different ways of conceiving politics in the Marxist tradition that, while still describable in terms of the possibilities opened by the metaphoric/metonymic distinction, are different from the hegemonic turn. It is to that history that we have now to address our attention.

4

We have spoken about a zero-degree of the rhetorical, whose attainment would ideally require that the syntagmatic differential logic is able to dominate the whole field of signification (in the expanded sense that we have given to this last term). The prerequisite for attaining such a zero-degree would be, of course, the ability of the syntagmatic logic to fully control paradigmatic substitutions (an ability about which we have good reasons to be rather sceptical). However, we have so far limited the question of the zero-degree to its structuralist version—i.e., to a purely *synchronic* system— while identifying the notion of diachrony with a retroactive fixation/transgression that would operate from "outside" the structural "inside." Is this, however, the only true alternative? Is it necessary that a purely syntagmatic/ combinatorial space is organized in a synchronic way? I think it is not. As long as diachrony is not conceived as a contingent, external intervention, but rather as structural by a teleology, a diachronic succession is perfectly compatible with a zero-degree of the tropological. Pure differentiality (our zero–degree) is not necessarily linked to either simultaneity or succession.

It is from this point that we have to start in our consideration of the Marxist tradition. For at the root of this tradition there is a discourse anchored in Hegelian teleology. We know the defining features of the latter: The essential determinations of any entity are to be found in its *conceptual* specificity; the *conceptual* contradictions inherent in this specificity force us to move to a new entity embodying a new *conceptual* stage, etc. Marx did not change things in the least with his "inversion" of Hegelian dialectics: If the ground is "matter" rather than the "idea," but matter has inner laws of movement that are *conceptually* specifiable, Marx's materialism is as idealistic as Hegel's. Ontologically speaking they are not, actually, different from each other.

The important point for our subject is that in the vision of History that emerges from this diachrony, the different stages in the succession are not conceived as *interruptions* of what preceded them but as *teleological fulfilments*. We are dealing with a pure combination in which each actor and task has an assigned place in a secular eschatology grounded in the "necessary laws" of History. It comes as no surprise that the main political consequence of this approach is to privilege "strategy" over "tactics." Long-term strategic calculations were considered to be possible because the teleologism of the premises opened the way to historical predictions, even if they were only "morphological predictions," to use the words of Antonio Labriola. And any unfulfilment of those predictions could be dismissed as a temporary aberration to be superseded once the "necessary laws" reasserted their long-term validity.

The most extreme versions of this teleologism are to be found, of course, in the orthodox currents of the Second International, but it is enough to read the preface to the *Critique of Political Economy* to realize that, although in less crude ways, it impregnates the whole of the Marxist tradition. That is why we can speak of a rhetorical zero-degree: In this syntagmatic succession there is no place for either metonymic displacements or metaphoric reaggregations. One could, however, ask oneself, but is it not precisely along the combinatorial succession of differential positions that metonymy operates? The answer is yes, but metonymy, as we know, involves a subversion of the principle of differentiality through substitutions grounded in contiguity, and it is precisely these substitutions that syntagmatic literalism tends to block.

Marxist literalism required the reduction of the process of historical development to a mechanism that had to be conceptually apprehensible as far as its laws of movement are concerned. But that conceptual apprehensibility also required that anything escaping what is specifiable by those laws should be discarded as historically irrelevant. "The changes in the economic foundation lead sooner or later to the transformation of the whole immense superstructure. In studying such transformation, it is always necessary to distinguish between the material transformation of the economic conditions of production, which can be distinguished with the precision of natural science, and the legal, political, religious, artistic or philosophical—in short, ideological forms in which men become conscious of this conflict and fight it out. Just as one does not judge an individual by what he thinks about himself, so one cannot judge such a period of transformation by its consciousness, but, on the contrary, this consciousness must be explained from the contradictions of material life, from the conflict existing between the social forces of production and the relations of production."[26]

Now, it is precisely this sharp distinction between what is relevant and what is not that is blurred during the first "crisis of Marxism" at the end of the nineteenth century. Capitalism recovered after a long period of depression, and the transition to the monopolistic phase and to imperialism started. In such a situation, the socialist faith in the collapse of the system as a result of its internal contradictions was shaken. Historical development had revealed itself to be far more complex than had been assumed, and such a complexity took the form of a contamination between social levels that, according to the classical theory, should have remained distinct. ("Organized capitalism" ceased to be explainable by pure market laws and an element of conscious regulation intervened at the very level of the infrastructure; imperialism led to the emergence of a "working-class aristocracy" and consequently to an attenuation of class conflicts, etc.) The consequence for our analysis is that the very terrain that had made accessible the zero-degree of the tropological was shattered and rhetorical movements became highly important.

This tropological turn, however, took a variety of forms and directions. As we anticipated, the first example that we'll refer to is the later work of Georges Sorel. As many other socialist thinkers of his time, Sorel, at the time of writing the *Reflections on Violence*, had lost faith in the perspective of capitalism bringing about its own collapse as a result of purely economic laws. So in order to keep alive the revolutionary vocation of the working class, it was necessary to appeal to something different from economic determinism. Some kind of subjective principle had to be brought into the picture. It is important to realize that, for Sorel, his support for the proletarian struggle was not grounded in the justice for the workers' demands but in his belief that the proletariat was the only force in society capable of preventing bourgeois decadence; the prospect facing contemporary societies was a general decline of civilization. The principle capable of maintaining the purity of proletarian identity was *violence*. For this purpose, it was essential that the working class did not intervene in politics, for that would co-opt it into the mechanisms of the bourgeois State. He opposed "proletarian violence" to "political violence"—the latter being epitomized by Jacobinism.

Proletarian violence had to be organized around a *myth*. "Men participating in great social movements represent to themselves their immediate action under the form of images of battles ensuring the triumph of their cause. I propose to call *myths* these constructions whose knowledge is so important for the historian: the syndicalists' general strike and Marx's catastrophic revolution are myths."[27] He counterposes "myth" and "utopia." While the latter is a pure intellectual construction, the blueprint of a future or ideal society, myth is just a set of images capable of galvanizing the masses' imagination and projecting them into historical action.

The myth around which proletarian identity should be organized is that of the *general strike*. "I understand that this myth of the general strike horrifies [*froisse*] many *wise people* because of its character of infinitude; the present world is very much inclined to return to the opinion of the ancients and to subordinate morals to the good management of public affairs, which leads to locate virtue in a just middle. As far as socialism remains a *doctrine entirely presented through words*, it is easy to make it deviate towards a just middle; but this transformation is clearly impossible once one introduces the myth of the general strike, which involves an absolute revolution."[28] And, again, "Today revolutionary myths are almost pure, they make it possible to understand the activities, feelings and ideas of the popular masses preparing themselves to enter into a decisive struggle, they are not descriptions of things, but expressions of wills."[29]

In a myth, the infinitude of the task goes together with the paucity of its contents. Its function is, precisely, to separate the militant from the concrete aim of his particular action. Let us suppose that a group of workers participate in a strike for higher wages. If the strike is successful, and its only aim was that particular demand, success leads to demobilization and to the integration of the workers into the status quo. However, if participation in that concrete action is seen as a simple episode, educating the proletariat for the final aim, the meaning of the political struggles changes altogether. But, for this, the myth of the general strike has to be operating from the very beginning. This explains the *infinitude* of the task, to which Sorel refers: It cannot be identified with any particular aim. And it explains also the poverty of its contents, which is actually more than poverty, for, as the name of an infinite task, it negates the very possibility of any content (which would necessarily have to be finite). The Sorelian myth is one of the purest examples of what we have called "empty signifiers." It does not matter whether the general strike is an event that could happen or not. Although Sorel is not entirely explicit in this respect, I think that the very logic of his argument leads towards a negative response, for any finite fulfillment would compromise the infinitude of the task. Its status approaches that of Kant's regulative idea.

How, however, to read this set of displacements that Sorel brings about against the sequence of categories of classical Marxism? Where and how exactly does the tropological turn take place? To start with, in Sorel there is not any syntagmatic plurality of places of enunciation because they all converge in reinforcing a unique proletarian identity. Whether we are dealing with a strike, a demonstration, a factory occupation, they are simply occasions for the rehearsal of a unique "future" event: the general strike. These occasions are certainly plural, but their plurality is present only to eclipse itself as a mere support of the single event that speaks through all of them. That is, we are faced with a pure metaphorical reaggregation that is not interrupted by any metonymical plurality. There is nothing to displace, because the sites of the metaphorical event are there just in order to be negated by the latter. To put it in clear terms: The revolutionary break does not proceed through equivalence but through absolute identity. So, in some way, Sorel is the symmetrical reverse side of the "rhetorics zero-degree" of the Second International. For the latter, there was no room for any tropological movement in the determination of the emancipatory subject. For Sorel, such a determination could only proceed through an extreme form of that tropological movement, namely, a pure metaphor that has eliminated all traces of its metonymical grounding. Analogy unconceals an essence that has broken all links with contiguity. Equivalence is replaced by pure identity. (As this identity, however, is constructed around an empty place—the general strike—whose discursive effects depend on its lack of content, its assertion is close to nihilism. Not surprisingly, Sorelianism fed very different currents of thought, from radical communism and ultra-leftism, to fascism.) We can go back here to Genette's analysis of Proust. According to him, as we have seen, there is narrative in Proust only because metaphors are inscribed in a metonymical succession; otherwise we will only have a succession of lyrical moments. Well, this last possibility is what Sorel's text enacts. Each revolutionary act does not find its meaning in a succession endowing it with its *raison d'être* within the series, but, rather, each of them is the expression of some sort of repetition drive constantly reinstating, in a Sisyphean way, a single identity. That is why Genette's notion of a succession of lyrical moments as an alternative to Proust's narrative—i.e., pure metaphorical flashes not inscribed in any metonymical succession—applies so well to Sorel's vision of politics. And, also, why there can be no Sorelian strategy based in a long-term calculation. While for a Kantsky or a Plekhanov such calculation was based in supposedly known laws of history, for Sorel the mere idea of a long-term prediction makes no sense. The assertion of a revolutionary subjectivity largely escapes strategical considerations.

5

If Sorel's discourse is structured in a terrain in which political subjectivity can only operate through a total metaphor that conceals even the traces of its metonymic locations, the experience of Leninism is different: The metonymic subversion of the differential space of Marxist teleology has to remain visible, to the point of making impossible the movement towards its metaphoric *telos*. Leninism emerges as a *political* answer to an anomaly in historical development. Russia was supposed to follow the pattern of the classical bourgeois-democratic revolutions of the West. The task ahead was the overthrowing of Tsarism and the opening of a long period of capitalist democracy, so that socialism was only a long-term prospect, to be achieved as a result of the contradictions of a full-fledged capitalist society. In that democratic revolution, the bourgeoisie was supposed to be the "natural" leading force. Tasks and forces were assigned roles according to a pre-ordained succession. The anomaly was that the autochthonous Russian bourgeoisie had arrived too late to the historical scene, when a world capitalist market was already well established, and as a result it was too weak to carry out its own democratic revolution. Capitalism, however, was rapidly developing in Russia as a result of foreign investments, so that there was the paradoxical situation—"anomalous" regarding the canonical pattern—of a country that was mature, and thus ready for a democratic revolution, in which, however, the "natural" agent of that historical transformation was incapable of carrying out its task.

As a result of capitalist development, however, a robust working class was emerging, which had none of the limitations of the indigenous bourgeoisie, and so—this was the thesis of the Russian social-democrats—it had to take up the historical task of leading the democratic revolution (in alliance with the peasantry, in the Leninist version) that its natural agent, the bourgeoisie, had left unfulfilled. This anomalous taking up of a task by a force that was not its natural agent is what the Russian social-democrats called "hegemony." So we have a fracture in historical development, a discontinuity in the sequence of its categories. The taking up of the democratic tasks by the working class was an event politically explainable by a set of historical circumstances, but not insertable as one of the necessary links of the canonical paradigm. It was an "exceptionality," to use the terminology of the time.

Now, if we study the structure of this exceptionality, we immediately see that it was the *presence* of the working class at the center of historical events at a moment in which the country was mature for a democratic revolution that assigned it to that role. It was a relation of *contiguity*. So we are dealing with the construction of a new link between task and agent, which can only be conceived as a metonymic displacement.

We know, however, that any metonymy has a natural tendency to shade into a metaphor, the relation of contiguity to become, through continuous association, one of analogy. So we could normally expect that the nature of the democratic task changed when taken up by the proletariat, and that the class nature of the latter was also altered as a result of taking up a democratic task. However, nothing of the kind happened. The whole Leninist strategy was designed to prevent the exceptional task from becoming the site of the construction of a new political subjectivity. The class nature of the proletariat had to remain unchanged. The Leninist motto was, "to strike together and to march separately." Why so? Various reasons conspire in it, but the main one was that for Russian revolutionists—the Bolsheviks included—Russian exceptionality was exactly that: an exception and, on top of that, one that was going to be short-lived. Neither Trotsky, nor Lenin—even after the "April Theses"—thought that a proletarian power in Russia, given its backwardness, had any prospect unless it found its natural continuity in a revolution in Germany and the other major and highly developed capitalist countries in the West. If that had been the case, the Russian "exceptionality" would have been quickly integrated into a "normal" process of historical development.

If we consider the matter retrospectively, we find here the root of the double discourse that will be inscribed in the Communist experience of the years to come. The canonical sequence of categories had to be maintained as an ultimate unsurpassable horizon—the Marxist syntagm was never formally questioned—but, as a counterpart, actual politics was going to be dominated increasingly by an empiricism of exceptionalities that eluded any theorization. Stalin's *Realpolitik* was the extreme expression of this divorce between theory and practice, but in more attenuated forms it was going to dominate the whole of Communist experience. The way in which both levels were combined can perhaps be seen at its best in the case of Trotsky. The whole logic of "permanent revolution" is only thinkable if the empiricism of the exceptionalities is articulated within the discourse of "normal" syntagmatic development. The argument runs as follows. Russia was ripe for a democratico-bourgeois revolution in which the bourgeoisie—Trotsky accepted the point—was incapable of playing the leading role. This would result in a democratic revolution led by the proletariat. But—Trotsky added—the bourgeoisie would not tolerate proletarian power—even if confined to democratic limits—and would respond with a massive lockout. The result would be that the workers' movement, in order to consolidate its power, would have to advance in a socialist direction. Revolutions always start with democratic banners, but their stabilization and consolidation requires their transition to the socialist stage. This model will be repeated *ad nauseam* by Trotskyites in all imaginable historical contexts.

The classic "stageism," although interrupted by an "exceptionality," is in full operation: The class nature of social agents is unquestioned as well as that of the tasks and of the succession of phases.

So the metonymic moment has to be frozen, preventing the construction of new identities through metaphoric reaggregations. Here we see the difference with Sorel. For him there is no narrative, only the sequence of metaphoric moments through which proletarian identity is constantly reinforced. For Leninism, the interaction between the two discursive levels forces it to engage in a permanent narrative, so that the metonymic moment is never abandoned. It is for that reason that Leninism is an eminently strategic type of discourse, whose difference with the strategy of the Second International is, however, visible: For the latter, strategic reflection was based on a historical prediction grounded in the necessary laws of history, while for Leninism, given the operation of exceptionalities, strategies have more the character of conjunctural analyses.

This notion of conjunctural analysis forces us, however, to move beyond Leninist frozen metonymies and, indeed, beyond the historical horizon of Marxism. For the question is: How exceptional are the exceptions? According to Lenin, the world capitalist market is not only an economic but also a political reality: it is structured as an imperialist chain. Crises can take place in one point of it that result—given that the chain is broken by its weakest link—in dislocations of the relations of forces in other points of the chain. This makes possible a seizure of power, even if the "objective" material conditions have not been met. In such situations there is no longer any question of either a pure combination of stages—as the one postulated by the theory of combined and uneven development—nor of a necessary class belonging of social agents, for what is at stake is the constitution of complex social identities constructed on the basis of practices homogenizing the heterogeneous. That is, we are dealing with metaphoric reaggregations. Frozen Leninist metonymies no longer do the trick. I think that Gramsci's notion of "collective wills" should be read in this light. But this incorporation of the metaphoric dimension does not lead us back to Sorel's camp either. For Sorel this is a unilateralization of metaphor, because the proletarian identity that he tries to consolidate is given in advance. No question for him of incorporating heterogeneous elements into a wider social identity. That could only lead, in his view, to undermining the class consciousness of the proletariat. However, once the political process is seen not only as a reassertion of an identity but as its construction—as in Gramsci's "war of position"—the metonymic dimension cannot be ignored. Hegemony means the passage from metonymy to metaphor, from a "contiguous" starting point to its consolidation in "analogy." But with this we are very close to the relationship metaphor/metonymy that Genette finds in Proust's text. Translating it into political language, we could say that because there is Narrative (*Récit*) there is strategy. But as the identity of the agents of that strategy is not given beforehand, we will always have short-term strategic movements, not anchored in any eschatology. They will exactly operate at the point at which metaphor and metonymy cross each other and limit their mutual effects.

CHAPTER 5

Answering for Sense

Jean-Luc Nancy
Translated by Jean-Christophe Cloutier

> Write me. Write anything.[1]
> EMMANUEL LOI

> The phrase—*literature*—is oral.[2]
> PHILIPPE LACOUE-LABARTHE

Whoever writes responds.

To whom or to what he or she responds, tradition has given many names. There's been the Muse, poetic Fury, Genius with or without a capital "G," inspiration, at times the mission or the vocation, at other times a necessity of the soul or of nerves, a grace from the heavens, a sacred injunction, a duty to remember or to forget, an auto-engendering of the text. But the most ancient name is *thea* in the first verses of the *Iliad*: "Sing, goddess, the anger of Peleus' son Achilleus...."[3] In this *incipit* of Western literature, the poet merely utters the first sentence—or at most the sentences that lead up to the question: "What god was it set them together in bitter collision?" and the response ("Zeus's son and Leto's") commits the entire poem, which, it must be well understood, is henceforth being sung by *Thea*.

Homer does not write himself: He lets the divine voice sing. Him, the *aede*, he sings in as much as he interprets the divine song—this song that he asks her to sing ("*menin aeide thea*"): He does in this way what he expects

---

Originally published as "Répondre du sens" in Jean-Luc Nancy, *La pensée dérobée*, pp. 167–78, copyright © Éditions Galilée, 2001. Reprinted with permission.

her to do in order for him to eclipse himself in this song—his own (hers) becoming his own (his), yet always remaining this divine song. He thus lets the voice sing, or else he makes it heard, he recites it. Always, since then, the one who writes writes in no other way than by letting himself be dictated in many senses of the term. *Dicto* is to say by repeating, by insisting; it's also to command, to prescribe. Whoever writes lets himself be directed to write: He responds to a command, if not an objurgation, or else an exhortation, of an excitation or a pressure. But also, he receives the dictation: He lays down in writing the text that another voice composes and recites to that end, a voice that does not write, a voice that archi-writes. From the word *dictare*, German has extracted, alongside *diktieren* (dictate), the additional verb *dichten* (to fashion a writing, particularly a poem). The one who writes responds one way or another, by echo or by execution, by transcription or by translation, to the *dictatorship* of a *dictatio*. That which, in the *Iliad*, appears to be *Thea*'s response—that of the *thea*, of an unnamed, unidentified *thea*—is in fact its total opposite, it is the *aede*'s response to the dictation of the divine voice, but more specifically, this response gives itself through its inverse form because, in truth, it's *aede* that responds—or else, more truthfully still, there is but a response to a response, and neither was the first to begin.

It responds itself: Such is the formula of what we call writing today. It responds itself: It responds in itself, it responds *to itself* and it responds *of itself*. *Res responsorial*, there's the subject that follows after *res cogitans* (unless it has always preceded it and inhabits it)—if we are willing to recall that *responsorius* used to designate the song by an alternation of *readings* (*lectio*) and *verses* (versus) or *responsories*. In writing, we are concerned with song, and with the alternation or the internal resonance that forms the song.

Aede and *Thea* don't respond like this in the sense that one answers a question, but in the sense that one responds to an expectation, or else in the sense that voices respond to themselves, that they correspond. They respond or they respond to themselves in the sense that the *re-spondeo* is to commit oneself in turn to a *sponsio*, in a religious and/or juridical commitment: to respond to a promise by a reciprocal promise (like a wedding engagement, a kind of *sponsio*, from which French has taken "épouser," Italian "sposare" and English "to espouse"). Whoever writes listens and commits himself in his listening, by his listening. Likewise in the German *Antwort* and the English *answer*, the "response" is the utterance that comes to the encounter. To write is to commit to an encounter: It is to go toward the encounter and it is to make a commitment to the encounter. To write is to set up a *rendez-vous*. (The encounter may be furtive, it can be but a simple crossing, a grazing, as much as it can be a long *tête-à-tête*—and it can also occur "counter-to," in a clash, in open defiance, in repulsion. But it's always about some kind of confrontation, and never does that come to pass alone.)

To listen is to resound: letting the sounds that came from elsewhere vibrate inside oneself, and to respond to them through their reverberations in a body that has, to that end, become cavernous. This cave is not Plato's: It isn't shut off and barely ajar to an outside that projects shadows, but it's the *opening in (it)self* in both senses that this expression can take on: It's the opening inside myself and the opening as such, absolutely. In fact, it is "me" as opening, me as box of resonance upon which the chords and the accents of the outside voices, the divine voices, come to strike, slide, and scrub. But the resonance is not a shadow: It isn't what's left of a subtraction, it's the intensification and the recalibration, the remodulation of a resonance. Whoever writes resounds and, in resonating, responds: He shares the commitment of an outside voice. He commits to it when his turn comes, he renders polyphonic the voice that came to him as a soliloquy. But without this polyphony, the soliloquy would not even be *heard*. That is, *we* would not hear it and *itself* would remain deaf to it(self).

The response is the reprise and the relaunching of the voice: of what it says, of its accent, of its articulation, and of its phrasing or its singing. But without reprise, thus without response, the voice would remain in itself. A voice in itself is not a voice: It's a silence that does not even have the space of an address, it's a muting enclosed in its buzzing, in its roaring or in its murmur (the repetition of a mute *mmm—mutum*). A voice is always two voices at least, always polyphonized somehow. Always must a voice call out to the other, "Sing! *Aeide!*" *Aeido*, from which *ôdé*, the song, the ode, is formed, also relates itself to *aude*, which characterizes the human voice by its distinction from *phoné*, which can also be said of the animal voice. *Audaô*, it's addressing speech, launching a reply or an appeal. The human voice always reverberates toward another voice and from another voice, or else in another voice. The resonance of its sound cannot be dissociated from a reverberation of address and of listening: Even when I speak alone and silently "in my head" (as we believe we can say), that is, whenever I think, I hear another voice in my voice or else I hear my voice resound in another throat.

"Writing" is the name of this resonance of the voice: the appeal, the encounter, and the commitment that the appeal assumes in the encounter. In this sense, all writing is "committed" in a sense that precedes the notion of a political or moral commitment that is meant to serve a cause. To write is to commit the voice in the resonance that makes it human, but "human" in this case means nothing else than "that which stands—or that which arrives—in the resonance."

Writing is thus the very resonance of the voice, or the voice as resonance, that is, as throwback into its own same self—through the distance of a "self," to the "sameness" that allows it to identify itself: each time absolutely singular for an indefinite number of encounters that are singular each time. Writing "fixes," as they say, the flux of the utterance (*verba volant, scripta manent*): This fixing is nothing else but the recording, the reserve, or the abode of the resonance's capacity. In the spoken utterance, or else in the utterance that speaks only to inform this very instant, without delay or appointment, the resonance is extinguished as soon as the information has reached its destination. In writing, the destination is first and foremost, from the onset and forever, the resonance as such: Homer did not write for fewer than his millions and millions of readers, each one by one and by peoples or by groups of singular cultures for roughly thirty centuries. And it's for this that he commits his poem into the appeal to the divine voice of which he makes himself, him the *aede*, the resonance. Fixed writing, engraved in wood, wax, rock or paper, pixilated on screen, but just as well registered in the speaking voice of an orator, a singer, a general addressor, if we could forge this term—writing is only immobile and invariable because it thus inscribes the space of an always-renewed resonance.

When Hegel claims that a written truth loses nothing by being kept outside of the singular circumstance of its enunciation—like "it is night" pronounced at noon—doesn't he mean that truth has nothing of the order of empirical verifiability, but is really of the order of address and of resonance? If I say, "It is night" at noon, then what do I mean to say and what kind of listening can commit itself to the encounter of my saying?

To say, "It is night" at midnight states something, but announces nothing, or else this phrase announces a sense that must go beyond the immediately attested referential signification. Moreover, this phrase said at noon—that is, this *written* phrase—announces a sense that at first subtracts itself of the reference and points to something else. This "something else" consists at first in the phrase's address and in the resonance through which it addresses itself. In fact, we could say in French that it commits its sense by its *phrasé* rather than by its signification. The *phrasé* designates the manner or the art of articulating, in writing or in music, the groupings considered as units of sense: It's the song of sense.

The song of sense is nothing else than the sense itself. The sense is not the signification or the designation—the throwback by a signifier to a signified concept, the latter itself supposedly outside-language—it is rather the opening of the structure and of the dynamic of the *throwback* in general, through which something like a signifying throwback can take place:

throwback of signifier to signified, itself accompanied by a throwback of signifier to signifier according to the play of differences in the language, and lastly, or to begin with, the throwback of a voice to a listening, without which neither of the two preceding throwbacks could take place on their own, since the one like the other and the one through the other, on the whole, assumes that *hearing* is possible (*hearing* as *entente*, in the double-sense of the word in French[4]—in German we might say the obedience or the belonging to—*gehoren, gehorchen*—other modes of the "response").

At first, what should be heard is not what the utterance *means to say*, in the sense where a willpower would have already produced the reality replete with its intention or its desire. We must, before anything else, hear this desire itself: We must hear the "meaning-to-say" *meaning itself* to be in its saying. (In German, we should hear the *deuten* of the *bedeuten*, hear in the "signification" the declaration, the announcement addressed to all—to the people, that is also *deutsch* or *dutch*, since here the name of the people, the one of its language and the one of the appeal or the announcement, resounds in a same semantic space.) To hear the saying desiring itself as saying, it's to hear it already resounding while hearing it desire the other as its place of resonance and throwback. The sense as song is not at all a setting to music of a remark or a text: It is the resounding primitive character of sense itself.

To say it all, the meaning-to-say, before saying anything, first says itself as meaning-to, and this meaning-to, before meaning-to something, at first means itself as can-say-itself, that is, able to call itself and respond to itself.

In other words, if writing is responding to an appeal by another appeal, or else giving way and giving form to the *appeal* as such—like Homer, appealing to the goddess who herself appeals from the bottom of language and of legend, the one inextricably tangled in the other—it is now discovered that the appeal or the address are themselves nothing else than the sense: the sense as opening of the throwback's possibility.

The sense can absolutely never be the fact of a sole subject of sense, since this subject itself should at the very least hear the sense it would produce or find. It would need to *hear itself* and to hear itself it would need to have *called itself* and to call itself it would need to be able to resound—and, at last, to resound it would need, in the very first place, to offer in itself the space, the interval or the spacing, the *opening* that is the condition of possibility of a resonance, since the latter demands a relation of vibration to vibration, a "sympathy" setting as the physicians who speak of "vibration by sympathy" say, or a "harmony" setting as the musicians say. But the resonance, such as it should be here understood, is not only the relation between two distinct sonic orders: It first forms the sonority in itself. The sonority defines itself precisely by the fact that "in itself" it is in a spacing of itself. The sonorous is its own dilation or its own amplification and its own setting into resonance.

The song is the human sonority of sound: The sense is itself formed and defined by the internal spacing of its throwback, and at first from the throw by which it destines itself and desires its very self as a response to its own throw. *In this sense*, we are never, each one next to the other, anything but singular points along a general throw that sense makes of itself toward itself, and that begins and loses itself very much on this side and very much on the other side beyond us, in the infinitely opened totality of the world. But at the same time, these singular points that we are (or the many singular points that drop off one by one under each individual or collective identity) are themselves the necessarily discrete or discontinued structure of the general spacing at the heart of which sense can resound, that is, *respond to itself.*

By communicating itself to all the singular points of listening or of reading, of understanding [*entente*] or interpretation, of recitation or of rewriting, the sense does nothing else than share itself with, or in, as many singular senses (here the word "sense" can be understood both in its value as "meaning-to-say" and in its value as "able to comprehend," as in "good sense" or "artistic sense"—and these two values, this is understood, are inseparable from one another: They are one and the other present in the very sense of the same sense. . . .). The sense taken absolutely or in itself is nothing else than the totality of the singular senses. The infinite sense is identical to the infinity of the singularities of sense. It is neither a general sense, nor a sense by the summation or by the end result of singular senses: It is the interlacing and the discontinuity of these singulars. It is *that there is* passing and sharing from one to the other, passing and sharing of a "meaning-to-say" and of an "able-to-comprehend"—of an activity and of a passivity—that are together one and the same thing, *the thing of sense*, but this thing is such that its reality is nothing but its dissemination.

If *I mean to say*, this means above all that I mean to say *me* and thus immediately that I mean to say *you*, that I mean to say *"I" to you* and thus immediately to say *"you" to you*, to you who in my meaning is thus already the one that says "you" to me to call upon me to say, and to say "I" to you.

Writing—whose name recalls incision (*scribo, skripat, scaripha*)—is most exactly the name of the disjunctive spacing in which, and thanks to which, sense can respond to itself: desire itself, throw itself and throw itself back, indefinitely from singular point to singular point—which also means from singular sense to singular sense (from Homer—who himself wasn't alone, no doubt—to his reader Plato, to his reader Virgil, to his reader Augustine, to his reader Joyce and so on to his millions and millions of readers and reinscribers, responders, and correspondents . . .). Writing incises the indistinct mass in which, without which, neither mouth nor ear would open. Each stroke of writing is a mouth/ear[5] that throws itself, that calls itself, that hears itself, and that responds to itself: *Aeide, thea!*

Whoever writes responds to sense: He is, in as much as he writes, the response to the call of sense, or rather the "response-on-call" of sense. But this sense—*thea*—to which it responds, answers for it as well. The *aede* answers for *thea*: He is the only one, in fact, who attests of her presence and of her voice. His appeal to her song acts as testimony for her presence, which has no other attestation. *Thea* needs the *aede* to answer: He responds in her place and is answerable for her, he is thus responsible for her—and with her, for all that we are able to hear of her.

If the responsible one is the one who responds not *to* but *of* or *for*, it's because he is the one who commits himself thus, indirectly or in a mediate or deferred manner—deferred, but promised, committed—to respond to that which could be demanded on that subject or of the one *for whom* the responsible one assumes responsibility. The responsible one takes the commitment of an other under his responsibility and does so by his own means—the commitment that an other could not take on himself—or else the commitment that the present state of things makes impossible to knowingly take on: By declaring myself responsible for a project, for example, I take on the unpredictability contained in it. Responsibility is anticipated response to questions, to demands, to still-unformulated, and not exactly predictable, interpellations.

Whoever writes makes himself responsible for absolute sense. He does not commit himself to less than the totality and the infinity of this sense. At the same time, he bears witness to *thea's* existence and he takes upon himself his desire: the desire he has for *thea* and the desire that *thea* is herself.

Witness to *thea's* existence, he declares his own self as being her *aede*, that is, also her hermeneut. The hermeneut is not first the one who deciphers and who decodes significations, even if he has to, at times, do just that—and to do it again and again without end, or else up to the point where all signification unravels itself into exhaustion and slips away by the very incision of writing. The hermeneut is not first the one who signifies *what is* said: He is the one who carries the desire to say further. The hermeneut supplements the subject with this desire: He presents *thea* and makes her be heard in the very voice—her own voice—by which he convokes her. He also makes this voice singularly heard each time.[6]

But in this way, the one who writes not only bears witness to *thea's* existence, he also bears witness to her nature, and to how the latter is entirely made of this sharing of voices of whom he, he who writes (or she), is a part, a moment, an accent, and a sense beside so many others.

By responding to the sense's desire, and thus to the sense as desire, by reaching this desire and by letting himself be possessed by it, the one who writes takes the responsibility of the totality and infinity of sense as a sharing of himself. Sense shares itself, and it does nothing else: It opens up the continued and discontinued circulation, the exchange of the each-time-singularly-inexchangeable desire to say. Inexchangeable is this desire, for what it desires is not the communication of a signification: It's the cut and the touch of a singular truth.

What happens to sense in each point or singular moment—in each writing—is not the accomplishment of a moment that a final instance could come valorize and capitalize in a terminal satisfaction of sense (finished exegesis, completed interpretation, sense forever up to date). It is neither a moment nor an end in the process of sense—and in this sense, there is no process of sense: There is only its desire and its sharing. What arrives at the singular point, it's the singular itself as scansion of truth in sense.

The one who writes cannot make his own, in the time he writes, Rimbaud's phrase: "C'est très certain, c'est oracle, ce que je dis" [It's very certain, what I say is oracle]."[7] He pronounces this phrase without any arrogance whatsoever, but also without shrinking it to the derisory angle of a subjectivity. Certitude is here the truth of the commitment and of the responsibility in sense and for sense. The oracle is the one that speaks in the name of the gods. This oracle here—the writing oracle—still speaks in the name of the same divinity, *thea*, the one who has no name, the one who does not even have the unpronounceable name, and who is "divine" in no other sense than in the sense where her truth shares itself, here and now, in this singular utterance that commits itself to opening the mouth (*oraculum*) in order to let sense pass—or better: that commits itself to opening the mouth to/of sense, in both senses of the expression.

The singular truth, no doubt, does not arise from all spoken and written occurrences. Is not "oracle" the one that thinks to be an oracle, not the one that decides to be oracle? (For these ones shut themselves up in the representation of a "me"—which is a generality under the guise of particular—instead of opening themselves to the singular throwback of an "I.")

The truth can come to sense only if it is given access to its cut and its touch. This touch that cuts, that incises in writing the undifferentiated space and the closed mouth, can only come from the outside. This outside is not one of an authority nor is it of a spirit that breathes. It is the outside in which and for which the responsibility committed itself: this outside in which, first off, there is nothing, and at the heart of which no god, no muse, no genius watches over—nor is on watch. It's the silence of the outside that holds all authority and that exhales all inspirations.

In one sense—in a very first sense—this outside is that of absolute silence itself insofar as it is foreign to any signification, and consequently to the language itself in the first place: to the language, in all cases, formed, composed and articulated in the order of received significations and even of possible significations.

The truth comes from the language already lost or still to come. It comes from the voice that desires itself and that seeks itself behind the voice—in the back of the throat, where the incision opens a first separation that goes up to the lips but that the lips have not yet known. It comes like a to-come of language: an unheard of language, a roll of the tongue that will only take place this one time, an inflexion, an accent, or a *style*—that is the incision engraved by a stiletto. It's not a chiseling, it's truly an incision practiced in the language made entirely by the blade of an outside that is made both of non-language and of language to come, or of language desire.

The "style" of truth, or truth as style, owes nothing to the ornament or to the solicitation and the exploitation of available significations. It can only come from the outside—touch and cut of an outside that is properly the outside of a signification, that is thus the sense outside of itself, the truth of sense as its infinite excess or as its bottomless lack.

In order to come from the outside, to respond to this outside and to answer for it, the incision must owe something to chance, to surprise and to *kairos*, the favorable moment whose favor consists in offering itself to the one who exposes himself to the outside, and who consequently *no longer wills-to-mean*: to let this desire be touched by the favor of an excess on all possible "saying."

But to let one's self be disposed to this favor, to its rarity, there must be a retreat of language. We must have been led to this side of language, where language itself already knows—always already knows, where it forms itself, where a being liable to sense, a being susceptible to sense, sketches itself—that there is nothing to say in the end, nothing that does not envelop in some way a nothing of signification, and that by this nothing touches the same thing, the thing *in itself*, that is, the outside thing and *the thing from the outside*.

Whoever writes responds to this thing and he answers for this thing. This thing is itself *thea:* It is the sense and it is the desire to say, it is this desire's infinite sharing. It is not the inert blob that would subsist outside of language like a "real" that language would not know how to attain. No: It is the outside that language itself incises in itself, and is present in each truth to which it gives rise, or to which it sets ablaze.

Language is a knowledge—and it is thus the knowledge proper to writing: not what writing knows how to do, nor what it would know in order to write (like an "art of writing")—but the knowledge that writing *is as it writes*. It is the knowledge of that whose testimony it carries. It carries the testimony of this, whether sense, since it is throw and throwback, since it is appeal and response, gives itself or raises itself in retreat or in excess: retreat or excess for all signification that comes to stop or appease the desire and its response, this response that can in turn only be another desire and the desire of another. *I* who desires *you* and who desires that *you* say(s) *I* to him and that, in saying *I* to him, you in turn say *you* to him.

In this vertiginous tightening hides the knowledge of writing—I mean the knowledge it itself is, or whose act that it is. Whoever writes knows the desire of the other, and he or she knows that this knowledge must be divided from itself to be what it is: response, commitment to the truth of this non-knowledge.

CHAPTER 6

"Human" in the Age of Disposable People: The Ambiguous Import of Kinship and Education in *Blind Shaft*

Rey Chow

> The most massive form of poverty in today's world is the one we see in *underdeveloped* countries, where the combination of the destruction of traditional activities, the domination of foreign financial institutions, the establishment of a so-called New World Order, and so on, leads to a situation ... in which millions of human beings are *superfluous*. Nobody needs them—they are, so to speak, disposable people ... they are facing—and we are facing once more—the prospect of an extermination whose forms are not only violent but specifically *cruel* ... [1]
>
> ÉTIENNE BALIBAR

> In China there is a shortage of everything—but no shortage of human beings!
>
> OWNER/MANAGER OF A COAL MINE, *BLIND SHAFT*

Homelessness as a Modern World Condition

In the essay "Letter on Humanism,"[2] published soon after Germany's defeat in the Second World War, Martin Heidegger refers to the condition of homelessness as "coming to be the destiny of the world."[3] By homelessness, Heidegger means something more than not having a roof over one's head, even though the notions of dwelling and shelter are not at all excluded from his thinking. Heidegger's assertion of homelessness as the condition—not merely of the defeated but also of the victorious—of the modern world is part of a critique of the status of

---

From *Sentimental Fabulations, Contemporary Chinese Films*, by Rey Chow Copyright © 2007 Columbia University Press. Reprinted (with modifications) with permission of the publisher.

humanism in the West. From Roman times to the onset of Christianity, to the Hegelian phenomenology of spirit, the Marxist theory of labor, and Sartrean existentialism, Heidegger writes, every type of humanism, understood "in general as a concern that man become free for his humanity and find his worth in it,"[4] has remained erroneously preoccupied with the "throng of beings unthought in their essence"[5] and thus mired in metaphysics. In other words, despite considerable efforts by devoted thinkers, the concern with humanism has hitherto been ensnared—and limited—by a consistent failure to engage with the question of Being, that reservoir or reserve of irreducible surplus presence that sustains every human undertaking but that forever exceeds rational human consciousness. Defined in these terms, humanism is seen by Heidegger to have a relation to Being that is negative—in the form of a forgetting, an exile, a closing off—hence the condition of homelessness, which he specifies as "the symptom of oblivion of Being."[6] "Yet Being—what is Being?" he asks. "It is It itself."[7]

My concern in this essay is not exactly to reconsider various notions of humanism in Western history as such, but rather to ask if and how the suggestive concepts proposed by Heidegger—specifically, homelessness and its implications for what it means to be "human"—can be brought into dialogue with the film *Mang Jing/Blind Shaft* (2003). Directed and produced by Li Yang, who wrote the screenplay by adapting it from the novella "Shen mu" (Sacred wood) by Liu Qingbang,[8] *Blind Shaft* appears in many respects to be just a Chinese story about the plight of migrant workers. (The film was released in early 2003 and won some major awards at film festivals around the world before an edited version was officially released in the People's Republic late that year.[9]) But the culturally specific locality of the story is paradoxically also what lends it its abstract, philosophical resonance. What can a story like this bring to the interrogation of humanism—as the corollary of homelessness—that Heidegger initiated over half a century ago? Does humanism—as a concern for human beings finding themselves and becoming free in their humanity—still remain valid for critical thinking and practice when we are faced with the tragedies of those who are described by Balibar as the "superfluous" and "disposable" people along the peripheries of the contemporary world? Or, are such human tragedies themselves the latest symptoms, as Heidegger wrote, of the oblivion of Being that in fact constitutes humanism itself?

Heidegger's austere deconstruction of the metaphysics of Western humanism, we should note, was framed by an affirmative urging, the urging that we remember, that we think of the "essence" of man in terms of what he calls *techne* and *poiesis*. However, as David Farrell Krell, the editor of Heidegger's *Basic Writings*, points out, this affirmative pedagogical reminder is not without its own problems. Krell puts it succinctly: "Why, for instance, insist that there be an 'abyss of essence' separating humanity from animality? Perhaps most disturbing, can Heidegger invoke 'malignancy' and 'the rage of evil' without breaking his silence and offering some kind of reflection on the Extermination? And how can Heidegger's thought help us to think about those evils that continue to be so very much at home in *our* world?"[10]

The point about the Extermination—that is, the European Holocaust of the mid-twentieth century—is especially salient because, in ways that resound with echoes of contemporary global conflicts, this is a point about the politics of dealing with human beings deemed to be lacking legitimate membership in a particular group, nation, or community—foreigners. Without question, Heidegger's silence on the Holocaust is deeply troubling; at the same time, if by criticizing such silence what we intend to underscore is the ineluctable urgency of racial/ethnic violence for any account of humanism, it would be equally crucial to move beyond an exclusive focus on the anti-Semitism of mid-twentieth-century Europe. In the twenty-first century and, indeed, long before then, racial/ethnic violence has far exceeded the bounds of the Holocaust, in such ways as to necessitate a rereading of Heidegger's universalist pronouncements with a much larger set of connotations. From the "ethnic cleansing" in Eastern Europe to the aftermath of 9–11 such as the American implementation of so-called "Homeland Security"; from the wars led by the United States in the 2000s on Afghanistan and Iraq, to the renewed reinforcement of "secularism" in France in reaction to the wearing of headscarves by Muslim schoolgirls, the question of the *boundary* between so-called "us" and so-called "them" continues to structure *collective imaginaries* and actions around the globe, from legislation and prohibition to penalization, mass resistance, and suicidal protestation and defiance. At once large and abstract, *and* quotidian and intimate, this question is also a question about homelessness and what it means to be human. It is from this perspective that I would like to discuss Li Yang's film.

The "Local" Tragedy

Blind Shaft presents the chilling tale of two wandering coal mine workers, Tang Chaoyang and Song Jinming, engaged in the scam of making large sums of money by murdering a coworker while in the mines, claiming damages by pretending to be kinsmen of the dead person, and then moving on to their next victim. The (privatized) mine owners/managers, who maximize profits by disregarding safety measures, are callously indifferent to the life and death of their workers, and often consent to some form of payment so as to be able to cover up an incident. After successfully performing their mournful acts of monetary transaction and receiving their "rewards," Tang and Song see to it that all evidence is removed by collecting the belongings of the dead as they depart. At the first opportunity they flush the cremation ashes down a toilet.

In this frame of mind, they next entice a sixteen-year-old boy, Yuan Fengming, into pretending to be Song's nephew and going off with them to a new mine. Everything happens as usual, except that this time Song is beset with doubt because of Yuan's tender age and because he suspects, after being shown a picture of the boy's family, that they have already killed his father.[11] As the time approaches for the murder to take place in the mine, Song becomes unable to act. Sensing that their conspiracy is about to dissolve, Tang takes matters into his own hands and whacks Song with a metal tool before proceeding to kill Yuan. Miraculously, Song regains consciousness and musters enough strength to strike Tang down before he is able to touch Yuan. The young boy manages to exit the mine just before a regular session of dynamite explosion begins, while the two older men are left behind. As Song's designated "relative," Yuan now must take charge of his remains—but the irony is that he is also, despite his reluctance, bound by the contract signed by the older men to accept a sum of thirty thousand *yuan* as compensation for the death of his "uncle."

Obviously, this film can be interpreted as a local tragedy with an unexpected "happy" ending. As the English synopsis on the DVD jacket indicates, for instance: "*Blind Shaft* presents a hugely ironic vision of the Mainland's inexorable thrust towards 'socialist' advancement with capitalistic characteristics. . . . The first half hour of the film is a stunning introduction into the dark side of China's industrialization programme—essentially an exposé of the country's reliance on and exploitation of migrant labourers. . . ." The synopsis in Chinese spells out the "meaning" of the ending more matter-of-factly: "The ending is contrary to expectations. Despite the brutality and hopelessness, a sense of humanity still remains."[12]

As exemplified by the managers in charge of the mines, the major culprits here are the structural deficiencies that pervade the entire industrial production system in China, where working in coal mines is notoriously dangerous and where the death rate of workers is by far the highest in the world.¹³ When the leaders are selfish, corrupt, greedy, and irresponsible, the film seems to say, can it be any surprise that the workers don't give a damn about moral compunctions? If socialism, as a form of modern humanism, is about honoring the contributions and rights—and thus the basic dignity—of the downtrodden classes, *Blind Shift* is first and foremost a stark portrayal of the bankruptcy of Chinese socialism at the turn of the twenty-first century, when China moves opportunistically forward, instead, in *capitalist* global networks of production and exchange. In one scene in which Tang and Song are entertaining themselves and prostitutes at a karaoke bar, they proceed to sing a familiar socialist song with which many Chinese mainlanders grew up, "Shehuizhuyi hao" ("Socialism Is Good")—only to be mocked by their companions as "hicks" because the lyrics have long since been rewritten to reflect China's current pro-capitalist thinking and lifestyles. The old and new versions go respectively as follows:

> Socialism is good, socialism is good!
> Socialist countries are high atop.
> Reactionaries have been overthrown;
> The imperialists have run away with their tails down!

> The reactionaries were never overthrown.
> The capitalists came back with their US dollars,
> Liberating all the people of China,
> Bringing about the orgasm of socialism!¹⁴

To this extent, when the two men carry out their murder schemes, they are, as Ban Wang points out, simply pushing the reifying logic of capitalism "to its grotesque extreme" by "using other human beings as a source of capital that can yield quick returns."¹⁵ At the heart of this local story is, of course, the typical Chinese intellectual's concern about the fate of China as a culture, as suggested in rather explicit terms by the names Tang, Song, and Yuan, which correspond to three major imperial dynasties in Chinese history.

Even as the film addresses the Chinese situation with details scarcely known to the rest of the world, however, the obvious locality of its significance quickly morphs into a much larger, even if not immediately visible, picture. No matter how enormous it is, China is simply one player in the unstoppable, transnational processes of exploiting and depleting the earth's resources so as to satisfy the insatiable demands of human consumption. China's unprecedented need for energy such as coal is, in this regard, simply part of a vicious circle of "world trade" in which we all participate, as is evidenced by the many goods in our possession labeled "Made in China." At the level of nature—as captured on the screen in the desolate, inhospitable landscape—a kind of violence and cruelty is thus being staged in muteness even as our attention remains focused on the human story. There is a way in which the wretched lives of the migrant laborers—not only the makeshift livelihood and deplorable living conditions to which they have been reduced but also the level of depravity to which they have sunk—are a reflection of the bleak environment around them. Together, the laborers and the land form a pool of reserve energy that the world (ab)uses and abandons at will. To this extent, *Blind Shaft* can be viewed as a gritty, unsentimental documentary of the cesspool that human history has become.[16] (There is, for instance, no music from beginning to end to soften things up.) China, where there is "no shortage of human beings," as one coal mine owner/manager in the film puts it—where, in other words, the goods *we* want can always be produced dirt cheap—is simply the most extreme and egregious showcase of this universal waste dump.

But wait, some readers may object, doesn't the ending of the story give us a modicum of hope, when goodness in the form of remorse (on Song's part) provides the unexpected twist and rescues the young man, who is symbolically a stand-in for future generations? No matter how small a turn it is, would it not be possible to reinvest a sense of humanism in Song's change of heart? Could this not be seen as the beginning of a different pathway, even if it is to things we do not yet know for certain?

In my view, all such approaches to the film, including the director's own—which see it alternately as being about local problems of abject migrant labor, global problems of capitalist avarice and environmental debilitation, or a humanistic quest for goodness—are entirely valid but inadequate in explaining the film's powerful affinities with modern world politics. While all these approaches tend to revolve around the assumption of a moral decline, of the disappearance of a viable value system that effectively monitors human behavior (toward other human beings and toward the earth), the film is, I believe, simultaneously performing another, much less comforting, kind of thinking that goes considerably beyond these more familiar moral concerns. Viewing the film from the domain of the West, it is especially important that we recognize this, and resist the temptation of readily deciphering the message of a film such as *Blind Shaft* as, simply, an other-culture-speak (or a kind of third-world-speak), with the kind of neo-liberal, egalitarian (but in fact discriminatory) undertone that comes across all too often in influential publications such as *The New York Times*. In this spirit, I'd like to suggest that despite Li Yang's conscious designs, *Blind Shaft* delivers nothing short of a dramatization, albeit on a small scale, of the predicament of human community formation in general.

Kinship as "Conscience" and Education as "Hope"

In a primary philosophical manner, the activity of coal mining reminds us of the inextricable relationship that humans have with nature, of the fact that it is through the excavation and channeling of nature's energies that human developments—industrial, commercial, cultural—are possible. (The title *Shen mu* [Sacred Wood] of the original story is, from this perspective, ecologically as well as fictionally suggestive: It refers to the mythic beginnings of the discovery of coal in that area by some villagers who mistook the inflammable quality of the black graphite-like material, churned up from the riverbed after a flood, for the presence of divine spirit.[17]) For Heidegger, this relationship between humans and nature is premised on a process of revealing, a bringing-forth (in cultural processes that he names *techne* and *poiesis*) that, importantly, never ends:

> The revealing that rules throughout modern technology has the character of a setting-upon, in the sense of a challenging-forth. That challenging happens in that the energy concealed in nature is unlocked, what is unlocked is transformed, what is transformed is stored up, what is stored up is, in turn, distributed, and what is distributed is switched about ever anew. Unlocking, transforming, storing, distributing, and switching about are ways of revealing. But the revealing never simply comes to an end. Neither does it run off into the indeterminate. The revealing reveals to itself its own manifoldly interlocking paths, through regulating their course. This regulating itself is, for its part, everywhere secured. Regulating and securing even become the chief characteristics of the challenging revealing.[18]

Following Heidegger's hints about revealing and bringing-forth, but not strictly complying with his insistence on the essence of humanity as such, we may ask: What is being unlocked, transformed, stored, distributed, and switched about in the events of *Blind Shaft*? Other than as a subject ordering the universe by various instrumental means, what kind of truth about the "human" is being revealed and brought forth?

On close examination, I would contend, the story of *Blind Shaft* is not so much about good versus evil (about, for instance, the murderers versus their latest victim, or the poor miners/laborers versus the capitalist system, and so forth) as about the politics of human group formation. In Tang and Song's practice of recruiting and murdering strangers, one feature repeats itself as an indispensable melodramatic ingredient: The person they pick must take on the fake identity of being related to one of them by blood (as Yuan has to become Song's "nephew"), so that their eventual claim for damages can be justified. The strategy key to the entire scam is, in other words, the fabrication of a particular unit of social organization—namely, the kinship family—that appeals to others as something natural and authentic.

Insofar as the accidental death of a kinsman is deemed a major loss, one that deserves due compensation, the kinship family stands as the inviolable basic social unit—what one might further specify as a kind of inalienable property or evidence of (self-) ownership—that rationalizes human relations. Hence, when this basic social unit is perceived to be threatened or harmed (as in the case of a death), it is assumed that it needs, somehow, to be made up for as though it were a fatal injury. What enables Tang and Song's scam to function smoothly, then, is not simply that they lie but that other people—the owners/managers of the mines in particular—are ready and willing to credit the nonnegotiable centrality of the kinship family. Tang and Song can get away with their murderous schemes because everyone else has always already been fully interpellated into the "reality" of kinship ties.[19]

Why is kinship so important?

Paradoxically, throughout the film these same men who kill non-kinsmen without compunction also reveal themselves as caring and responsible kinsmen: We see them chatting about their sons' progress at school, sending money home, and contacting loved ones by long-distance phone, promising to be home for the New Year. Despite having to drift from place to place to find work, these murderers have nonetheless not neglected their obligations to their families. Li Yang's interesting remarks on this crucial (because seemingly self-contradictory) dimension of the story are worth quoting at length at this juncture, as they point to what is perhaps most at stake in the interpretation of this film:

> When I was observing the miners, although their lives were hard, they were not morose or dispirited. They possessed a kind of humour, or a sort of magnanimous view of life—what the Chinese call *renming* (or an acceptance of fate). They want to change their lives but they can't do it. Being poor citizens

they are concerned about how to earn money safely and go home to feed their families.

> *I adopt a sympathetic attitude [toward the two lead characters].* Because one of them wanted to free himself from the evil but couldn't do it. Though we are confronted with his immense evil, humanity isn't entirely obliterated and he's capable of being touched by sentimentality or the benevolent side of humanity.
>
> [These two men] have a decent side—*they are thrifty* as shown by the fact that they are not willing to spend even five dollars watching a video, and they stay in cheap hotels—*the first thing they do once they have money is to send some back to their families.* Why are such people capable of evil? . . . Why are these two people on the road to destruction?
>
> *The family as a virtue has been passed down through thousands of years of Chinese civilization.* Our traditionalist culture in respect to the family, its ethical values, has withstood the Cultural Revolution and foreign invasion. Why has it continued to be passed down the ages? I have constantly thought about this question. *The family is a theme in the background, and because of this, you can't say that conscience has been completely eliminated from the two characters.*[20]

Although, in terms of its documentary-like film language, *Blind Shaft* is on first viewing quite different from other contemporary Chinese feature films, Li's reflections help clarify how it in fact shares with them a major tendency toward the sentimentalizing of kinship. By attributing to the kinship family—or more precisely, the emotional attachment to the kinship family—the foundational import of "conscience," Li returns us to what I would argue is the very core of Chinese sentimentalism, a sentimentalism whose residual pull is experienced even by the most ruthless of murderers, who are (for Li) themselves victims of the chaotic changes sweeping through China. No less important is the fact that these murderers express their sense of familial attachment in the form of a concern for learning—specifically, for making sure that their children receive a good education. Kinship bonds matter, then, not only as an age-old cultural legacy that has "withstood the Cultural Revolution and foreign invasion," as Li says, but also as a way to the future: Such bonds present the possibility of extending one's life through the secure (social as well as biological) survival of the next generation.

Insofar as a redeemable sense of "good" can be traced in the two evil men's commitment to kinship and education, *Tang and Song are not so distinguishable from Yuan*: The young boy, we are told, is interested in making enough money so he can return to school. In other words, despite their differences the three males are ultimately subscribing to the same value system in which it is believed that education is the best means of future success, and in which one should have no qualms about sacrificing oneself for one's kin.[21] Moreover, this value system is thoroughly steeped in patriarchy, at least insofar as it is enacted by Tang and Song (Yuan is working so that his sister can stay in school). Through the coal miners we are introduced to a world in which women function primarily as sex objects (prostitutes are a cheap form of entertainment in the towns near the coal mines); the males socialize by sharing cigarettes, drinks, food, baths, sex jokes, and even a hotel room for simultaneous acts of copulation; and a young boy like Yuan must, it is said, be given his initiation into sex (however reluctant he may be) before he can be killed off. The presence of good strong women (such as the young prostitute who was forced on Yuan and the older woman who sees him off at the end) notwithstanding, this is a world in which a projection of the future is made primarily through sons. In addition to caring about his own son's education, we should remember, Song's primary reason for hesitating to kill Yuan is that, with Yuan's father (possibly) already dead, killing the son might mean driving the Yuan family line into extinction.

As we move our attention to the vestiges of kinship as the moral—and ideological—backdrop of the story, the violence and cruelty that accompany group formation come into much sharper focus. For instance, although Tang and Song are not related by blood, they have in effect formed a secret, blood-like bond, which serves as the basis for their illegitimate undertakings. What makes their partnership work is none other than an implicit mutual consent to a demarcated *interiority* of relations, one that must remain firmly marked off from the exterior. The strict adherence to this differentiation between the inside and the outside, this boundary between "us" and "them," is precisely what coheres and sustains the aggression against the outsiders, even as the material wellbeing of the insiders (the "family" or "kin" group) is structurally dependent on—in fact, derived from—the labor, good will, and collaboration of these outsiders. Under this type of social organization, the survival of the insiders—the possibility for them of a future, so to speak—is contingent on the status quo, that is, the continued solicitation, exploitation, and extermination of the "foreign" bodies that are considered as excess and disposable once they have served their utilitarian purpose.

In Song's refusal to carry out the murder plot as planned, the blind and primal desire to continue an inside group's existence ad infinitum at the expense of outsiders is, notably, interrupted. In this interruption—what amounts to an unprecedented recognition of the outsider's equal right to life—lies a small but significant opening, whereby Yuan can, presumably, return home, resume his formal education, become a good citizen, and help transform his society. Following the logic of this briefly emergent, benevolent tolerance, it would perhaps be possible, finally, to view education as a type of human cultural activity that occupies the status of *techne* and *poiesis*, in what Heidegger would affirm as a *positive* instance of the challenging-forth of Being. Li, on his part, puts it in the form of hope: "As for the ending, vis-à-vis the boy's fate, I wanted something open.... A child is the hope of mankind.... He is also the hope of the story."[22]

Li's deliberate intentions notwithstanding, however, the conceptual trajectory taken by the film remains intriguingly ambiguous as to the precise connotations and implications of education as a "solution." For instance, the respect for education is, as I have noted, shared by all the characters, including the irrevocably "evil" Tang (who appears to be semi-illiterate). Yet, if education is unquestionably valuable—the film compels us to ask—how is it that some who believe in it can at the same time be so cruel and indifferent to others, the "outsiders"? *Can this simply be explained by, or blamed on, "causes" such as the capitalist mode of production, globalization, China's new social situation, etc.—or does not the answer need to be sought somewhere else?* How can a supposedly enlightened belief in the virtue of learning—as the hope for the future—coexist so matter-of-factly with the cold-blooded practice of extirpating those who are not "us"—simply for the sake of money? Is education really the solution to the magnitude of the problems unveiled before our eyes?

Reflected on these terms, the iterative references to education in the film are not unlike the refrains of humanistic platitudes that we encounter everywhere we turn, from the orations of politicians to the declarations of entrepreneurs and media personalities alike—even as the New World Order of inhumanity saturates international relations on a daily basis with incidents of torture, illegal detention, persecution, and numerous other forms of discrimination and brutality against helpless peoples. Exactly what are the power relations that sustain *this* alienation—not so much the existential alienation created by class or economic disparity (as is so poignantly portrayed in this film) as *the disjuncture between the sign of a collective ideal (such as "education"), on the one side, and on the other, the violence and cruelty of actual human interactions*? How do we come to terms with the co-presence of these incommensurate human realities—a co-presence that, to return to Heidegger's terminology, seems to be at once the symptom of a certain oblivion *and* a revelation/bringing-forth that seems nothing short of a fracturing of the continuum of the "human" as such?

I am therefore inclined to seeing *Blind Shaft* as a specifically Chinese sentimental allegory about the very mutation of the concept of "human"—that is to say, as the unconcealment of a process of species-differentiation that is happening at the rupture between the positive sign of human culture, "education" (read: humanity-as-progress, or hope), *and* the ubiquitous biopolitical warfare around natural and other resources, and above all around kinship and other types of group survival—all of which being, of course, inseparable from education. To bring our reading of Heidegger up to date, perhaps *this* unconcealment must be recognized as our contemporary global condition of homelessness.

In the context of Chinese sentimentalism, the most unsettling questions posed by this film's narrative and characterization are these: Is kinship, defined as an inviolable *interiority* of familial/familiar relations as I have specified, in essence the last vestige of morality (and of "humanity") left in an utterly amoral world—in the sense that except for the protection and preservation of one's kin, nothing else really matters? At the same time, is not such commitment to kinship bonds, so deeply rooted in Chinese societies as to be associated with, and reaffirmed as, "conscience" itself, precisely complicit with some of the worst xenophobic—indeed murderous—practices in the contemporary world? What kind of "conscience" are we talking about when *kindness* is literally—and exclusively—directed at advancing one's own kin(d)?

Ironically, then, the Chinese sentimental attachment to *home* (in the multiple senses of one's blood family, kin, house, and so forth—all those ties marked off as the inside of a particular group as opposed to the outside) stands in this analysis as an instructive case in point of the modern and contemporary world condition of "homelessness." As a defense against this dangerous and depressing condition, perhaps our only viable choice is to give allegiance after all to the collective cultural ideality of education (as the last-ditch custodian of Being). Even so, we should probably not forget Balibar's warning about the inevitability of violence:

> Supposing . . . that the counterpart to the experience of cruelty is always some sort of particularly demanding thirst for *ideality*—either in the sense of *non-violent* ideals, or in the sense of ideals of *justice*—how are we to deal philosophically and practically with what I consider to be a matter of incontrovertible finality: that there is no liberation from violence, no resistance to its worst excesses, especially no *collective* resistance . . . *without ideals*? However, there is no guarantee, and there can be no guarantee,

concerning the "good use" and the "bad use" of ideals—or, if you prefer, there are certainly *degrees* in the amount of violence which goes along with civilizing ideals; but nothing like a *zero* degree. Therefore there is no such thing as non-violence.[23]

PART III

Heteronomy and Futurity in Psychoanalysis

CHAPTER 7

The Foreign, the Uncanny, and the Foreigner: Concepts of the Self and the Other in Psychoanalysis and Contemporary Philosophy

Rudi Visker

Although the first and the last word in my title differ by only one syllable, it is this, at first sight, negligible difference that will be at the center of this paper's attempt to question one of the few themes on which today's humanities seem, by and large, in agreement: the idea that there is a link between the theme of the foreign (the strange, the other small "o") and that of the foreigner (the stranger, the Other capital "o"). This link seems to be so evident that it is hardly ever articulated—it is, more often implicitly than explicitly, itself linked with a number of assumptions concerning the role that psychoanalysis could play in a "progressive" contemporary philosophy. One of these assumptions is that, if one follows psychoanalysis in introducing the other into the self, the relation between such a self and the Other (the foreign*er*, the strange*r*) will become less tense. This belief in the possible results of combining psychoanalysis and a philosophical valuation of the Other is *exemplarily* formulated by Julia Kristeva, an author with a well-established reputation both in philosophical and in analytical circles, in a short passage from which I will start off my analysis.

However, before doing so, I should first like to stress again its exemplarity. Its authorship is in a sense of secondary importance; what matters is that a certain author, named Kristeva, and regardless of what she may have said elsewhere, gives voice in this passage to an *énoncé*, a discursive statement that isn't characteristically hers, but that points to the "archive" or the "order of discourse" from out of which we all, to a certain extent, speak.[1] It is not the fact that it is *Kristeva* who writes this that interests me, but that what she writes is something we all seem to underwrite, to the point of no longer even taking note of what it is in fact that we are in agreement with. Our disagreements in the humanities presuppose that first agreement that is not an agreement with or against a particular author, but rather something like an *episteme*, a discursive soil, a horizon that is operative in and presupposed by all the ongoing discussions that are made possible by it. Indeed, as Foucault has shown, in *The Order of Things*, for example, the tendency to focus on authors, on their auctorial mastery over their works, and hence the increasing parochialism and the partisanship that characterizes so much of the secondary literature,[2] shares with the history of ideas a common blindness: It focuses on what Foucault calls the "tines of a fork," and neglects that they have a common stem that is stuck in a discursive soil from the perspective of which the passionate discussions between the tines are no more than "storms in a children's paddling pool."[3]

Having said this, I hope the reader will for now be willing to bracket Kristeva's name and reputation and simply read the following passages taken from the end of her extremely popular *Strangers to Ourselves* in which she combines what I take to be a philosophical and a psychoanalytical argument to reach the following cosmopolitan conclusion:

> On the basis of an erotic, death-bearing unconscious, the uncanny strangeness . . . sets the difference *within* us in its most bewildering shape and presents it as the ultimate condition of our being with others. . . . By recognizing *our* uncanny strangeness, we shall neither suffer from it nor enjoy it from the outside. The foreign is within me, hence we are all foreigners.[4]

Hence, her conclusion that "the ethics of psychoanalysis implies a politics: It would involve a cosmopolitanism of a new sort that, cutting across governments, economies, and markets, might work for a mankind whose solidarity is founded on the consciousness of its unconscious—desiring, destructive, fearful, empty, impossible."[5] To summarize: if we recognize the foreign in us, we will no longer have a problem with foreigners.

As I stated before, I think that the conclusion to which Kristeva *jumps* in this passage is not warranted by what she has shown. But before coming to that, let me first show how the kind of reasoning to which we are invited here profits from the philosophical climate that is characteristic of our times. We live in an age of intersubjectivity that no longer approaches the existence of others as a problem, but is rather inclined to embrace it as a solution to the problems into which a solitary subject inevitably runs. Hence the popularity of expressions like "the other" (with or without capital) or "the other in me," which have the additional advantage of suggesting some sort of solidarity between what psychoanalysis shows and what philosophers are trying to advance. Instead of remaining hostile if not allergic to Freudian thought, contemporary philosophy's preoccupation with the other seems to welcome it to the point of no longer even being shocked by what in Freud once shocked philosophy: the attempt, for example, to think an unconsciousness that could not privatively be derived from consciousness, but that instead would force one to rethink consciousness itself! Whereas traditional philosophers, like Sartre, protested just that move, contemporary philosophers seem to find in it just the ammunition they need to further dethrone the subject from its once privileged position. One enthusiastically quotes Freud's "the I is no master in his own house" in one breath with Nietzsche's "man is riding the back of a tiger" to triumphantly conclude that the subject is a mirage one no longer has to believe in. A conclusion that would to psychoanalytic ears betray but another resistance—as if the truth would lie hidden in the Id, and as if the yoke that we would need to be emancipated from would be the Ego or the Superego. In the terms of Freud's first topology: as if consciousness would only be an obstacle that prevents the unconscious from exercising its therapeutic and liberating force. Though these are not exactly Kristeva's assertions, what she does assert seems to come dangerously close. Let us look in some detail at what Kristeva must be presupposing for her argument to work.

1. *Kristeva's Presuppositions*

On a charitable reading, Kristeva is recommending that the subject should learn to accept the strangeness or foreignness that it experiences in itself, so that it can also accept the foreignness it is confronted with from the outside. This acceptance is at the core of the psychoanalytic ethics she has in mind—an ethics in which she sees a cure for the tendency to blame others for what, from her point of view, they cannot and ought not to be blamed for. For the subject is split within itself—it bears the strange in itself—and this split is accordingly not something that others inflict upon it and that could be eliminated by eliminating these others. In other words, the irritation we feel toward the strangeness outside of us ("the problem of the foreigners") is, according to Kristeva, but the flipside of our *incapacity* to recognize the strangeness/foreignness in us. Inversely, solidarity with the foreigner presupposes that we should admit or allow the foreign within ourselves. Instead of closing ourselves off from the other/strange/foreign in us, we should open ourselves to it. And by thus opening ourselves, we would be able to overcome the very borders that divide humanity into natives (autochthonous) and foreigners (allochthonous). Hence the central statement: "If I am a foreigner, there are no foreigners."

Apparently the foreign within us has the capacity to give birth both to what is best and to what is worst in us. It all seems to depend on how we react to it—in a flexible acceptance or an anxious attempt to ward it off. The problem with this line of reasoning lies in its twofold premise: Firstly, why would the foreign within me be in harmony with the foreign of or within the Other? Why would the mutual contact between these two instances of the foreign lead to solidarity and not to, for example, fratricide? And, secondly, what guarantee do we have that even the foreign that I recognize in myself should be content with that recognition?

Expressions such as "the foreign within me" or "the other within the self," suggest that the "within" is self-evidently guaranteed. As if there would be a border between the foreign and the self that prevents that foreign from invading that self, and, eventually, from destroying it. In other words, one tacitly assumes that the relation between the foreign and the self ("the foreign within me") can be one of mutual respect: The other-within-me would respect the borders that assign it to the kind of place that is signaled by the word "within"—a kind of inner extraterritoriality. This is surely an all-but-self-evident assumption to make, especially bearing in mind that when Kristeva is talking about the foreign/strange, she means the unconscious, of which she herself states that it is "fearful, empty, impossible."[6] Freud's uncanniness—which Kristeva renders as "inquiétante étrangeté," discomforting strangeness—seems to have become surprisingly "canny," "comfortable," almost homey. Uncanniness gets a homeopathic function: Difference *in* us becomes a precondition for us living with difference *outside* of us. As if Freud had not remarked that the prefix "un-" in "uncanny" was "the token of repression."[7] The uncanny, Freud had learned from Schelling, concerns those situations where something that ought to have remained hidden and secret comes to light.[8] In other words, those situations in which what is repressed returns, and in which repression has been unsuccessful and the barrier that upholds it is "effaced."[9] What is so discomforting about the strangeness Freud is talking about is that it refers to a situation in which a border is *no longer* operative: In the uncanny, something comes to the fore which was not meant to show itself. What was meant to remain private suddenly appears in public. And instead of feeling solidarity, what Freud says we are experiencing is unease, a discomfort. We feel "awkward," and react to the uncanny with a (mild) anxiety.

In the light of this, it seems all but evident on exactly what basis Kristeva wants to erect her ethics. *Either* the foreign respects the borders that assign it a place within me, but then repression is successful and there is no uncanniness at all. *Or* there is uncanniness, which means that the foreign has invaded the self, but then it is unclear why that foreign would be kind enough to assign an enclave to the self instead of simply destroying it.

Clearly, what Kristeva needs for her argument to work is a distinction between a good and a bad other—where the good would not only be good for/to me, but also for/to the Other (capital O) outside me. Such a good other would bring me to open myself up for that Other outside of me and would perhaps even bring me to sacrifice my self-interest to that Other's well-being. There is at least one philosopher who has constructed a system around such a notion of a good "other-in-me" that can change me without crushing me.[10] But that philosopher—Emmanuel Levinas—has also pointed out the price one needs to pay for the introduction of such a good other, which he calls the soul:[11] one would need to agree that the subject, before it is tied to and vowed to itself, is tied to and vowed to the Other. And this in turn makes, as Levinas explicitly says,[12] notions like God and creation "necessary."[13] But there is no mention of these notions in Kristeva. Nor would they seem to inspire Freud. Which brings us to a second point, which will be brief: Freud's anti-cosmopolitanism.

2. Freud's Anti-cosmopolitanism

For all I know, there is nothing in Freud's texts that would favor the cosmopolitan ethics that Kristeva advocates. To the contrary, there are many passages that work against it. Let me just remind you of the pages in *Civilization and its Discontents* in which he sees in the command to love thy neighbor an "excellent example of the un-psychological proceedings of the cultural Superego."[14] For this command, says Freud, goes against human nature: "It issues a command and does not ask whether it is possible for people to obey it"; "it [the Superego] does not trouble itself enough about the facts of the mental constitution of human beings."[15] As for these facts, Freud is a follower of Hobbes: "Men are not gentle creatures who want to be loved, and who at the most can defend themselves if they are attacked; they are, to the contrary, creatures among whose intellectual endowments is to be reckoned a powerful share of aggressiveness."[16] He quotes Plautus's *homo homini lupus* and even

Heine's "one must, it is true, forgive one's enemies—but not before they have been hanged."[17] Freud does not doubt that a foreigner who does not respect what to his mind is strange/foreign about me, is, in his turn, "unworthy of my love"—worse: "He has more claim to my hostility and even my hatred."[18]

Freud's message seems to be the inverse of Kristeva's: Culture can attempt to restrict human aggressiveness but cannot eliminate it. If it denies such aggressiveness, it will turn against the individual subject and make it unhappy. The command to love one's neighbor as oneself rests on an assumption which Freud does not hesitate to call "a mistake":

> It assumes that a man's ego is psychologically capable of anything that is required of it, that his *ego* has unlimited capacity over his *id*. . . . Even in what are known as normal people the *id* cannot be controlled beyond certain limits. If more is demanded of men, a revolt will be produced in him, or a neurosis, or he will be made unhappy.[19]

One would do wrong to attribute the different attitudes toward the foreigner one finds in Freud and Kristeva merely to their different views on man—e.g., Freud's naturalistic sobriety versus Kristeva's rousseauistic optimism, which would lie behind her belief in the natural goodness of man. It would be a mistake to simply treat Freud as a naturalist—as Vergote once remarked, "Freud did not naturalise man, he humanised nature in man."[20] The drive is not an instinct, but something between the somatic and the psychic. Which is, no doubt, the reason the author of "Triebe und Triebschicksale" (Drives and their fate, commonly translated as "Instincts and Their Vicissitudes") was so interested in Greek tragedy. For the tragic hero's fate (*Schicksal*) is not that of someone who is either guilty or innocent. As is well known, Oedipus realized his fate by trying to escape it—was he guilty or not? If there is any ethics to be found here, it is a tragic ethics that takes into account human finitude. It is that finitude that Freud wanted to bring out by focusing on the unconscious. For the unconscious confronts us with a paradox: "It works behind my back and yet it comes from me . . . it seems to be something that just happens and yet it is not foreign to me."[21] Perhaps one should, to do justice to that paradox, resort to a double negation and admit that I am "not unresponsible" for it, that I am "not uninvolved."

In what follows, I should like to bring this apparent disagreement between Freud and Kristeva into further relief by connecting Freud's exploration of the uncanny to a number of his remarks on the "narcissism of minor differences." As these remarks will show, the psychoanalytic conception of the relation between the foreign and one's own cannot be rendered by a simple "in." Instead of introducing an other "in" the self, psychoanalysis rather points to the otherness of that self, to it being foreign to itself in the sense that the "own" should be understood as something that is both strange and related to the self that is supposed to own that "own"ness. Lacan coined a nice expression for that: He speaks of an "extimacy," a neologism derived from intimacy, which itself is derived from the superlative *intimus*, like in Augustine's famous *intimior intimo meo*. I would like to show how Freud's "minor differences" can be understood through such extimacy.

3. Two Hypotheses on Narcissism

Freud introduced the term "narcissism of minor differences" to point to the "phenomenon that it is precisely communities with adjoining territories and related to each other in other ways as well, who are engaged in constant feuds and in ridiculing each other—like the Spaniards and Portuguese, for instance, the North Germans and the South Germans, the English and the Scottish." He sees in this phenomenon "a convenient and relatively harmless satisfaction of the inclination to aggressiveness, by means of which cohesion between the members of the community is made easier." It is always possible, Freud writes, "to bind together a considerable number of people in love, so long as there are other people left over to receive the manifestations of their aggressiveness." An anti-cosmopolitan creed, if there ever was one! "The advantage which a comparatively small cultural group offers of allowing this instinct an outlet in the form of hostility against intruders is not to be despised."[22]

An example that immediately comes to mind is the European Union: The more it gets united, the more it gets divided by all sorts of particularisms that resist such unification and defend their differences, no matter how small and negligible they are. The same would hold for what distinguishes, for example, the Serbs from the Croats in former Yugoslavia (the differences that they now insist upon between their languages were once small enough to allow for Serbo-Croatian/English dictionaries).[23] But why does Freud link this phenomenon to narcissism and whence that omnipresent appeal to an aggressiveness that, as such, is never explained? And why is that "Aggressions*trieb*" (a *drive*, not an instinct!) triggered by minor differences rather than by big ones?

The answer seems obvious, although, surprisingly, Freud does not give it himself—according to him the term, which he coined, "does not do much to explain the phenomenon."[24] Indeed, it does not. At least as long as one follows Freud's views on primary narcissism where the Ego is at first a libidinally invested narcissistic object that gradually learns to decathect part of its energy and invest it in objects of the outside world. Narcissism, here, refers to the Ego that is at first closed in itself and that only gradually opens up to reality and leaves its protective shell. The movement thus goes from the inside to the outside.[25]

As is well known, Lacan in his famous paper on *The Mirror Stage* (1949) starts from an inverse hypothesis: Here the movement is from the outside to the inside—the child finds its Ego in and through the other. It is the body of the other child (or its own mirror image) that is perceived as the *Gestalt* in which the child finds something it itself does not yet have: unity, motoric control.[26] Strictly spoken, one cannot state that the child recognizes its self in the Other, for it is only by/through that other that the child comes to a kind of self. Identity ("self," "unity," etc.) is the result of an identification without subject.[27] And the subject that results from it finds itself in an impasse that is both structural and that gives it its structure. Since it only reaches itself through the other, it needs that other (it is the other's self that models its "own" self). But for that very reason the other is an obstacle that prevents it from reaching the unity that it aspires to. To put this differently, identity will always bear the trace of an exteriority that it cannot fully interiorize. I am another (*je est un autre*, literally: [the] I is another) means: I cannot do without that other through whom I get an I. That other becomes someone that I cannot expel. In other words, my alienation is original, for it is implied in my self-constitution. There is no "selfhood" without "foreignhood." The self is not something I possess, my "self" is irremediably infected with an otherness that prevents me from being fully at one with myself. Think of what happens in jealousy: One hates that other whom one admires so much that one is constantly trying to bring him down.

Interestingly, one finds the same sort of ambivalence in our reaction to foreigners: "too lazy to do anything, only here to profit from us" and at the same time "trying to steal our jobs." It is as if the foreigner provides us with a welcome outlet for the internal ambivalence (*je est un autre*) under which we *already* suffer.[28] Racism would thus, on this "Lacanian" reading, accommodate for an *intra*subjective problem. It could be a kind of therapy that offers the advantage of giving us control over what seemed without issue: If there would no longer be any foreigners, we would be alright again—without fissure, undivided, united. And this therapy offers the further advantage that it makes that ambivalence a bit less ambivalent, more manageable. For now the other has a quality that makes him different from me and in which I can find a reason for my hate and my aggression: "He is Mexican and lazy." Or "He is Mexican and wants to steal my job from me." The *intra*subjective problem can thus be projected onto an outside and thereby becomes *inter*subjective and hence manageable. One can give voice, as in the example just given, to two contradictory feelings but not at the same time. It takes time to express such sentiments, but by taking time (and place) it also *gives* time and place to the one who is in the grip of such passions. Instead of being paralyzed by an internal ambivalence that pushes him backwards and forwards and hence immobilizes him, the racist can now quite literally give himself "an" attitude, or even two, the one contradicting the other, but not at the same time.

For Lacan, then, the problem of the Ego is not situated outside of it, but inside of it. Aggressiveness feeds on an original introjection—it is the outside that gives rise to an inside, which it infects with an exteriority that such inside will subsequently try, but never manage, to expel. This goes against the common understanding of a narcissist as a person who always has already experienced whatever one is trying to tell him about oneself. In short, someone who is so occupied with himself that he is incapable of giving you attention, of opening up, and instead is only busy projecting his own experiences on whoever crosses his path. An unbearable person who should learn to show consideration for others beside himself! That is Freud's conception. Lacan's is exactly the reverse: Instead of having to learn to open itself for others, the subject should find a way not to be crushed by that other who, from the beginning, is already inside. On this conception of narcissism, it would seem that one would have to invert Kristeva's conclusion: There is only a problem with foreigners because there is already something foreign in me. Worse: It is because foreigners resemble me without being completely identical ("minor differences") that I am constantly at risk of being drawn into the vortex of that dynamic that is propelled by the "je est un autre"—by what is, necessarily, *constitutively strange* to me. Hence my aggressiveness—it originates in the very mineness of that "me" which I cannot fully be.

4. The Importance of Minor Differences

Let us return to the "minor differences." Freud has one or two things to add that may help us understand why exactly it is *minor* differences that come to irritate us. "Big" differences might not have the same effect—if they are big enough, we react differently to them, or not at all. I would, for example, remain indifferent if the cat is in the bathroom where my wife undresses, but I would not react likewise if it were not the cat, but another male. Unless, of course, if I were the president of the V.O.C. (the Dutch East India Company) and that other male was the local servant, whose job it was to hand her the warm water she needs to wash herself. Big enough differences are not threatening: A cat, a local servant, a slave are not at my level—I cannot possibly *mirror* myself in them. Such differences are, as Bernard Williams would call them, purely "notional"[29]—think of the Samurai culture or Neolithic civilization: I know that they constitute other ways of being human, but these possibilities are out of my reach; they are not "a real option" to me. They can at most arouse my intellectual curiosity, as when, for example, I read the Dalai Lama about death, but they do not constitute a threat. I do not experience them as relativizing my culture. There is only an intellectual, not an existential relation.

This seems different in the case of "minor differences." Listen to this passage from Freud's *Group Psychology and the Analysis of the Ego*:

> In the undisguised antipathies and aversions, which people feel towards strangers with whom they have to deal, we may recognize the expressions of self-love, of narcissism. This self-love works for the preservation of the individual, and behaves as though the occurrence of any divergence from his own particular lines of development *involved a criticism of them and a demand for their alteration*.... We do not know why such sensitiveness should have been directed to just these details of differentiation.[30] (italics added)

But a mere three years before this, he had written a line or two that can help us further. I am thinking of the opening passage of a text in which he sets out to discuss "a detail in the sexual life of primitive races"—the disgust they feel toward women whose virginity is still intact (!) when they enter marriage. These cultures have been very creative in finding means to overcome this "problem": ritual mating, artificial rupture of the hymen, *ius primae noctis*, and all sorts of other practices that led to the "defloration of the brides."[31] Freud even refers to a Roman marriage ceremony described by Augustine where the wife had to seat herself upon the gigantic stone phallus of Priapus. At the beginning of that same essay, "The Taboo of Virginity," in which he mentions for the first time our "minor differences," Freud wrote the following: "There are few details of the sexual life of primitive races which seem so strange to us as their [negative] attitude towards virginity, the condition in a woman of being sexually untouched. The high value set [by our own culture] upon her virginity by a man wooing a woman seems to us so deeply embedded and self-evident that we become *almost perplexed* and feel *as if called upon to give reasons for it* (italics added).[32]

The primitive taboo on virginity does not make Freud's contemporaries doubt the value they themselves put on it. But it embarrasses them, by demonstrating that this notion, which appeared to be self-evident, was only self-evident *for them* and not for others. In such situations, Freud says, there is a kind of perplexity that overcomes us—there seems to be something about what is evidently our own, like our own culture, that we are not or barely able to account for. That inability—that confrontation with the apparent unfoundedness of what is proper to us—perplexes us. Twenty years later, in his *Moses and Monotheism*, Freud relates such perplexity to "people's hatred of the Jews."[33] To be sure, Freud reasons, the Jewish people are one of those minorities against which larger groups can unite in self-love. But he does not believe that to be a sufficient explanation of anti-Semitism: "The Jews are ... different, often in an *indefinable* way different, especially from the Nordic peoples and the intolerance of groups (*Rassen*) is often, *strangely enough*, exhibited more strongly against small differences than against fundamental ones" (italics added).[34] And a bit later he mentions circumcision as one of those customs that makes a "disagreeable, uncanny impression" on non-Jews.[35]

One should no doubt relate the uncanniness, the strangeness, the perplexity, which Freud wants to understand, to "the *indefinable* character" of the otherness he describes. For it seems that it is not only the other that escapes definition, but also the self that is confronted with it—this self experiences its very selfhood as something to which it finds itself attached without being able to sufficiently ground this attachment, to lay out the reasons for it. As if there is something about the other that escapes the mirror-relation between us, as if there is a tiny spot or crack in the mirror, a small difference that points me back toward the structural aporia that was involved in my becoming a self, in my getting an identity. As if my own indifference is "represented" in that small difference, in that blind and hence indefinable spot where the mirror does not reflect my image back to me. But note that "represented" is clearly not the correct term. As Lacan helped us realize, the re"present"ation concerns something that was never present for me, that has always escaped definition because I grew out of it. Which is why its "presence" is experienced as a threat, as something uncanny, almost suffocating, closing in on me. This something has to do something with me, it defines in one way or another who I am, but it escapes de-finition (from the Latin *finis*, border, contour) by the I that it defines: It escapes its grasp. Unlike ordinary things or properties, it is not graspable in a concept. My self-hood, my "own"ness, what is proper to me, escapes me: I do not own it, it is not something *for* me or *of* me, it is rather something "about" me. It is too close for me to conceive or understand it: It is *that* about my being which makes it *my* being and not someone else's; it is the difference that differentiates me.

Such a "that" is not objectifiable; it is not of the order of normal objects.[36] But neither is it a mere nothing—not being something, nor nothing, this "thing" about me that I cannot place at a distance haunts me. Some "thing" returns here that ought to have remained hidden. The uncanny overwhelms me when this "thing" that is not a thing nor a nothing and that singularizes me is awakened by the foreigner outside me. However, and this is crucial, the affect that accompanies such an awakening is not an affect that I can assume. Unlike anxiety in Heidegger or shame in Levinas, it is an affect that I need to be protected from. *And for that I need help from the outside.* I need a frame that makes that experience bearable, by which I can locate it, frame it, and localize it. In short, I need a kind of story by which I can have it make sense. Not that I would with the help of such a narrative be able to understand it, but the story could help me bind it: By giving it a place in a narrative, I may be able to prevent it from being everywhere and nowhere, all around me. The story could help me contain what I cannot hold out on my own. It provides a stage, a theatre where I can sit and watch at a distance what otherwise would shake me up so profoundly that it could be the end of me. Such is, for example, the role of art (though not exclusively of art), which Freud perhaps did not stress enough in his analysis of the uncanny: There seems to be an essential difference between the uncanny in literature, movies, etc., and the encounter with it in real life where we bump into it outside of any such framing and hence are confronted with it without any protection. Imagine not reading about "Der Sandmann" but "meeting" him in real life—imagine "living" Hoffman's story! But art is only one example among many. A similar "stage-ing" happens in an analytic setting and—why not—in what Lefort calls the "mise en scène" of a political regime.[37] Politics, too, could be about a framework that allows us to bind to a certain time and place, the differences—not just between us, but inside each of us—that would otherwise destroy us.[38]

These last remarks bring us back to our societies' problem with foreigners. Perhaps the fact that they experience these problems should not be related, as Kristeva would have it, to them not sufficiently opening up to the foreign in themselves (cf. note 4). But to the contrary, to them being overloaded by what is strange, uncanny, and foreign to/about their very selves. As if the other, unbeknownst to himself, has rendered the very soil on which we move in our familiar ways, unfamiliar.[39] No doubt we should stop blaming the other for that, but the question is: What does it take, what do we need to stop doing so? Psychoanalytical practice suggests a politics indeed: not a politics based on the good will or the individual tolerance of a tolerant individual who has learned to accept the other in him/her self, but a politics that comes to aid what we cannot handle on our own. It suggests that we need to change the way in which we have arranged our societies. Not by expelling the foreigners, but by creating similar stages or theatres that show and contain what divides each of us in ourselves. Arendt in *The Human Condition* has a wonderful phrase that points in the same direction: "Passions," she writes, "lead an uncertain, shadowy kind of existence unless and until they are transformed, deprivatized and deindividualized, as it were, into a shape to fit them for public appearance."[40] If there is a lesson to be learned from psychoanalysis, it is that such transformation cannot be the work of the individual's own doing. Not just because he needs an ear that accompanies him, but because both analyst and patient can only come to realize the alchemy that Arendt demands with the help of a setting that allows them to meet.

CHAPTER 8

An Impossible Embrace: Queerness, Futurity, and the Death Drive

Tim Dean

> History is the concrete body of becoming; with its moments of intensity, its lapses, its extended periods of feverish agitation, its fainting spells; and only a metaphysician would seek its soul in the distant ideality of the origin.[1]
>
> MICHEL FOUCAULT

Is every vision of the future heteronormative? Must our thinking of futurity necessarily occur within a reproductive framework that imagines the future as a figurative child born from the union of past and present, thereby installing covertly heterosexist assumptions at the heart of any conception of temporality? Motivated by concerns about the normalizing implications embedded in received accounts of history, temporality, and futurity, research in queer theory lately has formulated such questions anew. In the wake of Nietzsche's genealogical critique of historiography, we are inclined to adopt an attitude of profound skepticism toward any historical narrative organized around

---

Thanks to Robert Caserio for initiating this essay through an invitation to present on his 2005 MLA convention panel, "The Antisocial Thesis in Queer Theory"; thanks to Teresa de Lauretis and David Marriott for inviting me to Santa Cruz to answer directly Edelman's argument in their Research Unit on Psychoanalysis and Sexuality; thanks to my coeditors, Ewa Ziarek and Jim Bono, for urging me to transform the Santa Cruz lecture into an article, and for their judicious assistance in the labor of transformation; thanks to Steven Miller and Mikko Tuhkanen for discussion of these issues and the inspiration of their own work. A redaction of my MLA paper appeared as "The Antisocial Homosexual," *PMLA* 121:3 (2006): 826–828.

principles of development, telos, or progress. Queer theory compounds this skeptical disposition through its insight that developmental narratives tend to couch their goals in terms of maturity, heterosexual union, and reproductive sociality. Responding to the normalizing developmentalism implicit in much social theory, critics such as Judith Halberstam have proposed various notions of specifically queer temporality, suggesting that "queer time, even as it emerges from the AIDS crisis, is not only about compression and annihilation; it is also about the potentiality of a life unscripted by the conventions of family, inheritance, and child rearing."[2] According to this perspective, queerness telescopes time while simultaneously unfolding less predictable futures.

More dramatically, however, there are some who contend that the political efficacy of queerness lies less in its capacity for imagining lives unscripted by normative conventions than in its wholesale destruction of any and every vision of the future. For Lee Edelman there simply is no vision of the future that is not heteronormative. Given the psychoanalytic terms in which his critique of futurity is cast and the intellectual capital that it has accrued, this paper investigates how Edelman's use of the notion of the death drive might be reframed for a different—one might say queerer—vision of futurity. It is a question of adjudicating not which political strategy (or critic) is queerer than another, but how the drive might be less unambiguously destructive than Edelman would like to believe. Understood psychoanalytically, the drive betokens neither what destroys nor what remains stubbornly invariant in any historical configuration. It is, rather, one of the principal categories through which psychoanalysis endeavors to describe a nonvolitional force, only equivocally human, that brings about change. In spite of Freud's propositions concerning the atavism of the drive, I want to reconceptualize this force as oriented as much toward an underdetermined future as toward an always already determined past.

The Melodrama of the Death Drive in Queer Theory

The wager that it might be strategic to exploit those aspects of homosexuality that threaten social reproduction has a genealogy that substantially predates the emergence of queer theory around 1990. For the purpose of situating Edelman's *No Future* in this genealogy, let's begin by reconsidering Leo Bersani's influential argument in "Is the Rectum a Grave?", an argument that has come to function within the contested terrains of queer theory and politics as a virtually traumatic opening.[3] By this I mean that Bersani's polemic has been unusually difficult to assimilate and therefore has provoked repeated returns to its disruptive force. What Edelman wishes to reconstruct from "Is the Rectum a Grave?" is Bersani's hypothesis that tactically it may be "necessary to accept the pain of embracing, at least provisionally, a homophobic representation of homosexuality."[4] Rather than contesting the pejorative representation of male homosexuality as feminizing, Bersani suggests that gay political struggle should consist in inhabiting this very representation. The painful "embrace" he advocates thus entails an internal struggle with gendered self-identification as a predicate of effective social struggle.

Behind his recommendation that we embrace "a homophobic representation of homosexuality" lies Bersani's counterintuitive proposal that it might be politically productive, rather than detrimental, to cease resisting the assumption that "to be penetrated is to abdicate power."[5] Of course, resistance to this culturally pervasive assumption has animated feminist critique from its inception. What interests Bersani are the erotic appeal of one's own powerlessness and the political implications of that appeal. Arguing against feminists (as well as against lesbian and gay critics) who lament the contamination of sex with power, he advocates a sexual politics that acknowledges the pleasure in giving up power and control. The problem is not that sex does not or should not involve power, but rather that struggles for sexual dominance obscure the profound erotic satisfaction of relinquishing mastery, especially self-mastery. For Bersani the pleasure to be found in surrendering power is dramatized especially well by the "bottom" in gay sex; "Is the Rectum a Grave?" thus construes the one who enjoys being penetrated, rather than the phallic penetrator, as the paradigm of specifically sexual pleasure.

In Bersani's reading of Freud, it is not the reproductive heterosexual couple but the man who takes it up the butt who exemplifies a distinctly psychoanalytic understanding of sexuality. Drawing on Jean Laplanche's notion of *ébranlement* (perturbation or shattering), Bersani argues that masochism is a tautology for sexuality—that, in other words, human sexuality originates in the excruciating pleasure taken when erotic stimuli overwhelm the fragile structures of the ego.[6] It is important to register that this overwhelming pleasure is "beyond the pleasure principle" and therefore that the account Bersani derives from Laplanche already aligns sexuality with the death drive. In accordance with this insight, Laplanche concludes his *Life and Death in Psychoanalysis* by characterizing the death drive as "the very soul, the constitutive principle, of libidinal circulation."[7] One quarter century later, however, in *Homos*, Bersani responds that "psychoanalysis challenges us to imagine *a nonsuicidal disappearance of the subject*—or, in other words, to dissociate masochism from the death drive" (italics in original).[8] Having recognized masochism as a tautology for sexuality and having aligned sexuality with the death drive, Bersani in *Homos* wishes to disentangle masochism from the death drive. The tension between these claims may be resolved by grasping how Laplanche and Bersani are referring to subtly different concepts with their apparently identical invocations of "the death drive." And Edelman refers to something different still by this term.

The possibility of distinguishing among disparate understandings of the death drive helps us account for the confusion, in *No Future*, about "embracing" the drive for radical political ends.[9] Whereas Bersani proposes as a tactic our embracing a particular representation of homosexuality as corrosive of autonomous selfhood, Edelman advocates our embracing—even identifying with—something that is not of the order of representation, namely, the death drive. While it may be possible, albeit painful, to embrace a homophobic representation of homosexuality for strategic purposes, I'm not convinced that it is possible, even were it deemed politically desirable, to embrace or identify with a drive. It is Edelman's recommendation that queers take on and, indeed, revel in the negativity with which the homophobic imagination associates us that most clearly distinguishes his position from others in queer theory. In *No Future* he goes beyond Bersani in advocating an impossible embrace of what he calls the death drive. I want to interrogate the viability of this as a political strategy by considering whether Edelman is discussing the death drive in a strictly psychoanalytic or a merely psychological sense, that is, whether he's thinking psychoanalytically or using recondite Lacanian vocabulary toward some rhetorical purpose that remains unstated.

It is neither psychoanalysis nor queer theory that associates sexual minorities with a force of radical destructiveness; rather, this association features prominently in right-wing fantasies about how "the homosexual agenda" threatens to destroy society altogether. The hyperbolic homophobia of religious conservatives, who see in the benign spectacle of lesbian moms or a gay wedding the end of civilization, has become dispiritingly familiar in the United States. This apocalyptic rhetoric attains a virtually camp quality in its melodramatic exaggeration of the dangers posed to the most powerful nation on earth by an act of sodomy. What I find striking about *No Future* is that, hearing in the delusional rants of homophobes the truth of queer sexuality, it comes across as equally melodramatic. In Edelman's view the sexual paranoia of the far right is well founded: "Conservatives acknowledge this radical potential, which is also to say, this radical threat, of queerness more fully than liberals, for conservatism preemptively imagines the wholesale rupturing of the social fabric, whereas liberalism conservatively clings to a faith in its limitless elasticity."[10] Far from delusional, then, sexually paranoid conservatives are in fact correct. Rather than arguing against these homophobic representations of homosexuality as sterile, anti-family, and death driven, Edelman insists that "we should listen to, and even perhaps be instructed by, the readings of queer sexualities produced by the forces of reaction."[11]

Edelman himself has been instructed thus. Indeed, the polemical ire that permeates *No Future* seems to have been appropriated wholesale from the right-wing rants to which he recommends we hearken. This polemical quality, producing an impression of barely restrained fury, helps account for the book's appeal insofar as it generates a *jouissance* comparable to that of Edelman's antagonists. In other words, the appeal of *No Future* lies less in its thesis or conceptualization than in its rhetorical style and the irrational passion that style conveys. Often it remains unclear whether the reader is witnessing the results of ventriloquism or spirit possession. As Edelman formulates his argument regarding conservative perspectives on queerness, his campy hybrid of fundamentalist rhetoric and Lacanian jargon conjures a spectacle of Slavoj Žižek demonically taking possession of the body of Jerry Falwell:

> Without ceasing to refute the lies that pervade these familiar right-wing diatribes, do we also have the courage to acknowledge, and even to embrace, their correlative truths? Are we willing to be sufficiently oppositional to the structural logic of opposition—oppositional, that is, to the logic by which politics reproduces our social reality—to accept that the figural burden of queerness, the burden that queerness is phobically produced precisely to represent, is that of the force that shatters the fantasy of Imaginary unity, the force that insists on the void (replete, paradoxically, with jouissance) always already lodged within, though barred from, symbolization: the gap or wound of the Real that inhabits the Symbolic's very core? Not that we are, or ever could be, outside the Symbolic ourselves; but we can, nonetheless, make the choice to accede to our cultural production as figures—*within* the dominant logic of narrative, *within* Symbolic reality—for the dismantling of such a logic and thus for the death drive it harbors within.[12]

In passages such as this, it is not only his rhetoric but also much of his conceptual framework that Edelman borrows from Žižek. Part of what has made the Slovenian philosopher such a popular exegete of Lacan is his tendency to explain the frustratingly abstract notion of the real through recourse to any number of memorable examples; in so doing, however, he has unwittingly authorized a less than salutary critical desire to lend form and content to that which is defined by formlessness and emptiness.¹³ Accordingly Edelman, invoking a structural opposition between queerness and the social, gives a content to the relations among imaginary, symbolic, and real: Queerness undermines the social order just as the real—that zone of nonmeaning or resistance to meaning—fractures the symbolic from within. By thus aligning queerness with "the gap or wound of the Real," Edelman renders the symbolic order as exclusively heteronormative. Further, he reduces the heteronomous relations among imaginary, symbolic, and real orders—which Lacan mapped topologically through figures such as the Borromean knot, in order to characterize relationality's incredible complexity and the various possibilities for its transformation—to a series of binary oppositions.

If the argument of *No Future* seems extraordinarily reductive, nevertheless we should not underestimate how seductive its simplifications are at an historical moment when the growing social acceptance of homosexuality elicits simultaneously reactive homophobia from the religious right and recurrent anxieties about our political relevance from the queer left. What feels invigorating about Edelman's critique is its melodramatic pitting of queerness against not only "the forces of reaction" but also the institution of the family, the symbolic order, the regime of reproduction, "politics as such," the possibility of futurity, and meaning itself. Hence claims such as the following: "By figuring a refusal of the coercive belief in the paramount value of futurity, while refusing as well any backdoor hope for dialectical access to meaning, the queer dispossesses the social order of the ground on which it rests: a faith in the consistent reality of the social—and by extension, of the social subject; a faith that politics, whether of the left or of the right, implicitly affirms."¹⁴ Never in the apocalyptic imagination of the most demented homophobe has queerness been attributed such spectacularly devastating power.

The Manichean universe conjured by *No Future* is oddly reassuring in its envisioning queerness as radically disruptive of heteronormative society and, indeed, of the world of established meaning. It lets us know which side the queers are on and how much potential queerness has. Whereas Bersani's thesis concerning sexuality's shattering effect on selfhood implicates all subjects, Edelman's thesis about the power of queerness to shatter the social makes some subjects the heroic agents—rather than the vulnerable objects—of that shattering. Some subjects' social positioning permits them voluntarily to "make the choice to accede to our cultural production as figures . . . for the dismantling of such a logic and thus for the death drive it harbors within." Some of us are sufficiently privileged to embrace and then deploy the death drive, instead of being simply subjected to it. In this way,

No Future offers certain readers a comfortably radical point of imaginary identification.

Embracing the homophobic equation of queerness with the death drive, Edelman aspires to harness the drive's negativity to his assault on "reproductive futurism." By *reproductive futurism* he means the dominant ideology of the social, which sees it in terms of a future requiring not only reproduction but also protection, and that therefore represents futurity in the image of the innocent child. Edelman's thoroughgoing challenge to the social and political investment in "family values" is welcome indeed. Mainstream cultural discourses frequently imagine futurity in the name of *a future for our children* and, in so doing, they construe futurity in reproductive, tacitly heteronormative terms. For example, one commentator, referring to declining birth rates that are especially prevalent in European countries, reasons that "if children are a sign of hope in the future, Europe—and to a lesser extent Canada, Australia, and the United States—is losing its will to live."[15] In the context of a critique of contraception, such claims interpret decelerating reproduction rates as symptoms of something like a death drive that threatens human futurity in toto.

Once the social is defined in terms of a future represented by the image of the child, then queerness (or perverse, nonreproductive sexuality) negates that future by fissuring it from within—just as, in Lacanian terms, the real fissures the symbolic. According to this perspective, queerness is structurally antisocial, not empirically so.[16] It is for this reason that Edelman's argument focuses on "the image of the Child, not to be confused with the lived experiences of any historical children."[17] His quarantining "the image of the Child" from any and every historical incarnation of that image enables him to overlook all those ways in which, far from the antitheses of queerness, children may be regarded as the original queers.[18] More than Edelman's disdain for the empirical and the historical is at stake here: Freud's theory of infantile sexuality, with its account of a universal predisposition to polymorphous perversion, long ago shattered the illusion of childhood innocence. We cannot protect kids from perverts because we cannot insulate any child from him- or herself. As Freud repeatedly discovered, sexual perversion comes from inside the family home, not from outside it. Thus, queerness, though it fissures the norm from within, does not simply negate futurity but, rather, unfolds incalculable futures by means of a vastly subtler set of determinations—a set that, I shall argue, remains irreducible to the terms of either reproduction or negation.

The Drive Returns

I have suggested that Edelman's critique of futurity launches a would-be psychoanalytic thesis concerning "the Child" that paradoxically requires him to suppress every psychoanalytic insight about children. In his effort to stabilize a dubious opposition between the image of the child and the figure of the queer, Edelman tends not only to schematize but also to essentialize the terms of his argument: the capital-C Child, so unlike the Rabelaisian infant of Freudian theory, morphs into a technical phrase, like the capital-S Symbolic. When it thus becomes unhinged from its living concepts and reduced to its often rebarbative vocabulary, psychoanalysis degenerates into a dogma whose principal function lies in producing the rhetorical effect of authority. This is acutely the case in Edelman's account of the drive. Drawing on an ostensibly Lacanian understanding of the drive, he defines it thus: "The death drive names what the queer, in the order of the social, is called forth to figure: the negativity opposed to every form of social viability."[19] Is the drive, even when considered as a death drive, really opposed to *every* form of social viability? Or are we witnessing here the deformation of a psychoanalytic concept by hyperbole, in the service of a distinctly melodramatic account of sexuality?

Freud, elaborating his theory of drives, distinguished the impulses and pressures that structure subjectivity according to their variant temporalities. Thus, in contrast to an unconscious wish, which can be momentary and fleeting, a drive is constant; its pressure is relentless. This is one of Freud's initial points in "Instincts and Their Vicissitudes," though it would not be until *Beyond the Pleasure Principle*, five years later, that he came to appreciate its full implications.[20] Differentiated from a wish, the drive also must be distinguished from an instinct, as Freud acknowledged by his use of the term *Trieb* (as opposed to *Instinkt*) when speaking about human sexuality. Strachey's ill-fated choice of the English word "instinct" to translate both *Trieb* and *Instinkt* has spawned misunderstandings that seem peculiarly difficult to dispel. In his commentary on this problem, Lacan notes that "the drive, as it is constructed by Freud on the basis of the experience of the unconscious, prohibits psychologizing thought from resorting to 'instinct,' with which it masks its ignorance by assuming the existence of morals in nature."[21] Invoking a commonsense assumption that the notion of instinct implies a natural object that is right and proper for it, Lacan insists that the drive has no such natural object. Understood psychoanalytically, the drive denaturalizes sexuality and thereby exempts it from all moralisms premised upon right or proper objects. This denaturalization of the drive comports with its peculiar temporality: Whereas instincts wax and wane according to their periodicity, a drive remains constant. Indeed, it is because no satisfaction of the drive reduces its pressure that the drive cannot be apprehended in biological terms. And I would suggest that it is only insofar as the attributes of the drive remain irreducible to those of an instinct that the drive qualifies as a psychoanalytic—as opposed to either a biological or a psychological—concept.

The same characteristic that differentiates a drive from both a wish and an instinct—the constancy of its pressure—indicates how a drive resists the regulation of the pleasure principle that otherwise governs psychic life. The relentless pressure of the drive compromises the pleasure principle, which seeks to reduce if not totally eliminate excitation. In recognizing that the drive's operation flouts a subjective economy organized around homeostasis, Freud finally realized that the drive, *any drive*, operates beyond the pleasure principle. Hence his "discovery," in the years following the First World War, of something he called the death drive. In their different ways, Lacan and Laplanche both elaborate how this discovery ruined Freud's late dualism of Eros–Thanatos, since, by virtue of the drive's persistence, human sexuality serves Thanatos as much as it serves Eros. "Every drive is virtually a death drive," maintains Lacan in "Position of the Unconscious."[22] The notion of the death drive thus constitutes something of a redundancy, one that serves to emphasize how human drives (unlike animal instincts) do not unequivocally support our well-being or even our survival.

Uncritically naming it "the death drive" essentializes the drive's negativity by implying that it leads always and only to death. More than as a redundancy, then, the notion of "the death drive" should be regarded as an instance of hyperbole in Freud's thinking—a point that Lacan makes in Seminar XVII, *The Other Side of Psychoanalysis*.[23] Insofar as it lends itself to conceptual redundancy, rhetorical exaggeration, and emotional responses typical of the genre of melodrama, perhaps we should not be surprised that a queer theorist of a certain generation should wish to embrace the drive without questioning its presuppositions.[24] However, the drive is not purely destructive; it also calls forth our inventiveness—as the concept of sublimation is meant to suggest.

Identified as one of the drive's vicissitudes, sublimation was notoriously undertheorized by Freud; both Lacan and Laplanche tried to compensate for this insufficiency by devoting yearlong seminars to the concept.[25] Arguing in Seminar VII that "the articulation of the death drive in Freud is neither true nor false," Lacan reminds his audience that the drive betokens infinite possibilities of creation as well as of destruction: "Freud's thought in this matter requires that what is involved be articulated as a destruction drive, given that it challenges everything that exists. But it is also a will to create from zero, a will to begin again."[26] There are not two separate drives, one to create and one to destroy, but a single, paradoxical mechanism whose results cannot be predicted in advance.[27] Thus although the drive is characterized by repetition rather than by development, nevertheless it can bring about change, can make something new.

In this way the drive may be understood as an opening to futurity, if not to the external world. Freud characterizes the drive as operating on the border between soma and psyche; its conceptual difficulty stems from this borderline function. In his well-known definition, "an 'instinct' [*Trieb*] appears to us as a concept on the frontier between the mental and the somatic, as the psychical representative of the stimuli originating from within the organism and reaching the mind, as a measure of the demand made upon the mind for work in consequence of its connection with the body."[28] The theory of drives constitutes psychoanalysis's solution to the mind–body problem, even as it raises a whole set of other questions by conjuring a picture of the embodied subject that defies the imagination. Here I mean something quite precise, namely, that the subject of the drive defeats imaginary capture. Freud's theory of drives makes human embodiment impossible to represent in an image, rendering it definitively unrecognizable to consciousness.

In his metapsychological paper on the unconscious (which dates from the same year as "Instincts and Their Vicissitudes"), Freud registers this impossibility in a manner that bears on Edelman's argument. Claiming that "the antithesis of conscious and unconscious is not applicable to instincts," he explains:

> An instinct [*Trieb*] can never become an object of consciousness—only the idea that represents the instinct can. Even in the unconscious, moreover, an instinct cannot be represented otherwise than by an idea. If the instinct did not attach itself to an idea or manifest itself as an affective state, we could know nothing about it.[29]

If a drive never can become an object of consciousness, it follows that it never can be embraced or deployed for political purposes. This does not mean that drives have nothing to do with political processes or that it is merely metaphorical to speak of what drives social and historical change; quite the contrary. It does mean, however, that any proposal about strategically embracing the death drive must be based on a fundamental misprision or a sleight of hand.

That the drive is amenable to sublimation yet constitutively unavailable for individual or collective identification stems from not only its function as an emissary between soma and psyche but also its related attributes of plasticity, multiplicity, and partiality. What is remarkable about "Instincts and Their Vicissitudes" is how Freud's discourse on specifically sexual drives elicits a description of the human body as so anarchic and fragmented that it makes surrealist anatomy appear positively classical. The Freudian body, subject to the drive, is as distant from any intuitive conception of embodiment as could be:

> This much can be said by way of a general characterization of the sexual instincts. They are numerous, emanate from a great variety of organic sources, act in the first instance independently of one another and only achieve a more or less complete synthesis at a late stage. The aim which each of them strives for is the attainment of "organ-pleasure"; only when synthesis is achieved do they enter the service of the reproductive function and thereupon become generally recognizable as sexual instincts. . . . They are distinguished by possessing the capacity to act vicariously for one another to a wide extent and by being able to change their objects readily. In consequence of the latter properties they are capable of functions which are far removed from their original purposive actions—capable, that is, of "sublimation."[30]

There is not one sexual drive but many; more precisely, the drive has a single (and singular) structure yet multiple corporeal sources. Each drive behaves autonomously and seeks nothing but its own satisfaction—what Freud here calls "organ-pleasure." Not only does each drive operate independently of the others, each is also originally independent of its object. This contingency of object, together with their homological structure, accounts for the drives' "capacity to act vicariously for one another"; their autonomy appears not to be compromised by their fungibility.

However, the relative autonomy of the multiple drives does compromise the ego's capacity to recognize the body as a totality or to apprehend it in a unified image. Freud's account thus raises not only the epistemological problem of how various anarchic drives "become generally recognizable as *sexual* instincts," but also the ontological conundrum of how various coexistent possibilities of pleasure render the body unrecognizable to itself. In Deleuzean terms the drives "deterritorialize" the body, generating an insoluble tension between bodily pleasures and the security of imaginary identity conferred by the ego. This helps explain why the drives' simultaneously sexualizing and dis-unifying effects on corporeality cannot be graphed in either two-dimensional or three-dimensional representations but require a different kind of mapping, for which Lacan appropriated topological models.

Having considered the drives' disorienting multiplicity and plasticity, as well as the unsettling constancy of their pressure, we now must grapple with what it means to characterize them as partial. Unified neither *among* themselves nor *in* themselves, the drives partialize the subject's body. Strachey's translation of the Freudian term *Partialtrieb* by the phrase "component instincts" implies that partial drives represent the constituents of a larger whole, but this is not the case. The paradox of the partial drives is that they do not form part of a whole or a totality; they do not operate synecdochally.[31] Any representation of the sexed body as a totality remains purely illusory. It is this fundamental impossibility that Lacan registers, in a crucial passage in "Position of the Unconscious," when he observes that "a drive, insofar as it represents sexuality in the unconscious, is never anything but a partial drive. That is the essential failing [*carence*]—namely the absence [*carence*] of anything that could represent in the subject the mode of what is male or female in his being."[32] As psychical delegations whose mission lies in translating demands from one register (that of the body) into another (that of the mind), drives always fail in their representative function. The drives are to be regarded as partial not so much because each body harbors many of them, but because their mode of representation remains by definition incomplete.

Freud proposed a solution to this troubling state of affairs. What allegedly redeems the marvelously chaotic body pictured in "Instincts and Their Vicissitudes" is "a more or less complete synthesis at a late stage"—a synthesis accomplished, if at all, in the service of reproduction. Freud's solution is, of course, the Oedipus complex—what Teresa de Lauretis calls his "passionate fiction" and what Edelman designates under the rubric of reproductive futurism.[33] As his "passionate fiction," the Oedipus complex organizes Freud's thinking in a manner akin to how it is supposed to organize and orient the subject's refractive sexuality. Freud's investment in Oedipus obscures some of his best ideas—even from Freud himself—by subordinating them to an ostensibly reassuring narrative of normalization. In order to interrupt that narrative, it helps to hold onto the psychoanalytic insight that, at the level of the unconscious, subjective synthesis and the organization of the drives fail permanently. What makes the psychoanalytic—as opposed to psychological—notion of the unconscious so challenging and yet so fruitful is its suggestion that this dimension of subjectivity possesses a virtually limitless capacity for displacement and condensation, but no capacity for synthesis or any grasp of finitude.

Just as Freud overcredits the normalizing power of the Oedipus complex, so Edelman believes too deeply in the power of reproductive futurism to determine every vision of the future and every notion of the political—as if the only solution to its totalizing grip were death and destruction. Although his argument appears as recognizably Freudian in its melodramatic misrecognition of the drive, strictly speaking it is nonpsychoanalytic, verging instead on a psychological idea of self-destructive pathology that derives more from Christianity than from psychoanalysis. In differentiating psychoanalytic from psychological conceptions of the unconscious, I am inferring also a distinction between psychoanalytic and psychological understandings of the death drive. Centered on the ego and its totalizing effects, psychological perspectives necessarily regard the death drive as destructive, whereas a psychoanalytic perspective sees in the drive a will to create as well as to destroy. As essentially impersonal, the drive proceeds on its itinerary indifferent to the moral valuations of creation or destruction. When one starts from the psychoanalytic vantage of the unconscious or that of the drive, he or she sees that the psychological assumption of an individual person is profoundly mistaken: Rather than a personal self, one faces libidinized bits and bobs, fragments without a whole. The concept of the individual self is a function of imaginary misrecognition, merely "a practical convenience," as Bersani puts it.[34]

In focusing on the characteristics of the drive as Freud lays them out in "Instincts and Their Vicissitudes," I have stressed the attribute of partiality as a way of clarifying how any drive can take on that self-destructive quality associated with "the death drive." The drive's partiality also makes clear why it cannot be embodied, identified with, or embraced. Although its partiality and its repetitive insistence help explain the drive's uncanniness and negativity, the same characteristics account for its providing the motive force behind creativity and inventiveness. The partiality of the drive, which makes it appear so dysfunctional by comparison with something like instinct, means that human subjectivity and sexuality are radically *under*determined. No form of bodily being is completely given in advance. The ontology that psychoanalysis derives from its theory of the drives is not one of lack but of incompleteness—an incompleteness that (once the myth of erotic complementarity has been discredited) makes of human sexuality a project of invention. It is thus thanks to the drive's partiality and the consequent underdetermination of subjectivity that a margin exists in which we can make a future that is not simply reproductive.

Becoming Queer

Having thus far engaged Edelman's thesis on its own psychoanalytic terms, I wish to conclude by examining it in terms of the philosophies of temporality, history, and futurity that it suppresses in order melodramatically to sustain its own negativity. Here should be mentioned the names of, for example, Spinoza, Nietzsche, Bergson, Deleuze, and Foucault—an entire philosophical tradition, crucial to the thinking of queerness and futurity, that goes unacknowledged in *No Future*. This absence is especially weird when one realizes that, in his critique of reproductive futurism, Edelman is attempting to write a version of *Anti-Oedipus* without the benefit of Deleuze and Guattari.[35] Since the Deleuzean project could be understood to consist in developing a non-Oedipal account of futurity, one cannot help but wonder at Edelman's disinclination to mention, much less engage, it. Whereas the latter insists that every notion of futurity remains hostage to heteronormativity, Deleuze elaborates through the concept of becoming what might be called a queer notion of futurity. As a ceaseless movement of being that is not coordinated by teleology or development, *becoming* never results in anything resembling an identity. In the process of differentiating becoming from evolution (and hence from the whole problematic of reproduction), Deleuze and Guattari characterize it in terms of "creative involution": Becoming entails not reproduction—reproducing in the future a version of what exists in the present—but what might be called nonreproductive, nonapocalyptic invention.[36]

The term *invention* implies an inventor, just as *creation* connotes (inappropriately in this context) a transcendental agent single-handedly bringing something into existence ex nihilo. What Deleuze has in mind, by contrast, is the emergence of the incalculable, that which is not fully determined—and so cannot be predicted—by present or past conditions. His term for what emerges in this way, by means of the complex differentiations of time, is *the new* (though the noun form should not be taken to imply a temporal durability, essence, or identity). As philosopher Paola Marrati explains in her contribution to the present volume, newness "anticipates neither the happy unfolding of history nor, for that matter, the certainty of a future apocalypse."[37] If newness entered the world in the form of new persons or new identities, as the fulfillment of a telos or the realization of dialectical change, it would be subject to Edelman's critique of reproductive futurism. Conversely, however, what Deleuze means by newness does not appear as the result of revolutionary destruction or social shattering. Were the new simply awaiting liberation, it would be vulnerable to a Foucaultian critique of the repressive hypothesis.

Here, as elsewhere, the thinking of Deleuze and Foucault resonates in ways that have enormous potential for critical projects associated with queer theory. At its most basic, Deleuze's account of *becoming* describes how life emerges and change occurs outside the circuits of reproduction. It thereby offers a nonheterosexist, anti-essentialist theory of futurity and even of biological life, as Elizabeth Grosz recently has argued.[38] However, to appreciate fully the subterranean influence of Deleuze on queer theory we need to trace a genealogy back to Guy Hocquenghem's 1972 book *Homosexual Desire*, a work deeply influenced by *Anti-Oedipus* and one that articulated a psychoanalytic critique of reproductive futurism three decades prior to Edelman's.[39] Indeed, so much more incisive is *Homosexual Desire* than almost everything published under the banner of gay studies or queer theory since then that perhaps we should not be surprised at how far from grasping Hocquenghem's insights queer scholarship still seems to be.

What Hocquenghem takes from Deleuze and Guattari is less the Nietzschean problematic of becoming than the radical psychoanalytic (or "schizoanalytic") critique of heteronormative familialism. Developing the implications of Freud's theory of partial drives in an anti-oedipal matrix, Hocquenghem shows how the drives' relative autonomy generates a libidinal disorganization that comes to be associated with homosexuality—homosexuality not as an identity but as tantamount to a counter-identitarian queerness that threatens social reproduction. In a discursive moment preceding the coinage and theorization of homophobia, heteronormativity, and affirmative queerness, he writes, "The great fear of homosexuality is translated into a fear that the succession of generations, on which civilization is based, may stop."[40] Hocquenghem thus diagnoses the anxieties of today's religious right as acutely as the phobias of his European contemporaries. Further anticipating Edelman's critique of reproductive futurism, he explains how, "From this point of view the gay movement appears basically uncivilized, and it is not without reason that many people see it as the end of reproduction and thus the end of the species itself."[41] This is the fantasy of homosexuality and its political affirmation as engendering a death drive.

More than simply a gay liberationist antecedent to Edelman's queer critique, however, Hocquenghem's book is analytically sharper on the relation between the death drive and nonnormative sexualities. What

Hocquenghem sees but Edelman misses is that "Homosexual desire is neither on the side of death nor on the side of life; it is the killer of civilized egos."[42] Edelman misses this because, though he mentions Hocquenghem once in passing, he declines to acknowledge his debt to him, feigning ignorance of the genealogy that makes his thesis possible. When Hocquenghem characterizes homosexual desire as "the killer of civilized egos," he is referring to those components of sexuality that remain oedipally unmasterable and thus perpetually threaten normative identities. Hocquenghem's argument is consonant with Bersani's understanding of the shattering effects of sexuality on selfhood, since the latter recognizes that, despite appearances, sexuality cannot be aligned exclusively with either life or death.[43] Further, if we define "life" restrictively (in terms of the reproduction of the species), then we see that Hocquenghem's argument about homosexual desire harmonizes also with Marrati's thesis that for Deleuze the new "anticipates neither the happy unfolding of history nor . . . the certainty of a future apocalypse." Although Deleuze explains the emergence of the new as a result of processes of differentiation whose paradigm is evolutionary life, nevertheless this conception of life remains distinct from a reproductive one. As with homosexual desire, the new is neither on the side of death nor on the side of life. Transposed into psychoanalytic terms, it would be through sublimation rather than through reproduction that newness appears.

No Future locates a version of "homosexual desire" resolutely on the side of death, envisioning the disruption of reproductive futurism—and hence the emergence of something new—solely by means of apocalyptic, nondialectical negation. The comparison with Hocquenghem enables us to grasp that, though queer desire disrupts the normative coordinates of selfhood, only in a paranoid fantasy can it be said to instantiate the death drive. And in thus drastically overestimating the destructive power of queerness, this paranoid fantasy falls victim to a repressive-hypothesis model of the relation between sexuality and power. Edelman's commitment to queerness as a nonrecuperable force of radical negativity represents the death drive not as exterior to discourse or the symbolic order, but as nonetheless capable "of undoing the Symbolic" and jamming the machinery of reproductive futurism.[44] For all its veneer of theoretical sophistication, Edelman's argument is rather naïve in its belief that by saying yes to the death drive, one says no to heteronormative power.[45]

This naïve conviction manifests itself most clearly in a sentence that several commentators on *No Future* have quoted with unabashed delight:

> Queers must respond to the violent force of such constant provocations not only by insisting on our equal right to the social order's prerogatives, not only by avowing our capacity to promote that order's coherence and integrity, but also by saying explicitly what Law and the Pope and the whole of the Symbolic order for which they stand hear anyway in each and every expression or manifestation of queer sexuality: Fuck the social order and the Child in whose name we're collectively terrorized; fuck Annie; fuck the waif from *Les Mis*; fuck the poor, innocent kid on the Net; fuck Laws both with capital *l*s and with small; fuck the whole network of Symbolic relations and the future that serves as its prop.[46]

The false sense of liberation conveyed by such a melodramatic utterance helps explain the *jouissance* of Edelman's rhetoric and the kick it gives certain readers. Yet it is necessary to bear in mind that such a sentence is possible to enunciate only from a position that has forgotten, whether strategically or otherwise, the most basic insights of queer theory's founding text. There is no small irony in *No Future*'s never once mentioning Foucault, since *La volonté de savoir* reoriented our understanding of sexuality precisely through its critique of negativity, arguing that the relation between power and sex should not be conceptualized primarily in terms of repression, prohibition, exclusion, or negation. To characterize queer sexuality as the privileged figure for a force that unequivocally negates normalizing power thus risks returning to an embarrassingly pre-Foucaultian conception of sex.[47]

Regrettably, Edelman is far from alone among queer theorists in his having failed to appreciate how normalizing power "is everywhere; not because it embraces everything, but because it comes from everywhere."[48] If one believes that reproductive futurism embraces everything, then perhaps it makes sense to imagine that the most effective source of resistance lies in a counter-embrace of the radical negativity associated with the death drive. However, Foucault's distinction between a conception of power that "embraces everything" and one that "comes from everywhere" fundamentally challenges this way of thinking. It does so not only because it contrasts a "top-down," centralized model of power relations with a "bottom-up," capillary model, but also because, by inferring a multiplicity of forces in play at every moment, it de-totalizes power relations. Far from deterministically construing social subjectivity and sexuality as mere epiphenomena of normalizing or disciplinary power, Foucault's thesis on power's omnipresence points to the microconflicts that constitute social relations, showing how every vector of relationality may be regarded as an axis of potential struggle in which no party ever is deprived entirely of power (or of what has come to be called agency).[49] To say that power is everywhere is to multiply sites of resistance and thereby to disintegrate the body politic into networks of conflict that cannot be apprehended—and therefore cannot be dominated—as a totality.

In this way Foucault de-totalizes power akin to how Freud de-totalizes the body. Throughout his analysis of biopolitical relations in *The History of Sexuality*, Foucault employs the same vocabulary that Freud uses to describe the multiplicity, plasticity, and partiality of the drives, speaking of the "polymorphous techniques of power," the "polymorphous incitement to discourse," "polymorphous causal power," and so on.[50] Rather than dismissing this vocabulary as purely figurative or ironic on Foucault's part, we might consider how it suggests the presence of a Nietzschean theory of forces in Foucault *and* in Freud. As Deleuze explains, in a formulation that pertains as directly to Freud's theory of drives as to Foucault's theory of biopower, "Being composed of a plurality of irreducible forces the body is a multiple phenomenon, its unity that of a multiple phenomenon, a 'unity of domination.'"[51] Is it a question here of the human body, discomposed by warring forces, for which the "body politic" stands as a metaphor? In fact, Deleuze contends that neither one is a displacement but rather each is an extension of the other: "Every relationship of forces constitutes a body—whether it is chemical, biological, social or political. Any two forces, being unequal, constitute a body as soon as they enter into a relationship."[52] Defined as a site of difference and conflict, the body thus cannot provide the ground for an essence or identity but only for transformation or becoming.[53]

It is this Nietzschean conception of the body that Foucault evokes when, in the sentence adopted as this paper's epigraph, he refers to history as "the concrete body of becoming; with its moments of intensity, its lapses, its extended periods of feverish agitation, its fainting spells."[54] This is neither a body that develops and matures nor one that remains stable over time, but rather an unruly, possibly hysterical entity wholly incapable of self-recognition or self-mastery. Subject to the perturbations of the drives, it is not primarily a reproductive body; the account of history to which it gives rise remains irreducible to reproductive futurism. Should this conception of the body and of history-as-becoming be understood as specifically queer? I think Foucault was getting at this possibility when, during interviews in the early 1980s, he characterized homosexuality as "not a form of desire but something desirable," suggesting that "we have to work at becoming homosexuals and not be obstinate in recognizing that we are."[55] Rather than representing a form of desire or an identitarian type, then, homosexuality offers an occasion for initiating ontological differentiations whose only assured outcome paradoxically would be the unpredictability of the new. Hence "becoming queer" is an interminable enterprise of not negation but invention, an adventure in becoming other to oneself independently of categories of gender or sexual identity.

CHAPTER 9

Luce Irigaray and the Question of Critique

Elizabeth Weed

The future of critique is one of the puzzles facing the critical disciplines. There is one mode of critical reading that attempts to trouble the text for what it is blind to or what it wants not to know. There is another mode of reading that explores some area in the domain of the known, thinks about it differently, casts new light on it, and in doing so, amplifies and clarifies. If the latter thrives to the exclusion of the former, there is a risk that a certain complacency might take hold, a renewed confidence in the reliability of language and thought. To neglect critique and its particular form of practice would be to forget something about the nature of change, for in order to approach change—something heretofore unseen—one cannot know in advance what one is looking for.

There has been much reflection on the fading of poststructuralist theory and the form of critique it represents. The very different kinds of critical work labeled "poststructuralist" have in common a certain set of practices that question the conditions of possibility of thought, examine the historical and symbolic elements constitutive of the seemingly natural and commonplace, and endeavor to expose conceptual and discursive blind spots. The rise during the past several decades of critical movements such as the new historicism and cultural studies has cast new light on poststructuralist practices and presented competing theories of critical practice and knowledge production. The question is, what is the status of critique in these competing theories?

This question is central to the current set of debates about psychoanalysis versus cultural construction. In *Read My Desire: Lacan Against the Historicists*, Joan Copjec characterizes historicists as those critics influenced by Foucault—though not necessarily Foucault himself—who read cultural phenomena with the understanding that the relations that pertain in those cultural texts can, with work, be exposed and known.[1] For the historicists, as she says, the regime of power relations at work in a society are seen as imminent within that society and ultimately knowable. It is against this "notion of immanence, this conception of a cause that is imminent within the field of its effects,"[2] that Copjec places psychoanalysis. By contrast, the psychoanalytic reading understands that there are generative principles that are, strictly speaking, "unspeakable"; it understands, in Copjec's words, that "every phenomenal field occludes its cause,"[3] that society is, in other words, external to itself.[4]

In a related but differently framed argument in *Culture and the Real*, Catherine Belsey positions a Lacanian poststructuralism against the culturalists.[5] For Belsey, the culturalists are concerned with what can be known, with what is there-for-a-subject, whereas the poststructuralists read culture as the instantiation of the gap between the symbolic and the real—the real, which, as Lacan says, "does not depend on my idea of it."[6] Belsey sees the culturalist reading, however seductive, as idealist and deterministic, as against poststructuralist materialist theories of the real, which ultimately open the way to insight: "And to the attentive observer, culture can . . . tell more than it thinks it knows about who and what we are."[7]

The terms of these debates are complex, as is the question they turn on of knowing and not knowing. The Foucaultians, Derrideans, and Lacanians, who challenged the ways traditional discourses of philosophy, mathematics, and the sciences construe the limits of knowledge, are, in these current debates, seen themselves to differ significantly in their theories of the not-known. Far from being forgotten, then, the question of critique is very much alive and central to the arguments.

While my aim is not to intervene directly in these debates, I am interested in a theorist who is neither a historicist, nor a culturalist, and who can be said to have always worked to theorize the real. Indeed, the continued and even increased attention to Luce Irigaray's work today seems to point to a sustained or renewed fascination with the powerful critique that drives everything she writes.[8] I am interested in that fascination, in why and how Irigaray is read, in the ways her critique succeeds but also how it falters and fails. My presumption is that critique as a mode of reading is very difficult to sustain, that everything, from language to the psyche to social formations, works against it, and that it is always in some sense on the wane. Certainly there are political and epistemological conditions that favor the practice, but even under those conditions, as in the France of the structuralist and poststructuralist years, it is difficult. Almost from the moment critique does its work—changing the way one sees a certain discursive field, whether in the sphere of subjectivity or philosophy or political economy—its power begins to lessen. The new way of seeing becomes naturalized and the thrust of the critique is folded into the familiarity of the new.

Critique purportedly reads the known, the self-evident, in such a way as to dislodge the premises, the assumptions to which that system of thought is blind: blind because those assumptions are so naturalized as to seem as true as the air we breath, or blind, as in the case of psychoanalytic reading, because the system is implicated in operations that are outside conscious thought. In its fully deconstructive mode, critique looks at how the very formulation of meaning produces unanticipated, unintentional effects that the stated meaning may know nothing about. Indeed, the lesson one learns from deconstruction, as from psychoanalysis, is that a definitive critique is an impossibility in that there can be no text that is not in some way blind to its own workings. And yet, the impulse to make meaning, to make sense, is so great that this impossibility is often easily forgotten.

What is required, then, for a text to maintain the play of difference that resists collapse into the already known? As Derrida comments with regard to the critique of metaphysics, "We have no language—no syntax and no lexicon—which is alien to this history [of metaphysics]; we cannot utter a single destructive proposition which has not already slipped into the form, the logic, and the implicit postulations of precisely what it seeks to contest."[9] Hence the many stylistic devices theorists use to thwart a too-easy understanding, such as Derrida's "paleonomy" (giving old words new meanings that defamiliarize the old) that he and Lacan use to such effect, or Irigaray's famous strategy of mimesis. Hence, also, the emphasis on *rigor* in the theoretical enterprise. Whatever else the rigorous text must do, it must always attend to the space of difference that critique requires.[10]

And yet, there is no theoretical critique that doesn't risk settling, in spite of itself, into the lure of its own meaning. One lure is what one might call the imaginary register of the text. Every well-developed text has its own imaginary register, a register that has to do with the logics, and tropes, and thematics of the work that adhere, and in adhering bind anew the reading that aims to unbind meaning. There are, then, theoretical texts with very high critical stakes that nonetheless yield to the lure of their own imaginary register. In such a text, one finds a figure, a thematic development, a rhetorical turn, or some other such textual element or combination of elements that begins to take on a life of its own. When this happens, there can be a slowing of the play of difference, a flattening of the textual space of critique. What this means is that even in the most rigorous theoretical text, critique can wax and wane.

I look at Luce Irigaray's writings with an eye to this instability of critique. On the one hand, Irigaray, the most radical of feminist theorists, undertakes to disrupt the known and provoke the unthought of sexual difference. On the other hand, her writing is consistently found by some readers to be essentialist, in other words, to be illegible as critique.[11] In this difference between the radicality of the project and its modes of illegibility lie not only the challenge of Irigaray's work, but also the challenge of critique.

Sexual Difference

Psychoanalytically, it seems oxymoronic to speak of a critique of sexual difference.[12] Sexuality in psychoanalytic discourse is figured as the very knot of not knowing, the knot of Oedipus and castration, through which the subject navigates the loss of the real and the entry into the symbolic. For Irigaray, however, the psychoanalysis that grasps so well what the subject can't know is itself blind to the way sexual difference operates in the symbolic register. Irigaray argues that sexual difference has yet to be thought in Western culture. As Heidegger claimed the need to think the unexamined relationship between Being and beings, she urges us to seize this historical time of feminist awareness to grapple with the unthought relationship between sexuate beings and sexual difference.[13] The theoretical stakes of the project are high. At issue is not just the call for sexual difference but the very question of the relationship between the social and the political. Irigaray argues that sweeping political and economic change is crucial and that it cannot happen without a change in the symbolic order. She refers here to the Lacanian term of the symbolic, a complex register in which subjectivity is structured with relationship to language and cultural Law, entailing sexuation in which the subject is positioned as masculine or feminine with relationship to radical alterity, or the field of the desire of the Other.

Irigaray, like Lacan, takes the symbolic register to be an important corrective to those theories more comfortable with the ego and the workings of the imaginary alone. Moreover, Irigaray is completely in accord with Lacan's portrayal of the feminine within the existing symbolic order. Woman, that is to say, *la femme*, cannot be said to exist as such. The universality designated by the article *la* cannot be applied to woman because she in her lack guarantees the fantasy of the whole, the fullness of being that castration holds out as a promise in its very denial of that fullness. Woman is thus other to man and other to herself. For Irigaray, this formulation amounts to a fantasmatic masculine universal posing as a human universal, a situation that has deleterious psychic and social effects, for women, for men, for social and political health. Where she breaks with Lacan is in her view that Lacanian psychoanalytic discourse is complicit in maintaining the symbolic order by not, as she says, examining its own historical determinants.

This is a critique that Irigaray first made thirty years ago, but she has continued to develop it and in her more recent work brings her call for an unthought sexual difference into such issues as citizenship, the European Union, and ecology. Her opus is an interesting one, then, in that it includes texts addressed to very different audiences in very different historical periods.[14] Throughout, she maintains that social and political change will come only when there is a different sexual difference and that that is dependent on a change in the symbolic. As recently as 2000, she writes that the horizon of thought must change before we have a culture in which the relationship between two different subjects, as opposed to the false universal male subject, comes about. "It won't just happen through social critiques and street riots," Irigaray says. "We need to go above and beyond: understanding that the human subject, woman or man, is not a mere social effect."[15]

As with all of Irigaray's arguments with Lacan, there is no simple dividing line between the two on the question of historical determination. It is not that Lacan has an ahistorical formulation of the symbolic. In *Seminar XX*, for example, he makes an off-hand comment that the idea of a Marxist "worldview" makes him laugh. A worldview, for Lacan, would belong to the realm of philosophy, presupposing something that *is*, existing outside of discourse. "Marxism is something else," Lacan says, "something I will call gospel. It is the announcement that history is instating another dimension of discourse and opening up the possibility of completely subverting the function of discourse as such, and of philosophical discourse strictly speaking."[16] And as early as *Seminar II*, Lacan discusses historical changes in structural orders, such as Socrates' inauguration of a new being-in-the-world, which Lacan calls subjectivity, the later advent of the concept of the ego, the discoveries of Freud, which he likens to the Copernican revolution.[17] Quoting Lacan, "When something comes to light, something that we are forced to consider as new, when another structural order emerges, well, then, it creates its own perspective within the past, and we say—*This can never not have been there, this has existed from the beginning.* Besides, isn't that a property which our own experience demonstrates?"[18]

It might be said that Irigaray bases her whole project on the argument that history is once again instating a new dimension of discourse, subverting the existing symbolic order and its structures of sexuation. Things have changed; the patriarchal social system no longer holds together in the West. It's time to apply critical pressure to discourses that serve to contain the status quo. Irigaray does this, through often brilliant deconstructive readings of canonical Western texts in her earlier writings, and in her later writing through formulations of a different sexual difference, in which much of the deconstructive work is concealed. It turns out that both these modes of critique are very hard to read, harder than the notoriously difficult later texts of Lacan. When it comes to simple legibility—or decipherability—Irigaray's are, of course, the more accessible texts. Which is not to say that they are without formal difficulty. Her earlier works make rich use of sustained indetermination and ambiguity, of a sometimes startling mixture of theoretical precision and lyricism, of wit and irony and word play. However, what I am concerned with here is not legibility per se, but legibility as critique. Because of its radical reach, Irigaray's project demands the most rigorous of critiques—a critique that turns the screw one degree tighter than Lacan's. But can it be read? In order to suggest the problems involved, I will briefly compare the styles of Irigaray and Lacan and the very different ways readers are drawn into their texts.

The Text of Jouissance

Lacan aims to rescue the psychoanalytic unconscious from the grips of any theory of the subject enthralled to the ego. Hence his expressed desire, particularly from the 1960s on, to thwart the tyranny of meaning. In the later writings, the relationships between sentences, even clauses within sentences, can make no sense, playing with adequation and with cause and effect so that things are never quite where one would expect them to be. The language games, jokes, ellipses, digressions, and bizarre transitions keep the reader unsettled and more often than not perplexed. The reader thus enters Lacan's text disoriented and remains disoriented, but without this estrangement from intelligibility as we know and imagine it, the text could not do its work. And it is, above all, work that Lacan wanted from his readers and from those who attended his seminars. As Bruce Fink comments, "Psychoanalysis, according to Lacan, is a *method of reading texts*, whether those texts be oral—the analysand's discourse—or written. And every text, whether doctrinal or therapeutic, is riddled with tensions and contradictions that must be read, reread, and pondered. Not necessarily *resolved*, but explored and worked on. Lacan even says that '[c]ommenting on a text is like doing an analysis.'"[19]

Nonetheless, it can come as a surprise to the student of texts—if not to the analysand—that the work Lacan aims to provoke must engage the *stupidity* of the reader. Early in *Seminar XX*, Lacan declares, "My sole presence—at least I dare believe it—my sole presence in my discourse is my stupidity."[20] Lacan's discourse is, of course, the analytic, a discourse that does not try to flee stupidity because it knows that any effort to represent a whole and complete subject can only end in *bêtise*, or nonsense. Its job is to address the subject who is never whole, the subject who never knows everything he knows.

Fink suggests that Lacan succeeds in evoking the analytic discourse in his published texts by a unique meeting of the written and the spoken. Something of the rich and reportedly charismatic and transferential speech of Lacan's seminars is rendered in the published texts, combined with the special kinds of difficulty the written text puts into relief: the bizarre look of written puns and other plays on words, the combination of conventional syntax with semantic incoherence, the lack of logical elaboration, demonstration, and examples. Added to these are Lacan's use of his mathemes and figures, which, he declares in *Seminar XX*, are the essence of writing. What Lacan achieves, Fink says, is something like the analysand's discourse: speech in its spoken address to the analyst, but a speech that is "based on or dances around a kind of writing," a kind of writing analogous to the inscription of psychic material in the subject's unconscious.[21]

The great student of textual seduction, Roland Barthes, offers a perspective on how one might characterize the experience of a text so constructed. In *The Pleasure of the Text*, Barthes writes that the pleasure can take the form of a drift (*la dérive*):

> *Drifting* occurs *whenever I do not respect the whole*, and whenever, by dint of seeming driven about by language's illusions, seductions, and intimidations, like a cork on the waves, I remain motionless, pivoting on the *intractable* jouissance that binds me to the text (to the world). Drifting occurs, whenever social language, the sociolect, *fails me*. . . . Thus another name for drifting would be: the Intractable—or perhaps even Stupidity.[22]

The stupidity of drifting would be something like analytic listening, and what would bind one to the analytic text would not be pleasure per se but a certain jouissance. For Barthes, as for Lacan, pleasure has to do with the law and with language whereas jouissance is, if not outside of both, at least not accessible to either. "Pleasure can be expressed in words, jouissance cannot," Barthes writes.[23] But jouissance *can* be expressed in writing, Lacan asserts near the end of *Encore*, "That which is written—what would that be in the end? The conditions of jouissance."[24] The writing Lacan refers to here is what he considers the essence of writing: mathematical formalization (or his adaptation of it), the formalization that alone approaches Lacan's notion of the real that cannot be expressed by language and symbolization. The penultimate session of *Seminar XX* closes with the following:

> Mathematization alone reaches a real—and it is in that respect that it is compatible with our discourse, analytic discourse—a real that has nothing to do with what traditional knowledge has served as a basis for, which is not what the latter believes it to be—namely, reality—but rather fantasy.
>
> The real, I will say, is the mystery of the speaking body, the mystery of the unconscious.[25]

The Voyeuristic Text

If Lacan grapples with the various determined ways discourses close off the unconscious, Irigaray struggles against Lacan's continual shoring up of the symbolic, even as he continually exposes its fissures. Hers is, as I suggested, a second-degree critique. She is a Lacanian who aims to expose the blind spot of psychoanalysis. She similarly aims to turn the screw of critique on other master texts such as Freud's, Nietzsche's, Heidegger's, and Derrida's. Like Derrida, her writing closely engages other texts, though her way of inhabiting those texts is quite different. She is famous for her mimetic style, for taking on the words, the concepts, the tropes, of the texts she reads, from the Greeks to Descartes to Hegel and so on. Her mimeticism is theoretically crucial for her given her understanding of woman's relation to language, an understanding that comes from the Lacanian theory of sexuation, but also her work in linguistics. Women are outside of language. They use it, of course, but what they use is man's language, a language forged by men, that reflects men, that is isomorphic with the male imaginary. "What claims to be universal," she writes, "is actually the equivalent of a male idiolect, of a male imaginary, of a sexed world—and not neuter. There is nothing surprising in this, unless one is a passionate defender of idealism. Men have always been the ones to speak and especially to write: in the sciences, in philosophy, in religion, and in politics."[26] Given the masculine nature of language, Irigaray mimes the male texts, inhabits them and shows from within their language a powerful and defensive shoring up of an economy of the same that is closed to the possibility of a radically other mode of sexuation.

Irigaray's project is unapologetically impossible: to think a sexual difference that has been banished from Western thinking, at least since Socrates, and this through deconstructive mimetic readings that put forth words like "woman," "femininity," "maternity," the "couple," the "divine," which all look familiar but mean something new, is a difficult task. This is what Derrida calls paleonomy, "the occasional maintenance of an old name in order to launch a new concept,"[27] the strategy of someone who attempts to dismantle metaphysics from within. With Irigaray, there is more than an occasional use of the new in the old; the practice is generalized and sustained from work to work so that there is scarcely anything that can be taken at face value. Instead of grappling with a text that displaces or short-circuits its meaning, Irigaray's reader is called on continually to read deconstructively and to keep the newly forged meanings in play. This task becomes even more challenging in many of the later works where there is no explicit deconstructive engagement with another text and where the language can seem more or less straightforward. The harder it is, as in these works, for the reader to maintain a deconstructive stance toward the text, the easier it is for the text to appear transparently referential. To maintain the integrity of the Irigarayan text, then, to hold it between the extreme poles of the impossibly difficult and the deceptively accessible, the reader is called on to practice a kind of askesis of reading, a rigorously disciplined stance something like a spiritual conditioning that opens out to the not yet fully thinkable.

But there is another problem for the reader: the question of textual intimacy. For those readers who manage to read Lacan's texts, the relationship between reader and the text of jouissance can only be characterized as intimate. With Irigaray's work, there is no easy intimacy between reader and text. It is blocked by the very mimetic technique crucial to its critical strategy. There *is* a site of intense intimacy in Irigaray's work, but that is located elsewhere, between the couple constituted by the feminist critical voice and the masculine text it inhabits. It is there that one finds the frisson of the writing, the libidinal energy that drives it. The reader may identify with the feminist voice or with the masculine text, but she is nonetheless called on to bear witness to the staged encounter. This is true even of a piece such as "When Our Lips Speak Together," where the feminist voice addresses itself to a woman—or to the woman in herself—in highly erotic terms.[28] Even there, or perhaps especially there, it is the power of the masculine foreclosure of sexual difference that calls forth the intensity of the lesbian imagery. How could it be otherwise? Irigaray does not speak of an existing femininity, of an existing relationship between women or between a woman and herself, but rather of something that might be brought forth, but only through this encounter with masculine language.

Irigaray is quite explicit about the erotized nature of her project. In the 1970s she claims that her only option is to have a fling—*faire la noce*—with the philosophers so as to find the blocked and contained feminine within their language and to return the masculine to itself.[29] A decade or so later she adopts a modified and even more loving style:

> Every text is esoteric, not because it hides a secret but because it constitutes the secret, that which has yet to be revealed is never exhaustively revealable. The only response one can make to the question of the meaning of a text is: read, perceive, experience.... *Who are you?* is probably the most relevant question to ask of a text, as long as one isn't requesting a kind of identity card or an autobiographical anecdote. The answer would be: *how about you?* Can we find some common ground? Talk? Love? Create something together? What is there around us and between us that allows this?[30]

Irigaray's styles of seductive engagement span a range of modes of address and intensity, from *Marine Lover*, an amorous dialogue with Nietzsche, to "The Envelope: A Reading of Spinoza."[31] The reader is positioned differently in these texts but in all, the main event remains the crucial encounter of the masculine text and the drive of the foreclosed feminine. Even in writings that seem expository—such as Irigaray's linguistic studies, or essays and lectures of the 1990s to the present that deal with questions like human rights, citizenship, ecology—even in those works where there is no staged meeting of the couple, the traces of that encounter are always there; they underwrite all theorizing and account for the startling formulations that can appear suddenly in the middle of what seems like conventional discourse. If this scene of the couple underlies all of Irigaray's writing, what can the reader be but a third party to the twosome? This third party position is something like what Barthes calls the "second-degree reader" of criticism. Citing Barthes, "How can we read criticism? Only one way: since I am here a second-degree reader, I must shift my position: instead of agreeing to be the confidant of the critical pleasure—a sure way to miss it—I can make myself its voyeur: I observe clandestinely the pleasure of others."[32] Of course, Irigaray's readings are not classical criticism in the sense of a commentary with a clear boundary between text and reader; her fling with the philosophers puts an end to all such boundaries. What Irigaray does is to expose the erotic dimensions of the commentary and turn them to her deconstructive ends. And the reader, somewhat like Barthes's second-degree reader of criticism, takes her pleasure, from a distance, as a voyeur.

The question remains as to whether Irigaray's critique can be read as such. Can such a project function as critique when the reader has both too much and too little footing in the text? Too much if she reads the deconstructive words—woman, the couple, mother, divine—as if they were old words; too little footing if her position as voyeur leaves her cold?

To Be Two

To compound the difficulty, there is the intimate theoretical entanglement entailed in Irigaray's writing. Her intense and ongoing entanglement with Lacan's *Seminar XX* is a good example. It is as if Irigaray aims to so fully inhabit Lacan's text that its shoring will no longer hold. I will try to give some small indication of what this theoretical intimacy involves. By *Seminar XX*, indeed since *Seminar XI*, Lacan has turned away from desire to the drive in order to grasp the intractability of some symptoms. Whereas desire finds its cause in the object a—the term that Lacan uses to figure the unsymbolizable residue of the part-object (the breast, the feces, the voice, the gaze)—the drive circles around and around the unsymbolized, or real, object a, drawing its force precisely from its resistance to symbolization. In *Seminar XX*, called *Encore*, Lacan returns to the woman question and, with that, to a knot of questions having to do with knowledge and sexuality, knowledge and jouissance, and most importantly with the relationship between the symbolic and the real.

It is there, in *Encore*, that he posits a feminine jouissance that differs from the phallic. Jouissance, for Lacan, is "enjoyment" more in the sense of sufferance than of pleasure and one that the subject doesn't let go of, dependent for his or her very being on the satisfaction that it brings. As Žižek says, it is the very density of being.[33] For Lacan, phallic jouissance always comes up short, to use Bruce Fink's words.[34] Because of the promise of wholeness that castration holds out, the masculine subject holds on to a belief in another jouissance. As Suzanne Bernard puts it, "One could say that while man is wholly subject 'to,' and hence 'in,' the symbolic, he is 'in it with exception,' that is, he 'takes exception' to it in some way. As a result, the fantasy of the subject not subjected to the Law—the fantasy of no limit—determines masculine structure in an essential way."[35]

As speaking subjects, women cannot *not* take part in phallic jouissance, but they do not share in the masculine fantasy, nor in the masculine anxiety. Through castration, the fundamental fantasy of the male subject entails his entering the field of the Other via the lost object, that object always to be sought. Bernard describes the male subject's dilemma:

> Within masculine structure, the drive remains haunted by the image of phallic presence, despite the fact that the masculine subject's place in the symbolic is fixed by its *exclusion*. Hence, one consequence of the masculine subject's attempts to realize the object of desire (to make it exist) is the (paradoxical) risk of dissolving the order in which *he* exists. As a result, he must remain at a certain distance from the object of his desire in order to maintain his sexual position. This is what Lacan refers to as the risk of annihilation the masculine subject takes in approaching the object. (p. 180)

Within feminine structure, on the other hand, the feminine subject *knows* there is lack in the Other, and this different fundamental fantasy allows her a jouissance beyond the phallic.

This difference between phallic jouissance and the Other jouissance turns out to be crucial to the relationship between the real and the symbolic, or in other words, to the way the real functions in male and female sexuation. For the male subject, the Other is constituted through the loss of the real, and the field of the Other is structured by this loss. The female subject, who does not take on the fantasy of the paternal exception to castration, and hence, the fantasy of full presence, has a different relationship to the Other. She is not *not* in the Law, but she is in the Law differently, not haunted by promised phallic plenitude, nor threatened by the dangerous annihilation it represents, not traumatized, in other words, by the lack in the Other.

In *Encore*, Lacan reminds us again that the sexual relation is not a fusion of the two into the one. He figures this by the trope of meiosis, that process of cell division that reduces the number of chromosomes in reproductive cells so as to produce the gametes capable of fertilization. Already in Seminar *XI* he had used meiosis to figure the lack in being that haunts the male subject's relationship to the Other. The lack in the field of the Other, he says, in turn takes up an earlier loss, "the blow of individual death" as he puts it, that the subject suffers at the time of sexed reproduction.[36] We are in the field of the libido:

> the libido, *qua* pure life instinct, that is to say, immortal life, or irrepressible life ... simplified, indestructible life. It is precisely what is subtracted from

the living being by virtue of the fact that it is subject to the cycle of sexed reproduction. And it is of this that all the forms of the *objet a* that can be enumerated are the representatives, the equivalents. The *objets a* are merely its representatives, its figures. The breast—as equivocal, as an element characteristic of the mammiferous organization, the placenta for example—certainly represents that part of himself that the individual loses at birth, and which may serve to symbolize the most profound lost object. I could make the same kind of reference to all the other objects.[37]

If the male subject suffers from lack in being, the female has a different relationship to the real, one of "not not being," as Bernard says. And this relationship has something to do with what Lacan calls "lalangue" or the m(O)ther tongue, to which the female subject has a different access. Quoting Lacan, "The unconscious evinces knowledge that, for the most part, escapes the speaking being. That being provides the occasion to realize just how far the effects of *lalangue* can go, in that it presents all sorts of affects that remain enigmatic."[38] It is this lalangue and not language that the unconscious speaks. And it is this lalangue, the (m)Other tongue—*en-corps*—that is heard in the Other jouissance.

One reason Irigaray's work tracks Lacan's so closely is because he continues to strain against his own categories and because those strains in his theorizing help to open up hers. In *Encore*, Lacan puts into relief as never before the pathos of the phallic sexual economy. Irigaray's frustration is that he stops there. For in the end, what becomes of those crucial formulations other than a mysterious suggestion, perhaps, of something different? From Irigaray's perspective, *Encore* might be seen as "yet again." All the figural straining required to produce the Other jouissance, all the double negatives, might be taken as signs, here more than ever, that the discourse can barely express what it needs to express. An analytic discourse that sets out to read a culture that fetishizes the mother's body must itself speak fetishistically. One might say that one is left with a sleight of hand: now you see it, now you don't.

It is here that Irigaray takes on a rhetorical impatience, here that she argues that Lacan should listen harder to what he hears from women. And it is here that she finds psychoanalysis complicit in furthering the very formations it reads so well. Her aim is to suggest that the subject's entrance into symbolization need not be structured forever within the pathos of male sexuation. She argues that psychoanalysis itself, in exposing this formation, leads us to see how women, but also men, might become subjects in a less pathological manner were there shifts in the symbolic. To say that the unconscious knows no history is not to say that the unconscious is ahistorical.

The force of Irigaray's argument lies in her reading of the lost object and all its attendant effects as symptomatic of the child's inability to symbolize its relationship to the mother's body. Much is made, she says, of the ambivalence Oedipus feels toward his father, but isn't this an ambivalence projected retroactively upon the primitive relation to the mother's body? "Now, it is true," she writes,

> that, in so far as it takes account of the drives, analysis does have things to tell us about the mother's breast, about the milk she offers, about the feces she takes away . . . and even about her gaze and voice. But analysis shows too little interest in these things. Furthermore, isn't it true that all this wrestling (*corps-à-corps*) with the mother, which has difficulties of its own, is part of a postoedipal phantasy projected backward onto the Oedipus phase? When the mother is cut up in stages, when each part of her body has to be cathected and then decathected if the child is to grow, she has already been torn to pieces by the hatred of Oedipus.[39]

Commenting on the importance of the Law, of language, the name of the father, she goes on:

> The social order, our culture, psychoanalysis itself, are all insistent that the mother must remain silent, outlawed. The father forbids any *corps-à-corps* with the mother. I am tempted to add: if only this were really true! We would be more at peace with our bodies if it were, and men need peace to feed their libido as well as their life and culture. For the ban does not prevent a certain number of failures of compliance, a certain blindness."[40]

The law of the father doesn't fully work, Irigaray says. If men were to effect real separation from the mother, their desire wouldn't depend on cutting her body into pieces; they wouldn't be threatened by the devouring vagina; they wouldn't need to find their mothers in their wives; they wouldn't need the woman as a guarantee that their body exists.

Irigaray has a strong rhetorical response to Lacan's trope of meiosis and to the placenta's role with regard to it. For Lacan, the placenta is a trope for the subject's—that is the male subject's—lost object. But seen from the perspective of female jouissance, it can also be read, as Bernard suggests, as the loss of a certain strange relation to the Other, a relationship of *not not one*, figured by the placenta's role in joining fetus and mother. For her part, Irigaray takes the trope out of the double negative. Let us read the placenta as it is, she suggests. The placenta is not a simple conduit of exchanges between two organisms and hence a fusion of them. It is a virtually independent organ that mediates a space between the tissues of the mother and the fetus and, at the same time, regulates exchanges between the two for the benefit of both, which includes moderating the mother's metabolism as necessary and secreting maternal hormones needed for gestation. Irigaray refers to biologist and theorist Hélène Rouch, who suggests that a cultural blindness to the relationship of mother and child as always already separated has to do with the total dependence of the child at birth, which produces the imaginary notion of the fusion of mother and child and the subsequent fantasy of the expulsion of the child from an undifferentiated paradise.[41]

Taking up the figure of the placenta, Irigaray is able to offer a different imaginary. Were there a way for the child to symbolize its relations to the mother's body, and were that relationship imagined as always already separate and at the same time life sustaining, the whole fantasy of fusion, triangulation, law, loss, and refusal of loss would be interrupted. The other imaginary would be the effect of a symbolic order in which what is now figured as castration would be realized differently. The double articulation of castration—into language, into sexuation—would be the work of what Irigaray calls negativity, the negativity of the absolute radical alterity of male subject and female subject. The female subject would be fully sexed in that her sexuality would be symbolizable, though without any fantasy of lost fusion. The interval between subjects would be productive of the field of the Other and of desire.

Knowing Too Much

It is impossible for me to do justice here to Irigaray's full theorization of a different sexual difference. But I can point to the obvious challenges it faces. How to evoke a change in the symbolic when one's thematization is so dependent on the imaginary? Any elaboration of a differently figured imaginary can easily be read as a hopelessly utopian and trivial project that makes the promise of a different social order seem dependent on our all being willing to embrace the trope of the placenta. It is to avoid such readings that serious critics of Irigaray never let her text stray far from the ones she inhabits—in this discussion, the text of *Encore*.

All critique is, of course, dependent on the text it reads: Critique is the disruption of the closure of one text by the critical work of the other. And it is this disruption of closure that makes critique so crucial to the critical disciplines. It is a reading practice (following, in particular, Althusser, Lacan, Barthes, and Derrida) that insures against authoritarianism and orthodoxy. But what to say of Irigaray's second-degree critique with its constitutive dependency on the texts it inhabits? In Irigaray's case, we are dealing with a particular kind of dependency that mirrors the very relationship of femininity and masculinity within the existing symbolic order. Can critique survive the proximity that the Irigarayan mimetic practice demands? Does this proximity not yield a too-comfortable familiarity? To theorize a femininity that is not the other of the masculine, the symptom of the masculine, is a tricky business. Irigaray more than anyone appreciates its trickiness and sees her work not as a utopian description of a future but as an intervention—a performative intervention—meant to stimulate change in the form of disruptive formulations. And, as in any engagement with the unconscious, there is no knowing the outcome in advance.

But in the reality of reading, doesn't everything work against Irigaray's project? The comparison with Lacan is illuminating. His texts are enigmatic because so much, in the sense of ordinary meaning, is withheld that the reader who is incited to produce meaning inevitably does so in the register of critique. Even the most reductive readings of Lacan have to perform contortions in order to reproduce the banality of the already known. In contrast, Irigaray's later texts, with their talk of placentas and couples and maternal genealogies, seem to inhabit the very register of the already known. If the reader of Lacan feels called on to produce intelligibility out of the impossibly difficult, Irigaray's reader feels impelled to restore the impossible to her intelligibility.

The Forgotten Mystery

Thus far I have emphasized the theorist whose texts demand a certain rigor to sustain a critique that continually struggles against the power of the already-known meanings of male and female. But there may also be ways to read Irigarayan texts that have more to do with stupidity and jouissance than with rigor. Consider, for example, her engagement with Greek mythology. In a 1989 lecture entitled "The Forgotten Mystery of Female Ancestry," Irigaray revisits the story of Persephone.[42] As Irigaray tells it, when Zeus gives Persephone to Hades without consulting her or her mother Demeter, Demeter finds ways to express her displeasure, as in rendering the earth barren. When mother and daughter are eventually reunited, Persephone recounts to her mother everything that has happened to her, telling her story from beginning to end. "In a way," Irigaray says, "she goes back in time, as must any woman today who is trying to find the traces of her estrangement from her mother. This is what the psychoanalytic process should do: find the thread of her entry into the Underworld, and, if possible, her way out" (p. 107).

The underworld Irigaray evokes is the hell of monosexual subjectivity and the ruin of sexual love, where the girl is estranged from her own virginity, deprived of all but the freedom to "seduce in accordance with male instincts." She "becomes a sort of puppet or movable object, reduced to being subjected to basic drives with passive goals." Irigaray goes on, "She thinks she needs to be 'screwed' by a man, she suffers from a basic oral need (partially an inverted projection stemming from male desire), Freud writes learnedly, without considering that this need might be symptomatic of woman's submission to male instincts. According to Freud, this need is a sort of relic of the initial chaos that male desire opened up in the earth's womb."[43] Concluding a pointed analysis of the bottomless hunger that psychoanalysis finds in women, Irigaray says, "None of this could happen if she had not been separated from her mother, from the earth, from her gods and her order. This is the original sin that makes woman a seductress against a backdrop of nothingness. But why abduct her from her mother? Why destroy female ancestries? To establish an order man needed, but which is not yet an order of respect for and fertility of sexual difference."[44]

What do I the reader make of this collapse of time so it is as if the separation of Persephone and Demeter happens in *my* time, with its deleterious effects on *my* desire? Rather than turn to Irigaray's ample theorization of the question of female genealogy, I suggest that one look simply at the effect of Irigaray's positioning the reader in mythic time. There is a way in which this very particular staging of the temporal registers of the psychic present is at work in all of Irigaray's writing, which is another way of saying that her mythical interventions are allegorical of her work in general.

To clarify, consider Shoshana Felman's reading of mythology and psychoanalysis in her book, *Jacques Lacan and the Adventures of Insight*. There Felman reminds us that Freud said: "the theory of instincts is so to say our mythology. Instincts are mythical entities, magnificent in their indefiniteness. In our work we cannot for a moment disregard them, yet we are never sure we are seeing them clearly."[45] And Lacan, following Freud, comments that "in the final analysis we can talk adequately about the libido only in a mythic manner."[46] What this means, Felman says, is that "insofar as it is mediated by a myth, the Freudian theory is not a literal translation or reflection of reality, but its symptom, its metaphorical account. The myth is not pure fantasy, however, but has narrative symbolic logic that accounts for a real mode of functioning, a real structure of relations."[47]

What is most important in Felman's discussion is her observation that this symptomatic or metaphorical rendering is not just a static gloss, an embellished narrative version of a serious scientific theory of the way things work. The myth is the *route* to theory and not the other way around, and the way that movement works is analogous to the analytic dialogue. What is involved in that dialogue is not an informative act (through statements or meanings), but a performative one. "The analytic interpretation in itself is a performative (not cognitive) interpretation in that it has a fundamental structuring, transforming function. At stake is not the accuracy of a particular reading but a relationship between the structuring address of the myth and the structuring reception."[48] And this is the relationship between reality and the psychoanalytic myth:

> The myth comes to grips with something in reality that it does not fully comprehend but to which it gives an answer, a *symbolic* reply.... [I]n much the same way as ... the analytic interpretation, within the situation of the dialogue, acts not by virtue of its accuracy but by virtue of its resonance (received in terms of the listener's structure), works, that is, by virtue of its openness to a linguistic passage through the Other, so does the psychoanalytic myth, in *resonating in the Other*, produce a *truthful structure*. The psychoanalytic myth derives its theoretical effectiveness not from its truth value, but from its truth encounter with the other, from its capacity for *passing through the other*; from its openness, that is, to an *expropriating passage* of one insight through another, of one story through another.[49]

Looking at Irigaray's mode of critique from this perspective, there might be more to be said about the voyeuristic text. Perhaps there is a double structure of address in these texts, two scenes staged and not just the scene of the feminist critical voice and masculine text. The second scene would be that of Persephone telling her story to Demeter. The reader of that scene might find critique, and, along the way, a route out of Hades.

PART IV

Inventions

CHAPTER 10

Parapoetics and the Architectural Leap
Steve McCaffery

This essay is divided into three uneven sections. The opening two are short. The first offers a "soft," manifesto-like exposition of parapoetics; the second discusses a related matter: the paralogicality of the frame. The final section comprises a part mapping of and a few suggestions toward areas of potential parapoetic investigation. Judged on the normative criteria for academic papers, it is premature, partial at best, and thoroughly inconclusive. Seen as an attempt to realize a parapoetic intervention, it will be judged to be an utterly abortive attempt—and quite correctly so. However, as the speculative and tentative tenor of the first part indicates, the third part is a probe into uncertainties and unknowns. Notably absent is any lengthy discussion of the important architectural contributions of the Situationists. That discussion can be found elsewhere.[1]

Parapoetics

Foucault reminds us that epistemic rupture, in radical breaks within power-knowledge machines, precipitates "endings." By contrast, the Deleuzean dynamic of "becoming" offers a kinetic, projective model. Becomings inflect trajectories and the geographic, offering "orientations, directions, entries and exits [with] no terminus from which you set out, none which you arrive at. Nor are there two terms, which are exchanged. . . . Becomings are not phenomena of imitation or assimilation, but of a double capture, of non-parallel evolution."[2] We are all heirs to this intimate inheritance of becoming—hardly an abyss and hardly the space of some grandiose Icarus effect—but a precise and fecund topological dynamic nonetheless. Unlike endings, becomings temporarily occupy an interstice; they are always realized in the between, in an uncertain transitivity and a transient inscription that for some might register an angst, for others the interstitial sublime.

The death of God, the end of man, the end of theory, the death of poetry, the death of the subject, the death of art, courtesy of Hegel, the death of man courtesy of Foucault, the death of Marxism courtesy of North American departments of English, the end of narrative courtesy of my friend with a smile like those horses in Picasso's *Guernica*. Having survived a tedious catena of such mortifications and eschatologies, I'll not add to the list the death of poetics. Crisis is a notion frequently complicit with endings, and I sense no crisis in poetics but do note complacency in matters of potentiality and scale. Accordingly I urge a shift into a purposefully fuzzy and still virtual discipline I call "parapoetics." Similar to David Carroll's notion of the paraesthetic, the term denotes a critical responsibility to approach poetry through its relation to extrapoetic domains. To borrow Carroll's own description, it's figured as "something like [a poetics] turned against itself . . . a faulty, irregular, disordered, improper [poetics]—one not content to remain within the area defined by the [poetic]."[3] Celan believed that naming occurs in the depth of language, and yet to accord to naming a definitional power is to end a being-as-becoming. Dr. Johnson warns that to "circumscribe poetry by definition will only show the narrowness of the definer,"[4] a sentiment endorsed by Schlegel in his oxymoronic definition of romantic poetry as poetry that can't be defined. Similarly, I want to avoid a specific predetermination of what constitutes parapoetics and leave it suspended as a non-determined concept and thereby allow critical desire to put mastery at risk. Abandoning the pursuit of theoretical dogmatism it will require that a negative capability be applied within the pernicious doublet Foucault concatenates as power–knowledge.

The *Concise Oxford Dictionary* offers numerous meanings for the prefix "para-": (1) beside, (2) beyond, (3) a modification, (4) a diametrically opposite relation, (5) a form of protection or warding off.[5] The larger *OED* adds further variations to these seemingly contradictory senses that strike me as particularly attractive to poetic practice:

In composition it has the same senses, with such cognate adverbial ones as "to one side, aside, amiss, faulty, irregular, disordered, improper, wrong": also expressing subsidiary relation, alteration, perversion, simulation, etc.[6]

"Para-" is appealing precisely because of its evasion of the janiform "post-," whose consequences, Derrida adverts, involve "a surrender to the historicist urge."[7] Among other things, "para-" provokes a shift from temporal to spatial conceptualization and positioning. Moreover, the lateral adjacency of "beside" offers a multiplicity of satellitic invocations: the friend, neighbor, relative, lover, guide, witness, and judge. "Beside" is also between, interstitial and intervalic, as well as extra, outside. Accordingly I'll be speaking more about the place of parapoetics than its ontology, on where it is and can be, than on what it is. Purposefully left undefined, the important step is to inscribe and activate its forces. Redirecting Derrida's call to architecture I write, "Let us never forget there is a poetics of poetics" and that poetics is beside poetics.[8] Heuristic rather than foundational, parapoetic desire does not seek to adumbrate upon the specificity of a discipline but rather to probe the fungibility and centrifuge always latent within the ontologically or intellectually discrete. As such it takes its place within the anti-Kantian lineage that denies the specificity of art and also offers a countermove within the current new "anxiety" of specialization rather than influence. Operating as a probe into uncertainties and as a force of disruption among stability, it aims to transform a total unity into multiplicity. Foucault and Blanchot encourage the "thinking of the outside" as a critical practice of transgression, one that refuses the stability of alterity while at the same time avoiding the incorporating move to totality. Parapoetics demands that singular disciplines or practices remove themselves in order to achieve a self-comprehension in a manner that avoids a transcendental installation of the theoretical attitude and submit to a voluntary disability. Assuming the burden of this kind of thinking, parapoetics works against the promulgation of any discursive formation as a complete and closed system and relatedly seeks to go beyond the discretion of Deleuze's "fabulation of a discipline to come."[9]

Free from a fixed definition it's also emancipated from a predetermined destination and able to install itself within the dialectical tensions and determinants of any number of target fields. Rather than serving as the critical mode of poetics, a species of self-policing and of external probing, parapoetics signals a shift in critical desire away from the poem as such toward other disciplines and discourses. Working between the seams and cracks consequent to the inevitable play between discourses, upon and without the hyphenated space of power-knowledge, parapoetics adopts more a contaminatory than a combative stance, marbling the smooth and certain propositional plane of discourse and ideas. Parapoetics does not support disciplinary cross-dressing and is not to be deposited in other disciplines as some governing metatheory. Deracinated and detached from poetics proper, and maintaining its distance from any discourse that seeks to master or explain, it can be likened to a hesitation within a caesura. For these reasons parapoetics will always be both a lot more and a little less than poetics.

The Frame-up

> All movements have direction. But why just one direction and not several? Movements can produce breakouts and new connections.
> YAGO CONDE[10]

Ronald Aronson encourages us to think of theory as a tool, not a framework,[11] and much of Derrida's *The Truth in Painting* explores the philosophical intricacies of working and engaging the frame. Frames both individuate and recontextualize, and their ultimate power is cartographic. We see the acute stakes of framing in our current geopolitical and sexual climates: on one hand, the melting of national boundaries and proactive deframings under the pressure of economic ideologies in Europe and North America (NAFTA and the EU), and on the other, a Balkanization of Europe and Africa from political and ethnic pressures to maximize territorial coding. The struggle toward legal ratification of same-sex marriages is a debate fought out in a judicial theater and hinges on the right to set up a frame within an existing frame.

Framing, of course, is the prime culprit in transforming objects *as such* into objects *of* theory, thereby guaranteeing a pacification of the chosen object field and the impossibility of the latter modifying the theoretical domain. For this reason theoretical endeavor is antipathetic to empiricism, whose method runs counter to such framing. Despite the fact that theory frames are designed to ensure a unilateral flow of power sufficient to preserve the integrity of its method, the logic of the frame moves against settled internal preservation. French architect Bernard Cache suggests that "the structure of the modern frame offers a certain amount of play.... The rigid parts of the frame still retain a certain geometry, but their articulation is mobile and their equilibrium results from the play of tensions that run through the system as a whole."[12] Frames are caught up in a contradictory logic insomuch as the boundaries they set out to demarcate are constantly threatened by external elements and forces. Rather than preservers of integrity, frames are conduits facilitating a promiscuous transit of forces from inside out and from outside in; they organize a contradictory yet mutual relation of an exterior to an interior that, like Foucauldian thresholds, construct an untenable divide between incompatible forces struggling for dominance. Derrida only pragmatizes this observation in his suggestion to "work the frame" as both boundary and conduit. Deleuze and Guattari emphasize the omniprobability of the frame reversing its function and serving to deframe in a process by which what is preserved internally finds a relationship to something external in a way that opens it up to the outside.[13]

The paralogicality of the frame bears comparison to the nature of dissipative structures, defined and investigated in the field of nonlinear thermodynamics by Ilya Prigogine and Isabelle Stengers. Dissipative structures are "forms of supermolecular organization requiring the continuous dissipation of energy and matter through the increase of small random fluctuations."[14] The theory of dissipative structures is emerging as a formative notion in numerous disciplines, provoking Fernández-Galiano to consider it "the new scientific paradigm of the age."[15] Both buildings and the city can be conceived as open thermodynamic systems dependent for their existence on nutritional elements and energy flows. As Prigogine and Stengers observe, in a cell or a city alike, we find "that these systems are not only open but live on their openness, nourishing themselves with the flows of matter and energy reaching them from the outside world . . . the city and the cell quickly die when separated from their mediums, for they are part of the worlds that nourish them and constitute a sort of local and unique incarnation of the flows that never cease to transform."[16] Likewise, both cell and city require the constant dissipation of energy, be it in the form of waste produce or the movement of populace, in a constant spreading beyond frames and boundaries. In sharp contrast to the practice of comparative poetics outlined by Earl Miner, parapoetics does not work to constitute and defend the discrete frame of the poem but rather explore how the frame can be challenged to open up a poetics without borders.

The Architectural Leap

The language revising its own architectures is the cloud palace and drift of your desire.
ROBERT DUNCAN, Notebook 31

Stein's call to "act so that there was no use in a center" is cannily prophetic of contemporary cultural desires, and in current poetics the ideas of rupture and multiplicity seem more attractive than the one of continuity.[17] Derrida leaves the fundamental nature of writing an open question and the same is required of poetics. Feeling that contemporary poetics has reached an impasse in *exclusively* poetic territories, I wish to propose a leap or "becoming" toward both urban texture and architectural theory as initial parapoetic domains. An exclusive focus on the poem-as-such severely curtails the potential critical range of poetics, and for the latter to maintain a vital critical function, then, a radical readjustment of its trajectories seems required. The purpose of this leap is not simply to obtain knowledge or display it in a different discipline, nor to plunder a terrain for concepts and ideas useful to one's own practice. The architectural leap involves *the knowledge of how and when to delay knowing*; how to be active in a state of suspended certainty. Via the poetic leap one is no longer beside but elsewhere. In the spirit of Bataille's oxymoronic formulation (that to love poetry one must hate poetry), the initial poetic leap will be a turn against its traditional object field and detach poetics from poematics. With explorations beyond affinities and analogies, parapoetics will situate interstitially, the way punctuation falls *between* meaning. Circumscribed within the broad thematics of disciplines and movings, parapoetics will focus on the interval where contamination, paralogicality, uncertainty, and misprision precipitate discovery, unforeseen collaboration, and contestation. As regards specific dynamics, in parapoetic logic, an entrance is the continuation of an exit by other means. And who knows, perhaps poetics after the postmodern might well be a parapoetics inside it.

Disciplines, like structures and language, are simultaneously closed and open, containing heterogeneity within a frame of the homogeneous. To insist on the specificity of both the poetic and the architectural is to seriously limit both research and the critico-creative enterprise inside, between, and across the two. "Why should 'literature' [*or* architecture] still designate that which already breaks away from literature—away from what has always been conceived and signified under that name—or that which, not merely escaping literature [or architecture], implacably destroys it?"[18] To repeat a well-known claim of Derrida's, "a writing that refers back only to itself carries us at the same time, indefinitely and systematically, to some other writing."[19] Beyond a critical engagement with this heterogeneity within the so-called homogeneous is an urgent need to shift not the mode but the target of poetics' transitivity.

Aaron Betsky has emerged as the popular theorist of that decentralizing condition and dissolution known as "sprawl." Sprawl shatters the tense logic of the frame. Not only an architectural and urban condition, sprawl is the essential condition of modernity. Pollution is sprawl, contemporary knowledge is sprawl. Sprawl is the authentic landscape of the contemporary but enters painting as early as Turner. Sprawl is the given condition, not the cursed share of architecture. Betsky insists, "The issue is not how to stop sprawl but how to use its composition, its nodes and its leaky spaces to create a kind of architecture."[20] As a blotting or formless spreading out from strategic nodes—malls, airports, and so forth—sprawl constitutes both the dematerialization of physical structures and modernity's urban given. It registers the contemporary city's tendency to heterology and centrifuge whose resonant inclination is to deframe. Betsky's name for this formless dystopia is "exurbia"—"where human forms meld into the remains of nature and where order becomes so thin that we recognize its most basic components." For Betsky urban sprawl may even provide a redemptive dimension that takes us "away from the high-rise tendencies of the city [and puts] us back on earth where we confront the realities of ground and weather." While declining the temptation to dangle such redemptive carrots I would insist, however, that in maintaining parapoetics as a deliberately nondetermined concept, we advocate a certain conceptual and creative sprawl.

Why the leap into architecture? From "stanza" to the "prison-house of language," architectural figures dominate within the very formulation of the linguistic. Architectural metaphors haunt writing to a degree sufficient to cause us to question a merely benign metaphoric presence. One of Heidegger's lasting insights is into how both language and architecture ground us in the world. In architecture, as in language, human beings dwell (poetically or not) whether in open mobility or confinement. Derrida observes, "We appear to ourselves only through an experience of spacing which is already marked by architecture."[21] Heidegger and Derrida alike suggest that prior to becoming social subjects, we are all architectural bodies.[22] We need, however, to add to Derrida's grammatological conception of architecture as "a writing of space, a mode of spacing which makes a place for events"[23] the facts that architecture too is the materialized conception of dwelling and that dwelling is fundamentally a relation of ontology to spaces. Architecture in that enriched sense serves to return being to its problems by way of *oikos* rather than *poiesis*. And if Bachelard is correct when claiming that all inhabited space bears the essence of the notion of home, then the link between reading and dwelling appears to be far from a strained analogy.

The myth of Babel implicates the two distinct phenomena of architecture and human speech, from which has developed an enduring complicity. The metaphoric saturation of architectural terms in other discourses (including both philosophy and literature) is well known: the "prison-house of language," deconstruction, the poem's fabric, foundation, and so on. According to Derrida, the architectural metaphor of ground constitutes the very core of philosophy.[24] But beyond a metaphoric presence, architecture has consistently offered writing a constructive model and, though hardly sister arts, architecture's intimate relation to the literary is historically tangible, even down to its grammatological contours.[25] Architecture provides the formal model for Saint Teresa's *Interior Castle*, Jeremy Taylor's *Rules and Exercises for Holy Dying* (figured in the preface as a tour through the rooms of a charnel house), George Herbert's *The Temple*, and Christopher Harvey's affiliate text *The Synagogue*. The arguments of Donne's magnificent sermon "Death's Duel" are built around the three prime architectural supports of foundation, buttress, and contignation: "The foundations suffer them not to sink, the buttresses suffer them not to swerve, and the contignations and knitting suffers them not to cleave."[26] In his 1850 Advertisement to *The Prelude*, Wordsworth recalls his conception in 1814 of the relation of his two earlier poems, *The Excursion* and *The Recluse*, in architectural terms that recall Herbert: "the two works have that relation to each other . . . as the Antechapel has to the body of a Gothic Church."[27] Even his minor pieces when collected and "properly arranged, will be found by the attentive reader to have such connection with the main work as may give them claim to be likened to the little cells, oratories and sepulchral recesses, ordinarily included in those edifices."[28] More recently, Ronald Johnson's long poem *ARK* adopts as its formal model "a kind of *naif* architecture on the lines of the Facteur Cheval's *Ideal Palace*, Simon Rodia's *Watts Towers*, or Ramond Isidore's mosaic house in the shade of Chartres"[29] with Johnson's earlier poem, *Radi os*, a selected textual deletion of *Paradise Lost*, envisaged as the final and one hundredth book of *ARK* and "conceived as a kind of Dymaxion Dome over the whole."[30] Mark Scroggins elaborates on *ARK*'s architectonic features: "[Johnson] calls his poem a 'model for a monument.' And its three major divisions reflect this spatial metaphor: 33 sections of 'Foundations,' 3 of 'Spires,' and 33 of 'Ramparts.' *ARK*, in turn, was to have been a 'dome' over the whole, a crowning and covering shell like that over Monticello, the U.S. Capitol, or the Roman Pantheon. The poem, then, is conceived of as in some sense a literal object, a literal architecture."[31] In *De vulgari eloquentia* 2.9, Dante offers a distinction between *stanza* (literally, "room") and *canzone* that illustrates the presidential status of architectural thinking:

> And here one must know that this term [stanza] has been chosen for technical reasons exclusively, so that what contains the entire art of the canzone should be called *stanza*, that is a capacious dwelling or receptacle for the entire craft.

For just as the canzone is the container (literally lap or womb) of the entire thought, so the stanza enfolds its entire technique.[32]

The interrogative crux structuring the entirety of Augustine's *Confessions* (a book that frequently addresses the infinite as a locus) is a *temporal* problem articulated as an architectural issue of impossible housing. I call on you, Lord, to you the Infinite to come and inhabit me, I who am but finite. Mark Z. Danielewski takes up this same impossibility in his recent novel *House of Leaves*, where the house on Ash Tree Lane is bigger on the inside than it is on the outside.

For its part, the materiality of language has provided an abundance of architectural possibilities. The dramatic and decorative possibilities of the letter shape as an interior space functions as the basic premise of the medieval "inhabitated" initial, but Johann David Steingruber brings about a more complex fusion of function and the fantastic in his *Architectural Alphabet* of 1773. The book's thirty-three plates constitute a veritable tour de force and show patently feasible functional designs. Steingruber's quintessentially baroque wit is retained as a trace element in Steven Holl's investigation into the intimate congruence of certain letterforms and architectural design in relation to context and urban syntax.[33]

Offering an attractive alternative to Bloom's anxiety of influence, Viktor Shklovsky argues for a deflection of influence. Put simply, the theory advances that artistic or disciplinary influence is transmitted not in an immediate and direct line within the same discipline but in an entirely different domain. The transmission of artistic and cultural influence travels like the knight's move in chess, not from fathers to sons but from uncles and aunts to nieces and nephews.[34] A recent example is Language writing's influence on musicology seen in Brian Ferneyhough's embrace of disjunction in his New Complexionism. Rather than literary continuity via canon and hierarchy, why not a deflectional move to geography, or architecture? (It's the trail of the transmission out of its current site that is important.) So in the virtual interrelations between poetics and architecture along a Shklovskian model, we might adopt an architectural configuration and rethink the concept of a poetic movement, and poetic practice in general, as the construction of a project in relation to a chosen program, itself relating to an actual preexisting site. Additionally, the programmatic ideology of architecture facilitates rethinking that socio-ontological problematic complex named "community" through the architectural notion of "site." Site as locus and topos has a fecund, aristocratic history stretching far back beyond Olson through the genius loci to Aristotle's claim that "place is something, but it also has a certain power."[35] Bernard Cache's Deleuzean-informed architecture lets poetics abandon the otiose binary of form and content and take up the triplet of frame, vector, and inflection. Cache's complex theorizing on the status of the image warrants careful scrutiny and perhaps, additionally, a bold application in *poiesis*. Similarly, it might be asked: How would catachresis find an architectural realization or, equally, an axonometric method in poetry?

Perhaps then we can learn more about the discourse of the poem by examining it from architecture's alterior position and through a purposeful displacement of poetics into architecture. The dialogue between these two practices occurs as much within as between each other, and the integrity of both practices should be risked. Parapoetic strategy seeks out not what is confluential but also conflictual in these two practices, as well as what each is displacing and becoming. Contemporary architecture shows a cartographic caution around establishing boundaries and domains. Indeed, it is coming to understand that discrete disciplinary issues can't all be raised in architecture itself (involving, among other things, the broader philosophical issues of ontology, presence, history, topos, memory, and mimesis); there are additionally the wider sociopolitical issues of urbanism, the city, and context, and perhaps most paramount, a relation to human bodies, as well as the broader matters of coordination, material, and scale, and the relation of interiority and exteriority.

Bernard Tschumi is not alone in stressing the conceptual nature of architecture as its paramount purpose. Tschumi compares it to Lacanian psychoanalysis whose goal is not curative, with the patient's recovery occurring as a felicitous indirect effect: "To make buildings that work and make people happy is not to [*sic*] goal of architecture but, of course, a welcome side effect."[36] I currently concur, however, with Robin Evans in seeing architecture as the construction of the preconditions that govern the way bodies occupy and negotiate space—a credo not far removed from Yago Conde's claim that "the habitual exclusion of the body and its experiences of [*sic*; from?] any discourse on the logic of form would be instances of the lack of any intertextual impulse."[37] Architecture is a form of action centering on users, and the key question of architectural form is a question of architecture's relation to the scale and matter of human freedom.

However, having said that, I have to admit that the question of what "is" architecture has become much more difficult to answer in recent times. Traditionally, architects are subject to the same constraints as a poet laureate. Forced into a species of contextual bricolage as a compromise formation, their profitable work is commissioned construction within predetermined spaces and for the most part within fixed, urban, and spatial exigencies. Owing to the governing economy of commission, the vast majority of architectural projects remain conceptual. With the rise of paper and information architecture in the 1960s, and subsequently virtual architecture, the practice was suddenly liberated from the binding functionalist mandates and found itself free to investigate numerous theoretical issues. As a consequence, contemporary architectural theorizing emerges not as a self-certain or consensual discourse but as a vibrant metamorphic terrain of dispute. In Solà-Morales's estimate: "At the present time, [architectural] criticism resembles hand-to-hand combat: a contest between information seeking public recognition and the power of collective sanction vested in those supposedly able to bestow it."[38] The impact of philosophy on recent architectural thinking has been consequential, precipitating both attempts at application and actual collaborations.[39] As early as 1970 Robin Evans envisioned an "anarchitecture" conceived to function as the tectonic of noncontrol,[40] and in 1973 architectural historian Manfredo Tafuri proclaimed "from now on form is not sought outside of chaos; it is sought within it."[41] Much contemporary architecture, like performance, seems to challenge its seemingly inescapable parousial condition by attempts to destabilize presence and orientation. Solà-Morales contrasts effectively the traditional locus of stability, durability, and memory with the contemporary locus of event:

> The places of present-day architecture cannot repeat the permanences produced by the force of the Vitruvian *firmitas*. The effects of duration, stability, and defiance of time's passing are now irrelevant. The idea of place as the cultivation and maintenance of the essential and the profound, of a genius loci, is no longer credible. . . . From a thousand different sites the production of place continues to be possible. Not as the revelation of something existing in permanence, but as the production of an event.[42]

These sentiments are echoed in Cache's tenet that "if the expression 'genius loci' has a meaning, it lies in the capacity of this 'genius' to be smart enough to allow for the transformation or transit from one identity to another."[43] The works and proposals of Peter Eisenman, Lebbeus Woods, Neil Spiller, and Bernard Tschumi appear extremely provocative in this area. Architecture's traditional investment in functionality includes, as its central desiderata, safety, stability, permanence, control, anesthesia, consumption, and comfort. All are called into question as requisite elements by the diverse works of Archigram, Daniel Libeskind, the late John Hejduk, and Zaha Hadid.[44] Indeed, early in 2001, the radical procedural architects Gins and Arakawa abandoned architecture for their newly formed practice of "Bioscleaveconfigurature." As well as a common belief that there can be a positive quality to disequilibrium and contradictions, what unites these architectural thinkers is the trenchant, uncompromising repudiation of architectural modernism's functional ethic and its attendant emphasis on problem solving over problem production.

Even though German romanticism is known to have avoided the linguistic in the simple complicity sought between architecture and music, and despite Victor Hugo's famous warning in *The Hunchback of Notre Dame* that "the book will kill the edifice"—(a prediction at the heart of this problematic relation between poetics and architectural theory)—current architectural thinking, via Derrida's impetus, is being redirected to the architectonic possibilities of language, textuality, and writing.[45] Preeminent is Peter Eisenman's advocacy of discursive rather than figurative architecture, opening up to the mirrored possibility of how writing can be inscribed in architecture and equally architecture in writing.[46] One aspect in his work readily lending itself to a parapoetic scrutiny is the virtuality of a diagrammatic model for writing. Eisenman himself believes (perhaps over ambitiously) that such a writing-as-diagram is possible and will provide "a means of potentially overreaching the question of origin (speech) as well as the metaphysics of presence."[47] Eisenman stresses the diagram's deconstructive potential, as the following vertiginous and typical sentence suggests: "The diagram helps to displace presence by inserting a not-presence as a written trace—a sign of the not-presence of the column—into the physical column. This trace is something that cannot be explained either through function or meaning."[48] However, the axonometric nature of the diagrams offers a more parapoetic potential. The chief feature of axonometric diagrams is parallel projection, which effectively collapses the governing dualism of vertical and horizontal planes, freeing up the possibility of thrusting the observer into decentralized disequilibrium.[49] Axonometric presentation maximizes presentational possibilities, showing more sides than it is ever possible to view. For Eisenman, "the diagram is a tactic within a critical strategy—it attempts to situate a theoretical object within a physical object [and is capable of producing] spatial characteristics that both blur iconic forms and produce interstitial spatial possibilities."[50] There are clear intimations that poetics is already exploring at least the effects of axonometry. The disjunctive poetics that emerged in the late 1970s produced texts by Bruce Andrews and Susan Howe whose immediate effects are decenteredness and readerly disequilibrium. Ron Silliman's and Barrett Watten's New Sentence (due to its paratactic emphasis and rule of nonintegrationing sentences) constructs precisely those interstitial spatial possibilities of which Eisenman speaks.[51] The white hiatus between letters, words, and sentences—what Silliman considers the twenty-seventh letter of the alphabet and marking the virtual space of nonintegration—makes reader intervention possible on the level of semantic construction and connotative tracking. A similar quality of axonometric distortion occurs in much of Clark Coolidge's poetry and in the systematic-chance-generated texts of Jackson Mac Low. In Coolidge's recent book *Alien Tatters*, which retains the sentence as its minimal unit of composition, grammar and syntax function in a superficially normative way.

> Monkey come down from that roof with my mother's dowry. These baleful scenes can be made to explain. It was just that dare of a day. Expediency Beranger they called for. A collided ice to the vitamin point.
>
> Mondo Pianissimo of the bulky Colorado. This is not as silly as might be turned to in times of expectancy, clearing right out. Pencil-thin silhouette just down the barrel from all aim. The cow made smaller by the light.[52]

Although the two most characteristic features of the New Sentence—parataxis and nonintegration—stylistically dominate in the passage, catachresis and grammatical transgressions help attain an intense quality of disequilibrium. Considered axonometrically, not as a text but an architectonic, we can say that the grammar and syntax function as the vertical and horizontal elements in an "angled" axonometric structure through which "diagonal" elements (in the form of catachresis and undecidability) provide informational and semiological distortions.[53]

Eisenman, too, is attracted to text and trace as ways of denying architecture both originality and expression. He seeks a radical incorporation of alterity in which a work is defined in terms of another author, a process involving "a search for the signs of absence within the necessary presence of architecture."[54] This incorporation of otherness in sameness is precisely the method of Tom Phillips in *A Humument*, Ronald Johnson's *Radi os*, and John Cage's various "writings through." All three employ a practice of treating a source text, using methods of written readings through which a latent text is exhumed and the source text partly deleted. Johnson's source is *Paradise Lost*, Cage's variously include *Finnegans Wake*, *Walden*, and Thoreau's *Notebooks*. To give one example: In *A Humument*, a text excavated from W. H. Mallock's forgotten 1892 novel *A Human Document*, Phillips paints over vast areas of the pages, creating efficacious rivulets of text that open up a latent content. Each page of Mallock's novel offers Phillips a reservoir of paragrammatic possibilities and a tactical opportunity for local improvisations within constraint. The exhumed text releases a difference in sameness, the result being a stunning intermedia work: part text, part pictorial transformation in pen, ink, and acrylic gouache. But beyond its visual impact, *A Humument* raises the proprietary question: Whose words are these? The Victorian Mallock's certainly, and reproduced in the same place on each line as he planned. Yet they serve to deliver a new text, a text out of a text, Phillips's text as the text by Mallock that Mallock never wrote.

Parapoetics might also address how applicable to poetics are the three deconstructive questions that Eisenman sees evoked by the diagrammatic: (1) Can the metaphysics of presence be opened up or displaced; is there another way to think presence other than through fullness? (2) Is there a way to rethink the relationship between the sign and the signified as other than a motivated relationship? (3) Is there a way to rethink the subject as other than a subject motivated by a desire to have architecture communicate a sense of place and ground?[55]

Let me digress briefly on a parallel but variant history of reception, specifically, the deconstructive and the folding turn in architecture and literature. Mark Wigley claims that architecture (circa the mid-1980s) was "the last discourse to invoke the name of Derrida."[56] Without doubt the strategic introduction of instability into stable structures and relations remains deconstruction's theoretical contribution to architecture. Jeffrey Kipnis clearly states the architectural demands of deconstruction: "The architect must find methods to simultaneously embody more complex organizations of multiple and contradictory meanings while at the same time meeting the responsibility to shelter, function and stand."[57] By 1993, however, the interest in deconstructive architecture had significantly waned, with interest shifting to the architectural implications of Deleuze's concept of the fold. Greg Lynn suggests that folding offers an alternative and preferable fluid and connective logic to the deconstructionist impasse of conflict and contradiction. Where deconstruction inspired architecture of brutal diagonals, plication encouraged curvilinear, folded, heterogeneous forms. "If there is a single effect," Lynn notes, "produced in architecture by folding, it will be the ability to integrate unrelated elements within a new continuous mixture."[58] Deleuzean curvilinear logic facilitates dissipative structures with porous movements of external forces into interior domains and the concomitant inclusion of noncolliding discontinuities. This proclivity to generative theory is generally absent in the literary field where deconstruction and plication (despite Rodolphe Gasché's warning that general textuality is irreducible to the properties of specific literary texts) have largely fostered a critical apparatus to be laminated over texts for interpretive purposes and has had a comparatively weak impact on the production of primary texts.

This linked but uneven development is not to be lamented but rather noted for opening the possibility of cross-disciplinary intercourse.

Shifting focus from predominantly theoretical matters, I want now to suggest that the most fruitful target for parapoetic attention is the city. Wittgenstein, a practicing architect himself, compares language to "an ancient city: a maze of little streets and squares, of old and new houses,"[59] while Sherwood Anderson writes of a postmelancholic, neglected city of words rebuilt and recast by Gertrude Stein:

> There is a city of English and American words and it has been a neglected city. Strong broad shouldered words, that should be marching across open fields under the blue sky, are clerking in little dusty dry goods stores, young virgin words are being allowed to consort with whores, learned words have been put to the digger's trade. Only yesterday I saw a word that once called a whole nation to arms serving in the mean capacity of advertising laundry soap. For me the work of Gertrude Stein consists in a rebuilding, an entire new recasting of life, in the city of words.[60]

Architectural theories and debate, however, provide more complex notions of the city than Wittgenstein's and Anderson's simple metaphoric rendition, civic theories that might modify literary encounters with the city. Architecture tells us how it frames light in space and is committed to creating photic and thermal as well as human circulation, and that the interior of its products marks its living history. In this way architecture emerges as a form of action. Buildings and their complex articulations onto, and relations to, towns and cities are characterized like language by defeasibility and lability; they assume and evolve through numerous functions independent of both architectural form and original purpose. This feature specifies the paragrammatic force of dwelling; the occupied house or building as a dissipative structure.

This specification, however, does not eliminate a certain perdurability of form. Reflecting on the Palazzo della Ragione in Padua, Aldo Rossi notes how "one is struck by the multiplicity of functions that a building of this type can contain over time and how these functions are entirely independent of the form. At the same time, it is precisely the form that impresses us, we live it and experience it, and in turn it structures the city."[61] Rossi's pragmatic observation allows us to return to Wittgenstein's description of language in a nonmetaphoric way. There is no city just as there is no language, only linguistic utterances, and architectural usage and events. The growing displacement of structural and general linguistics by pragmatics is symptomatic of a shift in interest from form to usage and to a sense of language as both a changing dwelling and a lived experience. In light of this shift, Barthes's highly competent semiological readings of the city appear less relevant to living than to obeying Lebbeus Woods's call to "build our buildings and then discover how to live and work in them."[62]

British architect Nigel Coates, founder of NATO (Narrative Architecture Today, aka "Nigel And The Others") emerged out of the Thatcherite design boom of the 1980s with an ebullient theory of the architecture of the city that combines filmic handling of space with collage and surprise. There is something of the flaneur about Coates's methodological approach to city architecture: "It's about getting under the skin of the city, about going with the flow, seeing where it takes you, and then responding in appropriate ways. A healthy city, or a city you want to be in, is always changing; it's an organism, not a machine running on fixed lines. This sense of a city being alive informs both our response to the city as architects, and the individual buildings we design."[63] Notwithstanding this laudable declaration of commitment, Coates's projects so far (apart from the proposed redesign of the sleazy environs of King's Cross) do not reflect a particularly positive response to the prevalent social predicament of poverty, the need for shelter, low-income domiciles, and the like. According to Glancey, Coates approaches the city "as a vibrant organism rather than a grid of geometric lines. It's about living, about meeting people, about accidental encounters, changes, risk-taking, sex."[64] Such sentiments would not be out of place in any number of Situationist texts on unitary urbanism.[65] However, that critical awareness of ideological or economic governing forces so apparent to Constant and Jorn is notably absent in Coates's notion of the organic, vital city and his neoliberal soft planning. The myopic range of Coates's vision becomes apparent when measured against the ominous backdrop of co-optation and global economic controls outlined succinctly by Richard Rogers:

> Despite all our new wealth—material and intellectual—most of the world's inhabitants are denied the opportunity to lead decent lives. The swollen stomachs and shriveled faces of Third World children, the cold and squalor that our pensioners have to endure, the increasing number of people who live lives in boxes and doorways stand as an indictment of a society which has the capacity to eradicate poverty but prefers to turn its back. And beyond the exploitation and injustice which is so central a feature of our civilization looms the prospect of ecological disaster.... The predicament in which we find ourselves has a direct bearing on our appreciation of architecture. For in architecture, as in other areas, an exciting surge of creativity, discovery and invention has been frustrated by the same selfish interests that now sustain global poverty and threaten the environment.... The despoliation

of our built environment is only a small part of a broader pattern—a pattern in which new advances in ideas and technology are harnessed not to public values but to private interests.⁶⁶

We must remain alert to architecture's ominous expansion in the hyperrealism of the neoliberal dream, alert to the colonizing force in which architecture is mobilized by a compound telos of planning-for-profit. It is an alarming fact that this link of architecture and building to property, ownership, and profit is not a recent discovery. In early medieval times Hildebert of Lavardin places architecture in the category of "ultra privatum pecuniae modum fortunae," that is, "mercenary" things and financial gain.⁶⁷

"Cities are in reality great camps of the living and the dead where many elements remain like signals, symbols, cautions. When the holiday is over, what remains of the architecture is scarred, and the sand consumes the street again."⁶⁸ Marked as it is by the philosopher's distance and transmitted from the transcendental position of the theoretical attitude, Rossi's meditation on temporality and decay here seems most akin to Gibbon's musing in the ruins of the Capitol in Rome that sparked in him the idea to write the *Decline and Fall*.⁶⁹ Yet elsewhere, Rossi realizes that cities are first and foremost a composite of artifacts, and that to ignore (as urban studies do) "those aspects of reality that are most individual, particular, irregular, and also most interesting" leads to useless, artificial theories.⁷⁰ Juvenal emerged as the critical conscience of Rome, starting a legacy of poetic scrutiny of the city as the dysfunctional hospice of incurables. Gay, Johnson, the Shelley of "Peter Bell the Third," Baudelaire, Aragon, and Eliot: all fascinated and repelled by the inoperability of the metropolis. From Dioce to Wagadu, the dream of civic construction haunts Pound's *Cantos* as a thematic counterstress to the lure of fragments and floating signifiers.⁷¹

Despite the digital information highway and the extended community brought about by electronic communication, Georg Simmel's 1903 reflections on the metropolis and mental life seem more pertinent than ever. What distinguishes the metropolitan inhabitant is a blasé attitude to life brought on by the collision of constant extrasensory bombardment with internal stimuli. Part as a product of, part as a defense against metropolitan overload, the blasé subject struggles for an autonomy and circulation homologous to the flow of currency and commodities.⁷² The fascinating power of the city can be specified in an economic, ideological irony: that the people who use the city are simultaneously and for the most part unconsciously used by it. Tafuri isolates and elaborates upon the capitalist nature of the Western city: "Objectively, structured like a machine for the extraction of surplus value, in its own conditioning mechanisms the city reproduces the reality" of the modes of production.⁷³ The soft city, transparent city, the wired city, the digital city. Whichever you choose, cities still need to be experienced as used and as the sites of consumption and production. Yet to resuscitate Le Corbusier's vision of architecture as the supreme mediator between realism and utopia seems as arrogant as it is ill advised.

In conclusion, let me suggest that you receive these rambling thoughts as a caveat against the fruit of that marriage of practical reason and the Kantian faculties we baptized some time ago as specialization. The current ideology governing graduate studies does not encourage attacks on thetic dogmatism. Rather, it supports the trenchant ideology of the frame. Doubtless an argument can be made that specialization safeguards the heterogeneity of discourses from domination by a single master narrative. However, the adverse consequences of the frame and the frame's governing contradictory logic have already been outlined. Aaron Betsky calls for an anchoring inside the amorphous vertigo of sprawl by means of slow space. Decelerate the speed of today and make the world stand still.[74] Against this moot tactic of survival I would suggest a *becoming* through agencies of difference, and so toward a spiral poetics, a clinamen architecture, a poetics of folding so as to construct free spaces that can only function as ephemeral interstices.

Hölderlin insists that the highest poetry is that in which the nonpoetic element also becomes poetic,[75] yet I wonder if the call in this claim to added negativity is pertinent to research. Let's attempt to problematize our specialist knowledge by placing it in a broader cartography, map antithetical and intersecting zones as a preliminary to nomadic practices, deframe and rethink research along spatial, not chronological, lines akin to Jed Rasula's notion of accidental research in which conceptual agility replaces a focused specialization. Experience at least the "internal drifts" of disciplines and even contemplate the possibility of random access research. In Marcos Novak's estimate "our understanding of territory is undergoing rapid and fundamental changes: with the scope of pragmatic experience both space and community are rapidly becoming non-local."[76] Random access is emerging as the most powerful virtual tool in epistemological capital. Novak believes it's becoming "a way of life characterized by precise and instantaneous affiliation. . . . Disembodied proximity implies the extension of random access to progressively larger parts of our experience."[77] I would extend the applicability of Novak's claim to the disciplines of knowledge. Novak further suggests that

> the virtual and cyber worlds form a continuum. . . . There is something of what we call cyberspace in virtuality and something of what we call virtual reality in cyberspace. . . . Cyberspace is always the "exterior" of virtual reality, because it always reserves the additional space of possibility, in contrast to

actuality. Possibility is the fundamental characteristic of everything that is "other," since possibility always contains the unknown.[78]

Derrida's essay on Tschumi's "Pont de Folie" introduces the term *maintenant*—"now"—a temporal indicator marking the time, the only time, when both endings and beginnings occur in the protracted space of a becoming.

That said as I'm ending . . . now. But perhaps as a poet, as the poet in me, I should add a coda: *The poem may well be dead, but as the architect said, one is never finished with the poem.*

CHAPTER 11

The Future of Literature:
Complex Surfaces of
Electronic Texts and Print Books

N. Katherine Hayles

Nothing is riskier than prediction; when the future arrives, we can be sure only that it will be different than we thought. Nevertheless, I will risk a prognostication: Digital literature will be a significant component of the twenty-first-century canon. Less a gamble than it may appear, this prediction slyly relies on the fact that almost all contemporary literature is *already* digital. Except for a handful of books produced by fine letterpresses, print literature consists of digital files through most of its existence. So essential is digitality to contemporary processes of composition, storage, and production that print should properly be considered a particular form of text for digital files rather than a medium separate from digital instantiation. The digital leaves its mark on print in new capabilities for innovative typography, new aesthetics for book design, and, in the near future, new modes of marketing. Some bookstores and copy shops, for example, are investing in computerized xerography

---

I am grateful to Nicholas Gessler for information on letterpress machines, for help with analysis of Apollonaire's visual poems, and for photographing Apollonaire's *Calligrammes*. I am also grateful to Special Collections of the University of California, Los Angeles, Young Research Library for permission to examine and photograph Apollonaire's 1918 edition of *Calligrammes*.

machines that produce books on the spot from digital files, including cover design, content, and binding.[1] Also available are electronic book-like devices that can be taken to a bookstore, where the electronic files comprising the text can be purchased, downloaded, and read at leisure on the device.

As these examples suggest, print and electronic textuality deeply interpenetrate one another. Although print texts and electronic literature—that is, literature that is "digital born," created and meant to be performed in digital media—differ significantly in their functionalities, they are best considered as two components of a complex and dynamic media ecology. Like biological ecotomes, they engage in a wide variety of relationships, including competition, cooperation, mimicry, symbiosis, and parasitism. These dynamic interrelations can be observed in the complex surfaces emerging in contemporary digital and print literature. As John Cayley remarks, "The surface of writing is and always has been complex. It is a liminal symbolically interpenetrated membrane, a fractal coast- or borderline, a chaotic and complex structure with depth and history."[2] Although complex surfaces are scarcely new, as Cayley reminds us, the surfaces created in the new millennium have a historical specificity that comes from their engagement with digitality. This engagement is enacted in multiple senses: technologically in the production of textual surfaces, phenomenologically in new kinds of reading experiences possible in digital environments, conceptually in the strategies employed by print and electronic literature as they interact with each other's affordances and traditions, and thematically in the represented worlds that experimental literature in print and digital media perform.

In discussing the surfaces of contemporary writing, Noah Wardrip-Fruin comments that "there is [always] something behind the surface." He continues, "Behind poetry, fiction, and drama on paper surfaces there are processes of writing, editing, paper and ink production, page design, printing and binding, distribution and marketing, buying and borrowing."[3] Wardrip-Fruin's main interest lies in "works that might be regarded as especially inseparable from some of their processes," that is, digital literature.[4] My focus here will be not exclusively on print or digital literature but rather on their interactions through complex surfaces that bear the marks of digitality. In the case of digital literature, computations continuously produce and reproduce the surface, as Wardrip-Fruin notes; in the case of print, computations produced the surface as durable inscriptions on paper. In both cases, the ontology of computation marks the surfaces of the texts discussed here, leading to complex interactions that bring into question the importance we might otherwise attach to the boundary separating digital and print literature.[5]

Complex Topologies of Immersive Electronic Literature

Good realistic fiction is often called "immersive," but the works discussed below are literally so, in the sense that they are performed in a three-dimensional CAVE (Cave Automatic Virtual Environment). Usually employed for scientific and mathematical visualizations, a CAVE costs well over a million dollars for a top-end apparatus (and thus is usually acquired through large scientific research grants). It uses high-speed computers to generate an immersive environment that employs virtual reality goggles and data glove(s) (or in some cases, data wands or joysticks) to mark the position of the user's gaze, hand position, and location within the CAVE, typically a four-surface room that includes three walls and a floor display. When the user moves her head, the computers generate the calculations that change the display accordingly, so she is given the impression that she is moving (or flying) within a complex, three-dimensional environment.

When the scientists at Brown University acquired a CAVE, Robert Coover went to them with a proposal to use it for his creative writing program, arguing that the writers would develop affordances that could create additional research knowledge, including immersive narratives, positional sound, and moving text. He then created a funding and instructional framework that allowed creative writers, sound designers, and student computer programmers to work together on projects. One result is *Screen* by Noah Wardrip-Fruin and his collaborators, including an introduction narrated by Robert Coover. As the work begins, the user hears Coover read the words "In a world of illusions, we hold ourselves in place by memories" and sees text displayed on the three vertical CAVE walls in billboard fashion. The texts, one by a female narrator and one by a male, relate memories that slip away even as the narrators try to hold onto them.

This narrative theme becomes enacted in a startlingly literal way when words suddenly begin peeling away from the walls and moving in the three-dimensional space. The user can try to bat them back into place with the data glove, but as she works, more words peel off faster than she put them back, despite her best efforts. Moreover, the batted words move along trajectories difficult to control, creating neologisms, nonsense words, and chaotic phrases that further make the text difficult to read. Eventually all the words lay jumbled on the floor, the text now impossible to recover for "normal" reading. In another sense, of course, the work has re-defined what it means to read, so that reading becomes, as Rita Raley has pointed out, a kinesthetic, haptic, and proprioceptively vivid experience, involving not just the cerebral activity of decoding but bodily interactions with the words as perceived objects moving in space.[6] Entering the narrative now does not mean leaving the surface behind, as when a reader plunges into an imaginative world and finds it so engrossing that she ceases to notice the page. Rather, the "page" is transformed into a complex topology that rapidly transforms from a stable surface into a "playable" space in which she is an active participant. "Playable media," a term coined by Noah Wardrip-Fruin to denote computer games and other interactive works such as *Screen*, accurately expresses the user's engagement with the game-like aspects of the work.[7] In effect, *Screen* performs a historical trajectory arcing from a print-like reading surface that invites the reader to enter an imaginative world to complex topologies that constantly re-enact, with every movement and change of spatial orientation, a computationally intense environment. In this environment, the barely perceptible lag times remind the user that nothing happens without the incredibly rapid calculations that are continuously generating the perceived environment, creating an interface in which a human user cooperates and competes with intelligent machines.

If memories hold us in place, as *Screen*'s introduction suggests, the engagement of human and machine cognizers shakes us out of our accustomed place of reading to an active encounter that hints at the place of the human in the contemporary world. In computationally intensive environments pervasive in urban areas in North America, Europe, Japan and other developed countries, most of the communication flows happen outside human awareness as embedded sensors send real-time data flows to networked computers, cell phones communicate with relay stations and satellites, Internet packets race along fiber optic cables, and international commerce proceeds at the speed of light. That in *Screen* the user is overwhelmed with falling text is one small indication that the circumstances in which reading and writing occur have radically changed in the new millennium, including now not only the reading and writing that humans do but the innumerably faster and vaster calculations performed by all manner of networked and programmable devices, from the chips in wristwatches to the computers generating the CAVE display at Brown University. At the same time, *Screen* reminds us that the invisible messages racing up and down the electromagnetic spectrum can enter our human world only through embodied experience that brings with it deep traditions of reading and interpretation. As Mark Hansen has noted about a wide range of New Media art works, embodied experiences inform our perceptions and actively constitute the complex meanings we derive from computational surfaces.[8]

When we encounter the playable (and playful) complex surfaces of New Media, we do not leave behind our long experience with print. In his recent work, John Cayley has focused on the ways in which our intuitive knowledge of letterforms can define space and inflect time. Working in the CAVE environment at Brown University, he and his collaborator Dmitri Lammerman created *Torus*, a virtual reality installation in which sixteen vanes of text are arranged like slices through a doughnut.[9] This torus shape is doubly virtual, for it is not imaged as such but rather is brought into existence by the text-slices that implicitly define it for the user. The play between what the user's imagination constructs and what is actually visible transforms the typical situation in literature, in which the user decodes words to create an imaginative space in which the action takes place. By contrast, space actually exists in the CAVE room, and the user explores it through embodied actions such as walking, turning, and listening. At the same time, the user can also read the text and re-create for herself the imagined world of Proust's *Remembrance of Time Past* that appears on the torus vanes.

Further complicating the writing surfaces is yet another dynamic, the relation between the virtual text and the massive computations generating it. Unlike durable ink inscription, here the text is a virtual image and so is capable of transformations impossible for print. In this installation, the text demonstrates its agency by moving in space, responding to the user's spatial orientation by always turning to face the viewer. Through this motion the user experiences a temporal dimension of the text—its motion so that it is always right-reading—acting in complex synchrony with the time of reading and the time of spatial exploration through the CAVE environment. These temporal interactions, as well as the virtual/actual spatiality of the textual surfaces, create an enriched sense of embodied play that complicates and extends the phenomenology of reading.

Influence can flow in the opposite direction as well, from the phenomenology of reading back into the installation. This effect was discovered when a glitch in the program caused letters that were proportionately smaller, and thus perceived as farther away, to be rendered over larger letters in the foreground. To reconcile the contradiction, users perceived the smaller letters as if they were inscribed on the back wall at the end of a corridor—a corridor that did not exist except in the user's perception. Cayley theorizes that our extensive experience with letterforms subconsciously affects perception, so users struggle to create a scene that preserves the integrity of letterforms while still making phenomenological sense. In this understanding, *Torus* becomes not only an experiment in the enriched phenomenology of reading but also in the complex interplay between our traditional experience with letterforms and our much more recent understanding of computation. Reading in this view becomes a complex performance in which agency is distributed between the user, the interface, and the active cognitions of the networked and programmable machine (or in Cayley's preferred terminology, the programmaton).

Cayley further explores the phenomenology of reading in *lens*, designed first as a CAVE installation and then transferred to a QuickTime maquette.[10] The pun suggested by the title hints that letterforms are not only figures we decode but also the lens through which (and by means of which) we perceive spatiality. The work creates a ground–figure reversal between large white letters spelling "lens" that, when zoomed into by the user, become the white ground against which dark blue letters become visible, previously unseen because they floated on a dark blue ground.[11] More zooming causes the blue letters in turn to become the dark ground against which more white letters become visible, and so on to infinity. Cayley summarizes the effect: "Literal graphic materiality is able to entirely and suddenly transform spatial perception and, at the same time, it creates an entirely new space for itself, for inscription and for reading. It creates the potential for a new experience of language."[12]

These experiments in the phenomenology of reading are interpenetrated by another kind of exploration: what it means for human cognition to come into contact with the cognition of the computer(s) generating the display. Cayley points to this interpenetration with a key question: "Is the display really a monitor of the programmaton's symbolic processing, or is it a window on computing's attempts to match and then exceed (through the incorporation of transactive or so-called interactive facilities) the illusionistic simulations of film and television?"[13] The question suggests that the monitor screen functions simultaneously in two different modes: It can re-create filmic illusions, in which case the screen reflects and reinforces conventional visual assumptions; on the other hand, it can also perform as a semi-transparent window through which we can intuit the algorithms generating the display. Experienced video game players are familiar with this duality, for even as they participate in the screen's video's illusions through the viewpoint of a first-person shooter, they also learn the patterns that are the visual trace of the algorithms dictating the computer's performance. The ability to discern these patterns is in fact the mark of a top player, for then she can anticipate what the computer will do and plan her strategy accordingly.

For text, the ability to function simultaneously as a window into the computer's performance and as a writing surface to be decoded puts into dynamic interplay two very different models of cognition. Traditionally, narrative text has been understood as a voice bringing into existence for the reader a richly imagined world. If that world is vibrant enough, a reader is apt to have the impression that the page has become a portal through which a world is called into being by the voice emanating from the book. That voice in turn is experienced as the in-dwelling of a distinctive personality; readers often speak of trusting (or not) an author's voice. The perceived voice connects the reader's own experience of interiority with a projected interiority of the author (and by extension, the narrator and characters), all of whom share a common bond in human perception and sense of self. The computer, by contrast, operates through commands often concealed from a user's direct inspection and that consequently must be intuited through the computer's performance. However well a computer can simulate text and thereby re-create the voice characteristic of narrative fiction, it remains a machine processing binary symbols as specified by the logic gates. Mediating between the brute logic of these machinic operations and human intentions is the program that, when run, creates a performance partaking both of the programmer's intentions and the computer's underlying architecture as symbolic processor.

Creating literature that functions as a site of negotiation between human desires and non-human forces has, of course, a history that precedes modern digital computers. Beginning in the 1950s, John Cage employed a variety of algorithmic procedures to create texts, for example, *Mureau*, produced by throwing yarrow sticks to construct a reading of the *I Ching* that he then used to transform Thoreau's writings.[14] Cage saw the computational nature of generative procedures as a way to circumvent human intentionality and open the work to the larger forces of the universe. When the computational device is a computer, the forces generating the visible surface perform a hybrid enactment that partakes both of human and machine cognition. These dynamic relationships are enacted in a digital environment by Jim Rosenberg's *Diagrams Series 4* poems, in which many textual layers appear to be superimposed over one another.[15] When the user mouses over the complex textual display, the layers separate and become legible as "stacks" of words, which can be combined in various ways as indicated by abstract shapes representing syntactical relations. The computer algorithms provide the flexible environment in which human play can make meaning from many different combinations and possibilities. Mediated through code, Rosenberg's designs are structured by the possibilities for textual overlays, separations, and parsings that the computer makes. Reading and writing, then, become in the Web instantiation of this work a complex performance of an extended cognitive system in which both humans and machines play roles.

A similar dynamic is enacted in a very different way in Cayley's *overboard* and *translation*, works in which an algorithmic substitution of letters cycles between different languages and/or different states of legibility. In *translation*, text on the right is complemented on the left by a visual display of glyphs whose changes indicate how the algorithm is proceeding, a process also enacted by the work's ambient music. In *overboard*, the text (taken from an account of the *Mayflower* crossing in Governor Bradford's *Of Plymouth Plantation*) describes a man who fell overboard and, clinging to a rope, was dragged along under the water until he could finally be pulled on board again. The text presents various stages of legibility, figured by Cayley as surfacing, floating, and sinking (or downing).[16] Here reading becomes unavoidably algorithmic, less a practice of re-creating an imaginative world than of participating in a rhythmic dance of letters and glyphs reflecting algorithmic transformations wrought by the computer.

As we know, the novel was instrumental in performing an interiorized subjectivity based on the relation between the sound and the mark. As literary forms change, the subjectivities they perform and inform change as well. What kind of cognitive state are these computational works helping to bring into being? We may find a clue in the connection Stanley Ambrose, an anthropologist at the University of Illinois, has proposed between the evolution of language in the Paleolithic period and the practice of fashioning compound tools (tools with more than one part that have to be assembled in sequential order, such as a stone ax with a handle, bindings, and a stone insert).[17] For 2.5 to 3 million years, early humans used simple tools without much change in brain structure. Then, about 300,000 years ago, compound tools were invented and things really starting hopping (relative to Paleolithic timescales). Evidence indicates that compound tools were contemporaneous with the accelerated development of Broca's area in the frontal cortex, the part of the brain involved in language use. Ambrose speculates that the sequential and hierarchical ordering required in the fashioning of compound tools co-evolved with language because language, like compound tools, requires the sequential ordering of reproducible and discrete units. In this scenario, the trait often identified with the essence of the human—our ability to use complex languages—was bound up at the dawn of *Homo sapiens* with the emergence of a relatively sophisticated technology (i.e., compound versus simple tools), initiating a co-evolutionary spiral in which language and compound tools developed together to bring about a new phase in human cognitive development.

Three hundred millennia later, another developmental spiral may be beginning. The computer, our new compound tool, is not only built using sequential and hierarchical order, it also uses the ordering of discrete reproducible units (ones and zeros) to create new kinds of temporal and spatial experiences. Reducing the semiotic toolbox from twenty-six letters to the binary distinction between one and zero is the crucial move that allows text, audio, graphics, video, and animation to be seamlessly integrated in the digital environment, which in turn gives text the potential for behavioral agency and active interplay. Interactive text stimulates, at the same moment, the language centers of the brain and other cortical functions not usually mobilized in conventional print reading, including fine motor movements involved in controlling the mouse, keyboard, and/or joystick, haptic feedback through the hands and fingers, and complex eye-hand coordination in a real-time dynamic environment. For humans who habitually interact with computers at a young age, such experiences can potentially affect the neurological structure of the brain.[18] Studies indicate that children exposed to long hours of interactions with computers show distinctively different cognitive styles than their parents who were raised largely with print.[19] Young people so exposed are more comfortable with multiple data flows, they often prefer to engage in many tasks simultaneously, and they can intuit the algorithmic patterns of computer processing much more easily than the older generation.

The interiorized subjectivity associated with print has certainly not disappeared, but it is being hybridized by a complex dynamic in which a subvocalized human voice, the characteristic mode through which print creates and performs its distinctive mode of subjectivity, is no longer the primary goal of screen displays. (Indeed, Robert Coover at one point decried electronic textuality precisely because it lacked the authorial "voice" of print texts.)[20] If the first compound tools accelerated language use, the new compound tools called computers are accelerating the cognitive mode I call hyperattention, characterized by a craving for continuously varying stimuli, a low threshold for boredom if stimuli decrease, the ability to process multiple information streams simultaneously, and a quick intuitive grasp of algorithmic procedures that underlie and generate surface complexity. This cognitive mode is distinctively different from that traditionally associated with the humanities, which by contrast can be called deep attention. Deep attention is characterized by a willingness to spend long hours with a single artifact (for instance, a 700-page Victorian novel), intense concentration that tends to shut out external stimuli, a preference for a single data stream rather than multiple inputs, and the subvocalization that typically activates and enlivens the reading of print literature.

Contemporary cultures in developed countries are currently in a period of active transition in which the cognitive mode of deep attention is still being fostered by formal education, especially humanities courses, and by parents who want their children to read books rather than surf the World Wide Web and play video games. Nevertheless, there is a clear generational shift in which preference for hyperattention is more prevalent the younger the age group, at least down to ages four or five, typically the developmental stage when the neural system has developed sufficiently to handle multiple incoming data streams. The effects of hyperattention are already being reflected in literary works, for example in Cayley's *translating*, where text is accompanied by glyphs visually indicating the algorithm's operation. With multiple data streams, constantly changing stimuli, and evocation of an intuitive grasp of algorithmic operation, *translation* appeals simultaneously to deep attention and hyperattention, in the process transforming what it means to read.

The uneven demographics of deep attention and hyperattention have created an environment in which various media compete and cooperate not only in terms of design, style, and thematic content, but also in terms of reader preferences and styles of engagement. Just as print is not left behind as we vault into the information age, so the cognitive mode of hyperattention is not put back on the shelf when the computer user pulls down a book and becomes a reader. The result is a complex and variegated landscape in which print literature is read for its ability to yield the traditional pleasures of deep attention but also for the ways in which it can appeal to the emerging cognitive mode of hyperattention. Without forgetting they are print books, contemporary novels are demonstrating that even print is not what it used to be. In many subtle and obvious ways, print novels are responding to, and themselves initiating, transformations of what it means to read. Not coincidentally, the new kinds of subjectivities they perform have much in common with those associated with digital technologies.

The Future of the Novel

To say that the novel is metamorphosing is nothing new. Almost since the genre's beginning, novels have been frustrating taxonomists by eluding fixed categories. Yet there *are* some new aspects to the transformations now in progress. The historical specificity of these contemporary changes have their origin in what Friedrich Kittler calls technical media: specifically, the digital computers that have changed the dynamics of twentieth- and twenty-first-century economics, politics, culture, and communication.

Digitization has also revolutionized the legacy media of print, the old technology that was so radically transformative when it was new.

Print's engagement with technical media has been accompanied by a persistent anxiety among print authors that the novel is in danger of being superseded, with readers seduced away from books by television, blockbuster films, video games, and the vast mediascape of the World Wide Web. Analyzing this trend, Kathleen Fitzpatrick in *The Anxiety of Obsolescence: The American Novel in the Age of Television* has argued that the *perception* of risk is more important than the reality.[21] She convincingly documents that anxiety about obsolescence is widespread, especially among younger white male writers. Rather than asking if there is evidence that the "literary" novel may in fact be losing audience share to other entertainment forms, however, she asks what cultural and social functions pronouncements about the death of the print novel serve. She argues they have the advantage of establishing the novelists as an at-risk minority (a state that Bruce Sterling satirizes in his novel *Distraction*[22]), while still allowing this putative minority to retain their hegemonic position as white male authors. In my view, the situation is more complex than Fitzpatrick allows. Empirical data indicate that young people are spending less time reading print books and more time surfing the Web, playing video games, and listing to MP3 files.[23] Nevertheless, Fitzpatrick is certainly correct in pointing to the perception of print authors that they are in danger of becoming obsolete.

This anxiety of obsolescence has a complex relation to the recent explosion of creativity in contemporary print novels. On the one hand, print authors fear that print might be regarded as old-fashioned and boring in the face of new media, especially electronic texts that can dance to music, morph to suggestive shapes, and perform other tricks impossible for the durable inscriptions of print. On the other hand, print itself is capable of new tricks precisely because it has become an output form for electronic text. If the seductions made possible by digital technology are endangering print, that same technology can also be seen as print-in-the-making: We have met the enemy and he is us.

The attempt of the print novel to one-up electronic textuality is thus inextricably entwined with the simultaneous recognition that electronic textuality makes possible many of its innovative developments. The complexity of this dynamic can be seen in the emergence of two apparently opposed but actually complementary strategies: *imitating* electronic textuality through comparable devices in print, many of which depend on digitality to be cost-effective or even possible; and *intensifying* the specific traditions of print, in effect declaring allegiance to print in contradistinction to other media. Recursively entwined, the two strategies often appear together in the same text. Moreover, they tend to morph into one another, much as a Möebius surface goes from inside to outside to inside, so there is necessarily a certain amount of arbitrariness in labeling a given instance as one versus the other.

Before listing the major characteristics of digital text that give it historical specificity, I will find it useful compare them to Guillaume Apollinaire's *Calligrammes: poèmes de la paix et la guerre, 1913–1916*.[24] These delightful, evocative, and wrenching poems with such titles as "Il pleut" (It's Raining), "Le petit auto" (The Little Car), and "La Mandoline, l'Œillet et le Bambou" (The Mandoline, the Eyelet, and the Bamboo) employ shaped text to create graphic forms that function as "textimages" (in W. J. T. Mitchell's phrase), with the text reproducing the shape of the object about which the poem is written.[25] Although Apollinaire claimed his calligrammes were new, in fact visual or shaped poetry comprises a rich tradition that dates back much further than even George Herbert's "Easter Wings," "The Altar," and other visual poems in the early seventeenth century, and it continues through Concrete poetry in the 1960s. As John Cayley remarks in distinguishing his "literal art" from Concrete, this tradition works by creating a visual correspondence between an object and letterforms, thus correlating the reader's decoding of text with the visual recognition of shapes representative of real-world objects.[26] Concrete poetry typically does not investigate the phenomenology of letterforms as such, nor does it use our habitual experience with letterforms as a basis for experiments in perception such as Cayley carries out in *Torus* and *lens*. Apollinaire's poems superficially resemble the novels discussed below in using mimetic text, but as Cayley's observation suggests, the way mimesis works and its relation to the text's materiality cannot be assumed to function the same way in all shaped literature but rather must be carefully assessed in terms of the work's context, production, and signifying strategies.

Apollinaire's work, for example, is marked by the state of printing in the predigital era. Close inspection of the *Deuxième Edition* (in contemporary terms, the second printing in 1918, by printer G. Roy, that apparently used the same plates as the first edition printed by Joudan) reveals that it was printed on a letterpress machine. The letterpress, typically employing zinc type and copper plates for images, produces books characterized by the physical indentation the press's pressure makes on paper, uneven ink distribution at the edges of letterforms or images, and slight irregularities in the metal type. To achieve more free-form effects than set type allowed, some of Apollinaire's *Calligrammes* were reproduced on copper plates from handlettered and hand-drawn shapes, which allowed for greater plasticity of form but with resulting unevenness in letters and other visual idiosyncrasies. The 1918 printing displays irregularities that indicate the typesetter was trying to follow Apollonaire's manuscripts as closely as possible, to the point of shaving the rectangular bases of some type elements when the spacing between letters was closer than normal setting allowed. This effect is particularly evident in "La Colombe Poignardée et le Jet d'Eau," sometimes translated as "The Fountain." (See Figures 11-1 and 11-2, particularly the nested *rr* in *guerre*.)

Consequently, the expressive quality of Apollonaire's manuscripts is largely preserved in this edition. Later editions, reproduced without attribution in Stefan Themerson's *Apollonaire's Lyrical Ideograms*,[27] show the typesetting of this poem becoming more and more regular, which perhaps looks more "professional" but actually results in a *less* expressive form than in the 1918 edition. Themerson had the good fortune to speak with Pierre Albert-Birot, in whose literary review *SIC* (*Sons Idées Couleurs*) Apollonaire's famous poem "Il Pleut" first appeared. Albert-Birot relates that the review's head printer, a man named Leve, was semi-retired but when he saw Apollonaire's original, he "liked it so much that he wanted to set it up himself, and he did. He started at once and worked on it all night, till the morning."[28] The result is a printed text not quite as irregular as the manuscript but aesthetically perhaps even superior.[29] (See Figure 11-3.)

These examples demonstrate that visual effects are highly sensitive to their physical instantiation. To put it another way: Form travels but materiality does not. Materiality (which I have defined elsewhere, in contradistinction to physicality, as physical aspects mobilized as resources by a work's signifying strategies) depends not only on the artifact's physical characteristics but on the ways in which the apparatus that created the artifact enters into the work's meaning through networks of production, storage, and transmission, as well as through the interaction of content with the work's physicality.[30] Another example is one of Apollinaire's calligrammes for Madeleine, "au front," originally penned in 1915 on the bark of a birch tree when Apollonaire was serving in the French army during the First World War. Even the most faithful reproduction, such as appeared in the 1918 edition, loses much of the poignancy of the original's materiality, to say nothing of the regularized typesetting of the Pléiade 1965 edition, which is so alienated from the original as virtually to constitute another work.

Like the contemporary print authors discussed below (although for different reasons), Apollonaire felt that the technology on which his calligrammes depended was in danger of becoming obsolete. In a letter to

André Billy in 1918, he wrote, "as for the calligrams [sic], they are an idealization of *vers-libre* poetry and of typographical precision at a time when typography is brilliantly ending its career, at the dawn of new methods of reproduction, the cinema and the gramophone."[31] Although his death pronouncement was premature, typesetting was, as we know, replaced in a historical progression that has now resulted in books printed directly from digital files, a transition that can be no less problematic in terms of aesthetic effects than the transformations in materiality that Apollonaire's calligrammes suffered. Raymond Federman's typewriter novel *Double or Nothing: A Real Fictitious Discourse*[32] was originally printed in 1971 using offset lithography, in which stones were made from photographs taken of each typewritten page, a process that preserved the look of the manual typewriter, including irregularities in keys, uneven pressure resulting in different ink densities, and uniform spacing of letters. A later edition used the less expensive method of OCR text and digital plate setters (which produce negatives for platemaking directly, thus eliminating the intermediate step of photographing an actual page layout), so that the typewriter's distinctive visual characteristics were lost and the novel's effect was diluted, to its detriment as a work of art.

It is not sufficient, then, to compare such texts as Apollonaire's calligrammes or Federman's typewriter novel with contemporary texts using visual effects without inquiring into the specificities of the technologies and their implications for the text's materiality. The point is simply this: Whether used for good or ill, the technology's historical specificity leaves visible marks on the text and inevitably carries with it assumptions deeply entwined with the embodied practices of production, storage, transmission and performance that create the text as a cultural-material artifact. Despite the fact that textual editors, bibliographic scholars, and book artists such as Jerome McGann and Joanna Drucker have been making similar points for several years, the literary establishment has yet fully to absorb the implications of materiality for critical practice and especially for understanding the issues at stake as electronic literature joins the twenty-first century canon and print literature moves into the digital era.[33]

For the novels discussed below, digital technologies have completely interpenetrated the printing process. Moreover, the novels are located within a robust media ecology increasingly dominated by digital representations, including CGI effects in films, audio CDs and video DVDs, digital projectors, the Internet, and the World Wide Web. Their historical specificity comes not only from the fact that digital technologies are deeply involved in their creation but also from the ways in which, as material signifying

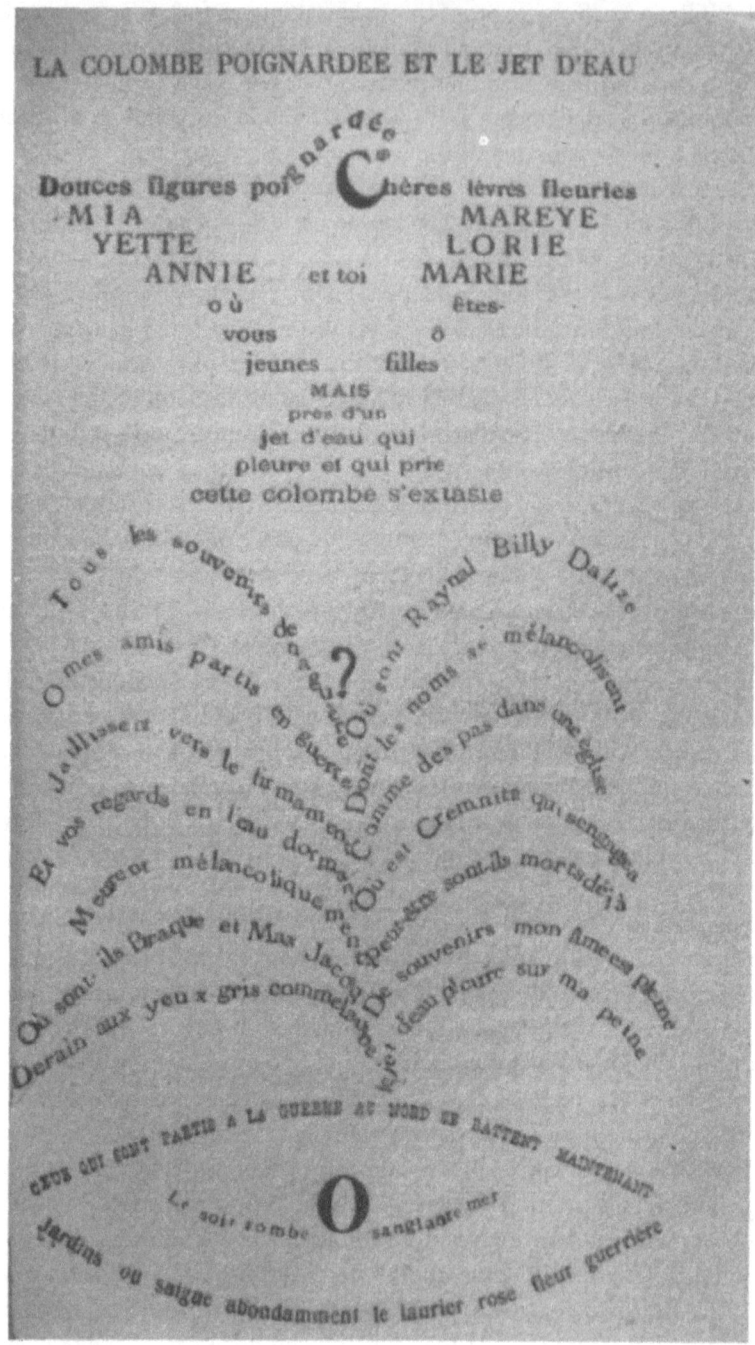

Figure 11-1

Figure 11-2

systems with graphic, textual, haptic, and kinesthetic components, they engage digital technologies on multiple levels while still insisting on their performance as print texts, specifically through strategies of imitation and intensification.

Below are listed the major characteristics of digital text around which the dance between imitation and intensification take place.[34]

1. **Computer-mediated text is layered**. Generating the text that appears on screen are several layers of computer code, from the hypertext mark-up language tags that format text on the World Wide Web, to compiled/interpreted programming languages like C++, down to the mnemonics of assembler, and finally to binary code and the alternating voltages with which it is associated. To distinguish between strings that the reader sees and strings that exist in the text, Espen Aarseth has suggested the terminology scriptons and textons. Although one can find some print examples where scriptons and textons appear as durable inscriptions—for example, stipple images (the scriptons) created by dots (the textons)—these tend to be unusual instances. By contrast, every computer-mediated text has this characteristic.

2. **Computer-mediated text tends to be multimodal**. Because text, images, video, and sound can all be represented as binary code, the computer becomes, as Lev Manovich maintains, the medium that contains all other media within itself. The increasingly visual nature of the World Wide Web vividly illustrates the point, as well as the growing number of Web sites containing QuickTime movies and video clips.

3. **In computer-mediated text, storage is separate from performance**. With print, storage and performance coalesce within the same object. When a book is closed, it functions as a storage medium, and when it is opened, as a performance medium. By contrast, with computer-mediated text the two functions are analytically and practically distinct. Files played on a local computer may be stored on a server across the globe;

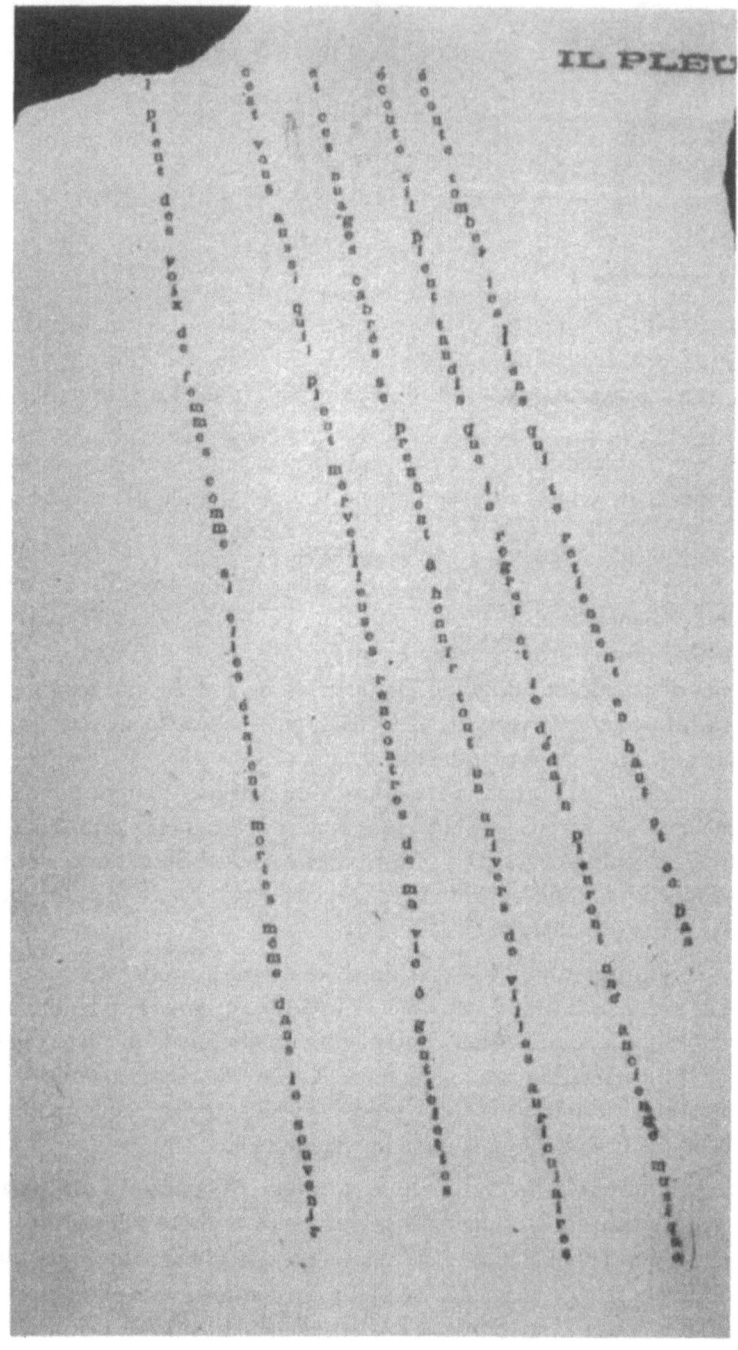

Figure 11-3

moreover, code can never be seen or accessed by a user *while it is running*. As Alexander Galloway has pointed out, code differs from human-only language in that it is executable by a machine. (While it might be argued that humans "execute" language in the sense of processing it through sensory-cognitive networks, they do so in such profoundly different ways than machines run code that it seems wise to reserve the term "execute" for processing computer code.)

4. **Computer-mediated text manifests fractured temporality.** With computer-mediated text, the reader is not wholly (and sometimes not at all) in control of how quickly the text becomes readable; long load times, for example, might slow down a user so much that the screen is never read. Moreover, even when the screen text is visible, as Stephanie Strickland has argued, the mouseovers, fine cursor movements, and other affordances of electronic display and reading fracture time into much more various and diverse scales than is the case with print texts.

To demonstrate how these four characteristics provide focal points for the recursive dynamic between imitation and intensification, I will use as my tutor texts three contemporary novels, which despite (or perhaps because) of their wild strain of exuberant experimentation, have attracted mass audiences: Jonathan Safran Foer's *Extremely Loud and Incredibly Close*, Salvador Plascencia's *The People of Paper*, and Mark Danielewski's *House of Leaves*.[35] The strategies employed by these texts show the print novel engaged in a robust conversation with electronic textuality. In this sense they stoutly resist the tendency that Lev Manovich sees for the "cultural layer" to be converted into the "computer layer" in an accelerating curve of assimilation.[36] At the least, they complicate what assimilation might mean by reinterpreting how the computer layer signifies. Beyond this, they demonstrate the resilience of print culture by responding to the predations of computerization with bursts of anxious creativity.

Digitality and the Print Novel

Imitations of the numerical representations of electronic texts appear in their most straightforward form when numerical codes appear as part of the linguistic surface of a print novel. In *Extremely Loud and Incredibly Close*, a particularly poignant moment arrives when Thomas Schell, now a grandfather who has lost his only son in the Twin Towers disaster, attempts to reconnect with his wife, whom he abandoned when she told him she was pregnant. He has not seen or talked with her for forty years. Traumatized as a young man by the firebombing of Dresden, he has lost the ability to talk and communicates through written notes, gestures, and "yes" and "no" tattooed on his hands. When he telephones his estranged wife after arriving in New York, he is still unable to speak, so in a procedure familiar to users of Moviefone, he taps out a numerical code using the keypad, in which a single digit can stand for any one of three letters.[37] Cryptologists call this kind of code a one-way algorithm: Easy to construct, it is difficult (and sometimes impossible) to decrypt. Lacking any indication of where the breaks between words occur and faced with mounting uncertainties about which of the three letters is the correct choice, the reader is confronted with possible combinations that increase exponentially as the message grows in length. And this message does go on, for some three pages of single digits separated by commas. An extraordinary amount of patience is required to work through this code; I confess that I have decrypted only the first page and a half. Nevertheless, the code is positioned at a decisive juncture when Thomas seems to realize what a monumental mistake he has made in abandoning his wife and unborn child. The stakes for the reader in understanding the dialogue, one might suppose, are considerable.

Why write it in code? Many reviewers have complained (not without justification) about the gimmicky nature of this text, but in this instance the gimmick can be justified. It implies that language has broken down under the weight of trauma and become inaccessible not only to Thomas but the reader as well (previously, even when Thomas was unable to speak, the narrative shared his thoughts with readers). Moreover, what his wife hears are the beeps to which the numerical codes correspond; "Your telephone is not one hundred dollars," she says. The comment hints that the text is performing a satiric inversion of Claude Shannon's information theory. In his theory, Shannon made a sharp distinction between the informational *content* of a message and its *meaning*, insisting that his theory was not concerned with meaning because meaning could not be reliably quantified.[38] Even at this moment of imitating the computer's numerical representation, the text operates so as to deconstruct Shannon's famous diagram of the communication circuit (which proved crucially important to the emerging science of informatics).[39] The diagram shows a sender encoding the message so it can be sent as a signal through a channel, the channel being subjected to interference by a noise source, and a receiver decoding the signal to reconstitute the message.

In Foer's scene, by contrast, there is no problem with noise in the channel: The machine transmits the encoded message with complete accuracy. Rather, it is the message's *human* import that is at stake. Each component is freighted with meaning that resides in the text but outside the communication circuit as Shannon constructed it. The encoding is undertaken not in order to send a message through a channel—its presumed function for Shannon—but rather because the message is too associated with trauma to be directly articulated. The channel, which normally would be vulnerable to noise, sends the message through perfectly, but Thomas's wife interprets the encoded signal as meaningless static. The reader has a better chance of decoding the numerical signals to reconstitute the message, but the decryption process takes so long to do by hand that it is probably feasible only if one were to create a computer algorithm that would correlate the letter groups with a dictionary to determine the possible words and then use information about syntax and word order to decide on the most likely choices for the message content. Since writing such a program would take considerable effort and programming skill, it is likely that message will never be decrypted, an outcome that could be read as the triumph of analog meaning over numerical representation.

Even without knowing precisely what the numerical code represents, however, we understand well enough the message's import: Thomas is laden with guilt, he wants to reconcile with his wife, and he wants to "reach YES" (in code, 7 3 2 2 4 9 3 7) so he and she can share what life remains possible for them.[40] Thus what initially appears as imitation of the numerical representation of language, the *modus operandi* of the digital computer, turns into intensification of techniques native to the print novel.

Layered text, another characteristic of the computer's hierarchical architecture, appears in Foer's novel at the climactic point when Oskar Schell, the precocious nine-year-old whose father died in the Twin Towers fire, makes contact with the man he knows only as his grandmother's "roomer," actually his grandfather Thomas Schell who has again taken up residence with his wife. Forbidden to reveal himself to Oskar, Thomas is discovered by the child and slowly begins making his acquaintance. Eventually Oskar shares with him his terrible secret. On the fateful day of 9/11, he was let out of school early and returned alone to his apartment to find on the answering machine four messages from his father, desperate to reach his family. While Oskar is in the apartment, the phone rings a fifth time, but he is so traumatized by the knowledge of what is happening he is unable to answer. The answering machine records his father repeatedly asking "Are you there?" as if he intuits Oskar is listening.

When Oskar replays the messages for his grandfather, the text visually breaks up on the page, as if imitating the noisy call imperfectly recorded by the machine. As the grandfather's narration continues, the lines are crunched closer and closer together.[41] They quickly become illegible but nevertheless continue on for several pages until the surfaces are almost completely black.[42] The text, moving from imitation of a noisy machine to an intensification of ink marks durably impressed on paper, uses this print-specific characteristic as a visible indication of the trauma associated with the scene, as if the marks as well as the language were breaking down under the weight of the characters' emotions. At the same time, the overlapping lines are an effect difficult to achieve with letterpress printing or a typewriter but a snap with Photoshop, so digital technology leaves its mark on these pages as well.

The recursive dynamic between print and digital technologies is apparent in the text's final pages. Oskar has found on the Internet a grainy video of a man falling from the Twin Towers. Although the resolution is too fuzzy to make out the man's features, Oskar speculates it might have been his father. Having more or less come to terms with his father's death, he cannot resist indulging in a final fantasy. He imagines that his father, rather than falling, flies upward through the sky to land on top of the building, goes down through the elevators, and walks backwards through the street until he flings open the door and returns to safety in the apartment. The novel remediates the backward-running video in fifteen pages that function as a flipbook, showing the fantasized progression Oskar has imagined.[43] On the one hand, the poor resolution makes clear the book is reproducing digital images, thus suggesting that the book is imitating electronic text. On the other hand, the flipbook functionality re-creates the distinction between storage and performance characteristic of digital media but now in a form historically specific to the print book. Once again, imitation and intensification cohabit these pages.

My next set of examples comes from *The People of Paper*, beginning with the passage in which the thoughts of the mechanical tortoise are represented as a square block of ones and zeros.[44] The reader is tempted with the possibility of decoding, for it is possible to take the series and, using the byte equivalents for ASCII, find out if it constitutes an intelligible message. That is probably not the point, however (how interesting are the thoughts of a mechanical tortoise likely to be?). Rather, as with the telephone keypad, the payoff comes precisely in *not* being able easily to decode the numbers, in the shock of discovering the witty and appropriate substitution of numerical code for human-only language. The mechanical tortoise enters the story because Federico de la Fe, disturbed that "Saturn" (the pseudonym by which the characters know the author) can read his thoughts, mobilizes a resistance movement that uses the tortoise's lead shells to shield the characters' consciousnesses from Saturn's prying surveillance. When the surviving tortoise's thoughts come under the same surveillance, we find they are in a sense already shielded because they register the bifurcation between human-only language and the binary code that is the only language intelligent machines can understand.

The introduction of the author-as-character sets up an ontological hierarchy dramatized within the text by Saturn's position in an upper world whose bottom forms the sky of the other characters. Disrupting this hierarchy, the lead shields reproduce within the story world the distinction between a linguistic surface and underlying symbols, hiding the characters' language and thoughts as a computer screen of text hides the code generating it. Like the silicon chip, the metal functions as a synecdoche for the encounter of the human with the intelligent machine, an analogy reinforced by having the mechanical tortoise's stream of consciousness rendered as binary code. The text thus enacts two different ways of ordering the chain of signifiers: on the one hand, an accessible linguistic surface; on the other, a layered hierarchy that makes language differentially accessible in a scheme that correlates access with power. This contrast provides the plot's central conflict, as Saturn tries to make Federico de la Fe's thoughts appear as a linguistic surface, whereas Federico de la Fe struggles to have them become subtextual and thus invisible on the page. The values associated with the different ordering schemes are complicated by the fact that Federico de la Fe, chief of the EMF (El Monte Flores) gang, interprets his "war" with Saturn as a fight for independence, understood by the EMF resistance movement as the quintessential human value.

Further complicating the ontology implicit in the book's materiality is the partitioning of some chapters into parallel columns, typically with three characters' stories running in parallel on a page spread, as if imitating the computer's ability to run several programs simultaneously. Significantly, the columns portraying Federico de la Fe's thoughts are typically headed not with his name but with Saturn's. When Saturn cannot see his thoughts, the column is blank. In columns headed by other characters' names, by contrast, the reader has access to the characters' thoughts even when Saturn does not. But one character is able to hide his thoughts from both author and reader even without a lead shell—a drooling infant boy so unresponsive that most people assume he is severely retarded. In actuality, we are told, he is the reincarnation of the prophet Nostradamus, gifted with the ability to see the past and future as well as the present. His consciousness appears within the text as a solid black column, a shield of ink hiding the text that presumably lies underneath, just as computer code is hidden by the text it generates.

Within the narrative world, however, this apparent imitation of computer code's hierarchical structure is interpreted as the baby's ability to hide his thoughts from the reader as well as Saturn, an interpretation that locates the maneuver within the print novel's tradition of metafiction by playing with the ontological levels of author, character, and reader. Moreover, when another child, Little Merced, manages to communicate with the baby and learn from him how to shield her thoughts as well (a process visualized on the pages by uneven blobs of black that slowly grow more regular and extensive as she becomes more proficient), the blobs are figured not as computer layering but as the very human process of one child learning from another how to negotiate an adult world of differential power relations.

Another characteristic of electronic text that the narrative appears to imitate is mutability. In contrast to durable ink marks, electronic text can easily be deleted and replaced by other letters or spaces; with a touch of a key, it can appear in different fonts, sizes, and shapes. That the page can also become mutable (and mutilated) becomes apparent when Saturn encounters Liz, his ex-girlfriend, and hears her utter the name of the white man for whom she dumped Saturn. We never learn the rival's name, however, because the places on the pages where it would putatively appear have been replaced by die-cut holes, Saturn's revenge on the name he cannot bear to hear. In a now-familiar pattern, a technique that at first appears to be imitating electronic text is transformed into a print-specific characteristic, for it would, of course, be impossible to eradicate a word from an electronic text by cutting a hole in the screen.

In *House of Leaves*, the recursive dynamic between strategies that imitate electronic text and those that intensify the specificities of print reaches an apotheosis, producing complexities so entangled with digital technologies that it is difficult to say which medium is more important in producing the novel's effects. All four characteristics of digital text are rampantly evident throughout. The text is richly multimodal, combining text, graphics, color, and non-linguistic sound effects, along with many other media. Divided between Zampanò's critical commentary on the film *The Navidson Record* and Johnny Truant's footnotes on Zampanò's manuscript, it offers multiple data streams, including footnotes on Johnny's footnotes as well as interjections by the editors, not to mention some two hundred pages of exhibits, appendices, and index. Layered text appears on many pages, for example as square brackets signifying indecipherable inscriptions or literal holes in the manuscript that hint at unseen text-behind-the-text; on other pages, text is overwritten onto other text, for example in Pelafina's letters in which overwritten words mimetically perform her disordered psychological state.[45] Supposedly typed, these pages were obviously composed in a digital program such as Photoshop and printed from digital files, thus testifying to their previous existence as electronic text. Code also runs riot on the pages, including signal flag codes used instead of Arabic numbers on some footnotes, astrological signs on other footnotes, dots and dashes of Morse code, and even a page of dots representing Braille. Responding to the digital environments that are affecting cognitive modes, this extremely complex book requires deep attention at the same time that it titillates the most ravenous appetite for hyperattention multitasking.

As if positioning itself as a rival to the computer's ability to represent within itself other media, this print novel remediates an astonishing variety of media, including film, video, photography, the telegraph, painting, collage, and graphics, among others. This implicit rivalry came close to the surface in Danielewski's long interview with Larry McCaffrey and Sinda Gregory.[46] Asked if the computer was important for the composition of this unusually designed text, Danielewski replied:

> I didn't write *House of Leaves* on a word processor. In fact, I wrote out the entire thing in pencil! And what's most ironic, I'm still convinced that it's a great deal easier to write something out by hand than on a computer. You hear a lot of people talking about how computers make writing so much easier because they offer the writer so many choices, whereas in fact pencil and paper allow you a much greater freedom. You can do anything in pencil![47]

When McCaffrey pressed him on the issue, however, Danielewski admitted the necessity of digital technologies for the book's production:

> There's no doubt computers, new software, and other technologies play a big role in getting any book ready for production these days. They also make it easier for a publisher to consider releasing a book like mine that previously would have been considered too complicated and expensive to typeset by hand. Yet despite all the technological advantages currently available, the latter stages of getting *House of Leaves* ready for production involved such a great deal of work that Pantheon began to wonder if they were going to be able to publish it the way I wanted. So I wound up having to do the typesetting myself.[48]

Digital technology functions here like the Derridean *supplement*; alleged to be outside and extraneous to the text proper, it is somehow also necessary. The construction suggests that at issue is the text's ability to posit its origin without digital technology and that, conversely, including digital technology would alter the text's fundamental view of its own ontology.

These suggestions become explicit in the text's consideration of how other media have been threatened, and implicitly transformed, by the interpenetration of digitality. Particularly revealing is Zampanò's discussion of digital photography. Distinguishing between films representing fictional stories and documentaries, Zampanò notes that documentaries "rely on interviews, inferior equipment, and virtually no effects to document real events. Audiences are not allowed the safety net of disbelief and so must turn to more challenging mechanisms of interpretation which, as is sometimes the case, may lead to denial and aversion."[49] The film at the book's center, *The Navidson Record*, purports to be a documentary, but the main object of its representation, the house on Ashtree Lane into which Will Navidson moves with his partner Karen Green and their children in an attempt to shore up the couple's shaky relationship, turns out to be an impossible object whose inside is bigger than its outside. At first the surreal excess measures a mere quarter of an inch but then stretches into distances greater than the diameter of the earth and older than the solar system. With its shifting walls, ashen surfaces, and labyrinthine complexities, the house's interior is not only impossible to map but also impossible to inhabit, for it destroys any artifact left within it. Combining an unrepresentable topography with an uninhabitable space, the house confronts those who enter its mysterious interior with the threat of nothingness that, far from being mere absence, has a terrible ferocious agency, figured by the beast-like growls Will and others think they perceive issuing from its interior. Moreover, even the film that putatively records this impossible object has an indeterminate status, for as Johnny Truant informs us in his introduction, the film probably does not exist—which does not, however, prevent Zampanò from writing some 500 pages interpreting it.

In a brilliant article, Mark B. N. Hansen has equated the house's unrepresentable space with digital technology, arguing that the digital image, unlike photography, needs no original object to anchor its representation.[50] The digital in Hansen's terminology (following Bernard Stiegler) is "postorthographic" because it is not compelled to represent actual events but can seem to record the past while not in fact doing so. (In this somewhat idiosyncratic terminology, orthography, whose etymology means "straight writing," designates "the capacity of various technologies to register the past as past, to inscribe the past in a way that allows for its exact repetition."[51]) Simply put, Hansen's article sets up a kind of syllogism: The house is unrepresentable; digital technology does not need a preexisting object to create its representations; therefore the "house is nothing if not a figure for the digital: its paradoxical presence as the impossible absence at the core of the novel is a provocation that . . . is analogous in its effects to the provocation of the digital."[52] The final twist is to argue that in the face of the abyss created by an unrepresentable object, meaning can be recovered only through the effects of the house on embodied observers, effects registered first on the body as preconscious experience and then brought back into articulation as the characters' experiences.

In Hansen's argument, a slippage occurs in the equation of the house as an unrepresentable object with digital technology's ability to create simulacra; in his formulation, the house "reveals the digital to be a force resistant to orthothesis as such, to be the very force of fiction itself."[53] Although it is true that digital technologies can create objects for which there is no original (think of Shrek, for instance), the technology itself is perfectly representable, from the alternating voltages that form the basis for the binary digits up to high-level languages such as C++. The ways in which the technology actually performs plays no part in Hansen's analysis. For him the point is that the house renders experience singular and unrepeatable, thus demolishing the promise of orthographic recording to repeat the past exactly. Because in his analogy the house equals the digital, this same property is then transferred to digital technologies.

Here one might object that, on the contrary, digital technologies render repetition more exact than has ever been possible before, allowing endless copies to be made with precision. If digital simulacra disrupt the tie between the object and its representation, thus breaking one-half of the orthographic promise to capture and repeat the past, it reinforces the other half, i.e., exact repetition. The arrows of digitality's relation to orthothesis do not, then, all point in the same direction. More important, in my view, is an aspect of digital technology that Hansen's elision of its materiality ignores: its ability to exercise agency. In his account, meaning can be recovered only in the holistic effects of embodied experience because all that the digital can do is break the tie between representation and referent. In fact, however, the layered architectures of computer technologies enable active interventions that perform actions beyond what their human programmers envisioned. In the field of artificial life, for example, programs have been constructed that produce species capable of mutating and evolving in unpredictable ways. Genetic algorithms go further in evolving not just the output of the programs but the programs themselves. Programmable gate arrays go further yet in evolving the hardware, changing the patterns of the logic gates to arrive at the most efficient way to solve certain problems.[54]

In *House of Leaves*, the house's agency occupies an indeterminate status figured by the beast whose presence (and absence) seems to haunt the house's interior. Never actually seen, the beast can be inferred from the deep claw marks that Johnny Truant finds beside Zampanò's body; the seeming growls recorded on *The Navidson Record*; and the "fingers of darkness [that] slash cross the lighted wall and consume Holloway."[55] Everywhere the beast is mentioned, the text wavers between representing it as an actually existing creature and a consensual hallucination created by the characters. Typical is the passage where Johnny reproduces in the edited manuscript the unexplained burn holes that pepper Zampanò's notes, creating a play between the letters actually inscribed on the page and the absences signified by square brackets. Zampanò argues:

> It seems erroneous to assert . . . that this creat[ ]e had actual teeth and claws of b[ ]e (which myth for some reason [ ] requires). [ ]t d[ ]d have claws, they were made of shadow and if it did have te[ ]th, they were made of darkness. Yet even as such the [ ] still stalked Hall[ ]way at every corner until at last it did strike, devouring him, even roaring, the last thing heard, the sound [ ]f Holloway ripped out of existence.[56]

Even as we reconstruct the noisy message for ourselves by supplying the missing letters, the brackets puncturing the text evoke the nothingness that the beast paradoxically signifies in its very presence.

This play between the absence of presence and the presence of absence is intimately related to the house's ambiguous agency. Perhaps it acts on its own, or perhaps, as the fictional critic Ruby Dahl cited by Zampanò claims, the house merely reflects the personalities of those who venture inside it.[57] Significantly, immediately after the beast consumes Holloway's body, the house goes crazy and eats Tom, as if infected by the psychosis that drove Holloway to hunt his comrades, murder one and wound another, and then commit suicide.

Following Hansen's key insight that there is a deep connection between the house and digital technologies, I arrive at a somewhat different explanation for its operation. Increasingly, human attention occupies only the tiny top of a huge pyramid of machine-to-machine communication, including cell phones, networked computers, ATMs, and RFID (Radio Frequency Identification) tags that give every indication of spreading faster than mold in New Orleans. Often these digital machines, ranging from the obvious to the nano-scaled, are coupled with sensors and actuators that carry out actions, from something as mundane as raising a garage door to the world-shaking launch of a nuclear missile. We would perhaps like to think that actions require humans to initiate them, but human agency is increasingly dependent on intelligent machines to carry out actions and, more alarmingly, to provide the data on which the human decisions are made in the first place. *House of Leaves* reflects these ambiguities in attributing the house's actions both to the humans who enter it and the beast that can seemingly act on its own, a nonhuman creature whose agency is completely enmeshed with that of the characters, the author, and the reader.

For digital technologies, the initiation of action ultimately translates into binary code. From the brute simplicity of ones and zeros, the successive layers of code build up constructions of enormous complexity, from genetic algorithms that produce advanced circuit designs[58] to the digital typesetting programs that produced *House of Leaves* as a material artifact. Although humans originally created the computer code, the complexity of many contemporary programs is such that no single person understands them in their entirety. In this sense our understanding of how computers can get from simple binary code to sophisticated acts of cognition is approaching the gap that yawns between our understanding of the mechanics of human consciousness—the neural structures, chemical transmitters, networked cells, and molecular interactions from which consciousness must emerge—and the apparent autonomy and freedom of human thought. The parallel with computers is striking. As Brian Cantwell Smith observes, the emergence of complexity within computers may provide crucial clues to "how a structured lump of clay can sit up and think."[59]

Yet human cognition is unlike machine cognition in being mediated through emotions and the complexities of bodily processing. Despite similarities in the layered architectures of neural nets and coding languages, huge differences remain between human thought and machine processing. In particular, humans seek meaning while computers execute commands. As noted earlier, Shannon's information theory marked a fateful juncture where information was separated from meaning. Shannon's theory was instrumental in the creation of information technology, for it provided a way reliably to quantify information and minimize noise. Instantiating many of the premises of Shannon's theory, computers process, store, and transmit data without any comprehension of its meaning in human terms. Although research in such fields as artificial life, emotional computing and artificial intelligence is ongoing to create computers that can achieve some sense of meaning, it remains to be seen whether an intelligent machine capable of sentience can ever be built. The nothingness with which the house—and the beast—are consistently associated in *House of Leaves* functions not only to deconstruct orthographic inscription but also to provide a figure for the absence at the core of the text's multiple layers and acts of inscription—an absence that draws into the question the very possibility of meaning and, at the same time, paradoxically provokes a riotous excess of meaning-making.

As the litmus test separating human and machine cognition, meaning in *House of Leaves* may be recovered through the multiple layers of remediation that this print novel creates (as I have argued elsewhere),[60] and linked to embodied human reading (as Hansen argues). Yet another implication lurks in the layered complexities of this print novel. An ambiguous agent, the beast both threatens and mimics the agency of the human characters. Above all else, the characters in the text, like the humans who read the text, are meaning-seeking animals. Nevertheless, they (and we) cannot determine the meaning of the beast's actions, or even if it exists. Its elusive presence that, like an equivocal figure, takes only a slight shift in perspective to transform into absence, stands in for the digital technologies that, ignorant of meaning, nevertheless initiate actions that often have consequences for humans across the globe.

Like the nothingness infecting the text's signifiers, a similar nothingness would confront us if we could take an impossible journey and zoom into a computer's interior while it is running code. We would find that there is no there there, only alternating voltages that nevertheless produce meaning through a layered architecture correlating ones and zeros with human language. From the nothingness of alternating voltages emerges the complexities of digital culture, including effects that are shifting the balance among the human cognitive modes of deep attention and hyperattention. In this sense *House of Leaves* performs within its fictional world the banal miracle that produced it as a material artifact and that also produces us as readers of the complex surfaces of contemporary literature.

The subjectivity performed and evoked by this text differs from traditional print novels in subverting, in a wide variety of ways, the authorial voice associated with an interiority arising from the relation between sound and mark, voice and presence. Overwhelmed by the cacophony of competing and cooperating voices, the authority of voice is deconstructed and the interiority it used to authorize is subverted into a series of echoes testifying to the absences at the center. Natural language is put into dynamic interplay with a wide variety of mechanical codes, and textual surfaces are littered with the marks of digital machines. As this text along with the others discussed above demonstrate, digital technologies do more than mark the surfaces of the contemporary print novels. They also put into play dynamics that reconfigure the relations between authors and readers, humans and intelligent machines, code and language. Books will not disappear, but neither will they escape the effects of the digital technologies that interpenetrate them. More than a mode of material production (although it is that), digitality has become the textual condition of twenty-first-century literature.

CHAPTER 12

Crisis Means Turning Point:
A Manifesto for Art and Accountability
Doris Sommer

> When I feel trapped, I ask myself, what would an artist do?
> ANTANAS MOCKUS

If the humanities are in crisis, this is no time to lament a cruel fate, but to make choices, fast. In common usage, crisis can mean stagnation and festering, a present so oppressively present that it crowds out the past and stifles the future. It is paralysis, or the kind of revolution that moves in vicious circles, like the ones associated with Mexico's Institutionalized Revolutionary Party until its first national defeat in 2000.[1] What response is possible except a derivative criticism, since there is nothing to do but disengage and denounce? Humanists have become adept at this face-saving gesture in the face of impossible odds. But crisis has another, more engaging, and obliging, meaning if you follow the etymological precision that enables Antonio Gramsci's interventions, despite the scientific Marxists who would have stopped him: Crisis means the opportunity, and therefore the obligation, to choose, quickly.[2] Acknowledging the danger of the other meaning—a static equilibrium imposed by a

---

I am grateful for the advice of Professor Arabella Lyon in preparing this essay. Among her contributions is the reference to Robert Scholes. "Presidential Address 2004: The Humanities in a Posthumanist World." *PMLA* 120 (May 2005): 724–733.

strong leader that can preempt an organic resolution to crisis—Gramsci exhorts his readers to think on their feet and seize the opportunity to redirect history.[3]

What are our choices now, while policy makers, foundations, social scientists, and other fellow citizens train a polite gaze on the humanities? Meanwhile, waning support for students and teachers of the arts alarms and offends us. Don't we deserve support, almost by birthright, as guardians of artistic and spiritual values in a world that keeps contracting the focus of education to narrowly rational and technical training? Yet training in arts interpretation, as much as in the cultural studies that address a broad range of creative practices, feels the pinch of purse strings drawing closed. Let us consider the predicament and possible responses. Critique of ungenerous others is not enough, and despair amounts to self-defeating inaction. Surely humanists can muster more creativity.

Common Sense

Quite early in the development of modern civility, intellectual narrowness had worried Immanuel Kant. He hoped to contain "the scandal of reason" that dismissed other human faculties by capping his major work with exercises to develop judgment.[4] Reason would reduce judgment to mere calculation, so Kant located that faculty for thinking freely in the unreasonable evaluation of beauty and the sublime. Aesthetic experience is a second-order pleasure. It judges immediate pleasures in order to distinguish self-serving enjoyment of an object that may be physically or morally useful from the freely conferred admiration for the form of an object, regardless of use or meaning. The exercise of judgment requires practice in locating aesthetic pleasure beyond external purpose and existing concepts. Unlike other philosophical activities, aesthetic judgment for Kant assumes that all evaluators will reach the same conclusion, since their exercises should be equally free from interest. Positing intersubjective agreement, Kant resignified "common sense" as the sense of judgment derived from freedom that we have in common and that can develop into an aptitude for free citizenship. Kant did not follow up on this ethico-political consequence of art for art's sake, Hannah Arendt explains, because it might have been risky to engage political philosophy and it was, in any case, redundant.[5] Judgment leads to political deliberation, she concludes. But the corollary between examined private pleasures and enhanced public sphere is news to most scholars today, good news that humanists might explore through programs that develop a taste for active (i.e., creative) citizenship.

Some artists and city governments, along with business interests, are already at work forging cultural citizenship and creative economies.[6] And research in education consistently links the practice and appreciation of arts with enhanced cognitive and social development.[7] Perhaps these links are worthy of more attention from the humanities, where the focus on aesthetic practices could include the ripple effects from pleasure to judgment and consequently to the common social sense that can sustain deliberation and collective action. Humanists who dedicate careers to identifying and teaching the particular enchantments of art make significant social contributions, whether or not they make conscious connections to politics and economics. Without drills in evaluating immediately pleasurable experience to determine whether it is free of interest or seduced by it, the faculty of judgment would remain as undeveloped as in premodern societies, where subjects are not obliged to judge but rather to obey within reason.

All the more reason for traditional humanists to stand firm, you may say, on the clearing of public ground that aesthetic education had pioneered. Any defense of that ground with arguments beyond the arts might, it seems, risk capitulation to the scandal of reduced faculties. But my point is that refusing allied arguments leaves the field almost defenseless today, paradoxically indifferent to the very claim of humanizing effects that follow from art and interpretation, effects that should justify financial support and moral standing. I am saying that it is misguided to refuse, on principled or disinterested grounds, to be reasonable about public and private fiscal priorities. For one thing, refusal confounds the disinterested experience of beauty with the scholarly meditation on its form and its effects. At a remove from art, scholarship is evaluated through its engagement with existing concepts, its rigor of argumentation, and display of erudition. For another thing, the rebuff of reason shrivels Kant's ambitious project to link a love of form with respect for reflexive common sense. The rebuff, consequently, answers the scandal of reason with an equally scandalous reduction of human faculties to the one exercise of good taste.

In line with Kant's aesthetic formalism, Victor Shklovsky dismissed the academy's sententious defense of great ideas. Art has nothing to do with content, but everything to do with technique. Here as in Kant, the pleasures of art have indirect ethical and therefore practical effects, not through ideas but through pleasure: Aesthetic experience rekindles a love for the world, reviving objects, events, and people deadened by habit. Without art, "life is reckoned as nothing. Habitualization devours works, clothes, furniture, one's wife, and the fear of war.... And art exists *that one may recover the sensation of life.*"[8] I underline the commanding subjunctive construction. Humanists surely feel that ardor of purpose, but feeling will stay limited and subject-centered if it ignores Kant's lead toward grounding civil society in free judgment, and Shklovsky's invitation to care passionately for the world. One paradoxical result of rejecting practical arguments for the humanities is, as I hinted, to forfeit some credit for significant contributions that humanists normally make to society, credit we might invest in making more contributions. The guardians of human values can be curiously indifferent to our own effects on fellow humans.

To See Unseen

Another paradox is the practically positivist posture that humanists assume before a work of art, imagining that we are not seen in the act, as if observation could avoid participation and interference. Any good literary or cultural critic might comment on this lack of reflexivity in another discipline, say anthropology. David Stoll, for example, is reprehensibly blind to his effect on Guatemala's peace process, and Elizabeth Burgos Debray is naïve about her relationship to Rigoberta Menchú.[9] But literary criticism's generally carefree move from observation to commentary passes with hardly a notice. Humanists do indeed ask about the effects of teaching and scholarship on the poem or painting they study, but scarcely ever about the ripple effect of the study on readers or on the general social environment, unless the humanist does cultural studies.[10]

Then the answers are characteristically critical and cautionary. Artists, scholars, and policy-makers seem invariably to do more damage than good when they try to intervene in policy, because culture is not expedient.[11] If resistance were possible, without folding back into an oppressive system, opposition would at least be laudable in this view;[12] but artistic contributions to existing systems look worse than suspicious. Although some distinguished authors show that cultural practices, such as micro broadcasting or traditional arts and crafts geared to nontraditional markets, are complex enough to demonstrate agency by participants,[13] cultural studies more often dismisses even the agency to resist power as a self-defeating illusion. To celebrate popular practices, or give voice to voiceless subalterns,[14] ends up for this dour tone of cultural studies as complicity with repressive forces, including the very studies that privilege the poor in a polar distinction from the rich.[15] Nothing good can come of it, apparently, except for the pleasures and privileges of performing academic feats of argument about some cultural disaster and counterarguments about even more disastrous practices, such as the exercise of cultural studies itself.

The perspective squints at evidence of democratizing contributions through arts and interpretation. Critique and denunciation practically exhaust the range of results, as if creativity were always doomed to reinforce the political and economic constraints from which it presumes to wrest some freedom. The closed system in which friskiness necessarily bites its own tail suggests a systematic rejection of capitalist society. Whatever ingenious creations or interventions make the system tolerable are thereby guilty of complicity and deserving of critique. I confess to less systematic thinking and to finding strength in small judgments about art and its aftereffects. Reformism may seem undignified to some critics, but I remember Rigoberta Menchú's response to dignified academics: "Only the privileged stop at critique," she taunted, "the rest of us need to develop solutions." If humanists today feel the pinch of tighter purse strings and the squeeze of losing institutional ground to economists, political scientists, and other social scientists whose questions beg practical answers, it may be time for cultural studies to consider socially useful contributions by developing best cultural practices along with exposing the worst.

For scholars of literature, painting, music, theater, and other arts, the question of social effect of interpretive work, as I said, hardly comes up. This makes the question worth asking, to take a lesson from Pierre Macherey, who identified the silences in literature as indicators of basic assumptions.[16] Widespread assent signals cultural foundations so solid that exposition becomes unthinkably redundant to writers and to their ideal readers. Other readers notice that something is missing. Think of literature students today. Do they ask, as mine do, why James Fenimore Cooper's gallant soldier preferred bland Alice over enchanting Cora in *The Last of the Mohicans*, or what the big deal is if Samuel Richardon's *Pamela* keeps her virginity or not, or how come the Inca Garcilaso de la Vega reports Old Testament rituals in ancient Peru? The archaeologically reconstructed answers are what Macherey listens for as the clearest indices of ideology, in Louis Althusser's sense of the word as a lived relationship to society.[17]

Perhaps one effect of the increasingly estranged field occupied by the humanities can be a fresh, defamiliarized perspective on our own silent assumptions about what we do as humanists. The silence, I think, amounts to assuming that we do not, should not, and probably cannot, do much. Outloud humanists say with confidence that we study and report on culture and the arts. One unspoken assumption for the field is that culture refers to individual creativity, which can miss ritual or collective practices. Familiar questions about creativity focus on an object of study: What rhetorical devices make a poem worth re-reading? Or, how do novels make mischief with more properly called literary genres? Where do brushstrokes call attention to the process of painting? Or, when silent movies ceded to sound, which transnational charms got lost in translation and which were found in new layers of language arts? The range of existing research agendas and their often-fascinating results stay relatively fixed on an object in order to render observations that have more or less descriptive power, are more or less right or wrong, true or false. J. L. Austin called this use of language "constative," practically the only use that philosophy had recognized for language, even though we do many more things with words. By naming performatives (e.g., a promise, a vow, a curse, or blessing), Austin moved philosophy beyond description toward recognizing the uses of language as intervention. He knew that the distinction between description and agency would blur, because naming has a constitutive effect, but the theoretical difference kept both functions in focus.[18] The lesson about what words do in the world, beyond vying for credibility, seems lost on the study of language arts. Surely it will be found when these arts include anticipation and accounts of the work words do.

For now, though, even when cultural studies breaks academic taboos about what counts for art, little evident reflection asks after the social effects of research and teaching. Add hip-hop to musicology, spoken-word poetry to belles letters, graffiti to art history, and scholarship can break out of an ivory tower but stay stuck behind an unremarked and therefore unexamined line between cultural products and interpretations of culture. Scholarship's binary business of seeing art and saying interpretation imagines that it proceeds without being seen. Shuttling between the poles of art and report, alternating between point and click, humanist scholars silently assume that that movement doesn't *interfere* with the context of study. When anthropologists noticed that imaginary line a generation ago, the result was to locate a blurry area of study where self-ethnographies develop along with collaborations between scientist and subject.[19] The penchant for reflexivity has generally upset the practices of positivist social science that had rejected earlier romantic impressionism by holding the line between colorful culture and black-and-white reporting. Even earlier, natural science had to consider how experiments interfere in studies.[20]

Interpreters of art seem strangely stiff and straight alongside these reflexive neighbors. Humanists don't worry much about what we do with words. But since interference is unavoidable, the relevant questions should be about desired effects and about choices among research options. I am insisting a bit, but the issue of effects has apparently seemed doubly irrelevant: either they are negligible, or too patent to argue, given the humanizing value of humanists. On the one hand, the social consequences of making and interpreting the arts are barely worth considering in a world where art has become ornamental and commentary is demoted to adjusting the worth of ornaments. On the other hand, we sometimes defend the apparently impractical or apolitical quality of art and interpretation as a spiritual refuge for thinking and feeling beyond the technocratic narrowness of contemporary society. The economic viability of art is not at issue, as I said, now that defenders of the "creative economy" document the revitalizing capacity of artists (and gays) on struggling cities.[21]

The urgent issue today is the role of art and the humanities in civic development. Art's socially constitutive appeal needs more advocates; otherwise, citizens may not appreciate art, including the art of interpretation, as the precious foundation of democratic life. This is no exaggeration. A disposition toward creativity, which acknowledges different points of view and more than one way to compose available material, resists authoritarian single-mindedness. Constitutional democracies that confer rights and obligations are themselves collective works of art.[22] And constitutions remain open to performative interventions, obliging citizens to remain creative.

Either way, affirming that art and interpretation are among humanity's signature activities or doubting the effects of disengaged interpretation, humanists might pause for a self-reflexive moment: What exactly is the social value added by inquiry in the arts? It is time we engage the question, now that many others are asking it, as a preamble to budget cuts that threaten the foundations of free society.

An Exemplary Crisis

Pedro Reyes had an ambitious idea for an art show and then he despaired. The idea was to fill Harvard University's Carpenter Center galleries during the spring of 2006 with projections of the future. But, on second thought, the project conjured such bleak visions of violence, scarcity, disease, and death that the distinguished young Mexican multimedia artist felt stuck between wanting to be honest and not wanting to spread gloom. Then something happened to revive his faith in art along with his hope in the future. Reyes discovered two cultural agents, "connectionists" to use his neologism, who show how to link creative practices to social and democratic development.[23]

The first and most spectacular agent today is Antanas Mockus, a mayor who thinks like an artist. The second is Augusto Boal, an artist who acts in city government. Discovering them was an invitation to think otherwise about things to come and about one's own contribution to forging the future. It was also a burden of responsibility to be ingenious and accountable. So Reyes got back on an active track where he recognized more fellow travelers among the artists he most admires: Alejandro Jodorowsky, for example, whose range of creative interventions (poetry, psychomagic, film, and plastic arts) may well serve as the third inspiration for the cultural agency of Reyes's future show. "Latin America may be politically unstable and poor by economic measures," he concluded, "but it is incredibly rich in creativity." That richness can pay off in public gains. It's not that creative arts lack intrinsic value, but that this very autonomy triggers fresh perceptions and unclogs procedure in ways that make it a social resource to reckon with.[24]

Exemplary creative agents can spark recognition of agency in others who artfully engage the world, as Reyes demonstrated by spotting Jodorowsky in the company of Mockus and Boal. The point is worth making in order to connect the intrinsic value of art to the added value of humanist commentary and interpretation that are now increasingly discounted by funders and policy-makers. Like writers, composers, painters, and playwrights, humanists who interpret and teach about art can also raise expectations that creativity may contribute to democratic social change. So much depends on the delicacy and skill of interpretation that often determines the pleasure and aftereffects of others. "There is nothing either good or bad," says the artist Shakespeare, "but thinking makes it so."[25]

Teachers are agents of culture who multiply the lessons they learn by reaching masses of students, whatever the reigning taste in art may be. To make good on this broad-based power of persuasion, humanists may want to add a reflexive question to research agendas and to lesson plans: How does our interpretive or pedagogical work affect the world? On this count, ironically, the humanities lag a bit behind the social sciences after inspiring them to develop levels of analysis beyond supposedly objective or positivist reporting. Humanists seldom investigate the social effects of interpretation. The silence is curious, because humanists obviously do something to the social environment by affecting the values and hopes of students and general readers, whether we feature work that builds society or art that undoes it. In fact, all of us are cultural agents: those who make, comment, buy, sell, reflect, allocate, decorate, vote, don't vote, or otherwise lead social, culturally constructed lives. The appropriate question about agency is not if we exercise it, but how self-consciously we do so: that is, to what end and what effect.

Agent is a term that acknowledges the small shifts in perspective and practice that can turn artists and teachers into first movers toward collective change.[26] The option of agency released Reyes from the familiar double bind of expecting too much from art and too little: On the one hand, artists and critics can make the radical and impractical demand that art replace a bad social system for a better one; on the other, they may stop short of expecting any change and stay stuck in denunciation, irony, cynicism, melancholy. Between frustrated ambition and helplessness, agency is a modest but relentless call to creative action, one minute step at a time.[27] It enables artists like Pedro Reyes and his models to engage the existing social world, instead of either discarding it or despairing altogether.[28]

Two Models and More

Antanas Mockus, the magus of Bogotá, is an international beacon of creative administration. Philosopher and mathematician, twice elected mayor and now presidential candidate in Colombia, he knows and teaches the value of artful responses to crime, corruption, and violence. During more than a decade before Mockus assumed office in 1995, general chaos had kept the capital off limits for tourists and had tormented residents. The situation seemed hopeless, given the level of corruption that turns investment against itself. More money for economic recovery deepens the pockets of drug dealers, and more armed police escalate the number of guns and the level of violence. What intervention could possibly make sense in this stagnant but volatile situation? I have asked this question of economists and political scientists who admit they are stumped by the challenge. But Mockus took action by engaging culture to connect the body and soul of the city.[29] If the body politic had grown too weak to process fiscal cures or to expect security, the first treatment was to revive a democratizing desire for civility through art, antics, and accountability.

For example, the municipality's inspired staff hired twenty pantomime artists to replace the corrupt traffic police. Each artist trained another twenty amateurs and soon the urban space became a stage for daily merriment that celebrated the rules of red lights and crosswalks. Daily spectacles of mimes directing traffic created a public, a res-pública to enjoy and to reflect on the law as an enabling structure of civility after citizens had been avoiding one another during years of lawlessness, mutual suspicion, and fear. The mayor's team also printed thousands of laminated cards with a green thumb-up on one side and red thumb-down on the other, for citizens to signal approval or disapproval of traffic behavior and help to self-regulate a shared public sphere. Engaged citizens don't simply follow laws; they also participate in constructing and adjusting law to changing conditions. Vaccination against violence was one citywide performance-therapy against the "epidemic" that had become a cliché for rampant aggression. Another playful interruption of murderous routine was "Women's Night Out." Unlike the direct demands for women's rights in the Anglo-American movement "Take Back the Night," Bogotá's politics were indirect and playful, encouraging sociability among women who took to the streets, the bars, and dance clubs while the men stayed home. The next day, newspapers reported no homicides the night before. Respect for life and for the law evidently did not sacrifice fun for women. In fact, Mockus taught us at Harvard University that without pleasure, pragmatism shrivels into a poor support for politics.[30] Arts programs in schools, rock concerts in parks, a "ciclovía" on Sundays, and holidays that close streets to traffic and open them to bikers and walkers have, together with tough law enforcement and fiscal transparency, helped to revive the once-desperate metropolis.

The documented results of the program called "cultura ciudadana" show that despair is unrealistic, a failure of determination and creativity. The dramatic reduction of homicides, alongside an equally striking increase in tax revenues, register successes that outstripped everyone's expectations, including the mayor himself and his advisors. When admirers from other cities wonder if the particular programs of cultural citizenship could possibly work on their home bases where people behave differently, Mockus recommends inventing games that will work better and learning to think counterfactually. Without imagining the world otherwise, change is unthinkable. And thinking otherwise is an invitation to play.

Augusto Boal has been playing all his life. Founder of "Theater of the Oppressed" as a companion to Paulo Freire's "pedagogy of the oppressed," Boal developed interactive theater, first in Brazil and then throughout the world.[31] As a young actor, Boal learned that theater runs ethical and aesthetic risks by replacing the real-life subjects of a play with a script written by someone else and then acted by others. When he played a hired farmhand in a rustic production that called on peasants to take up arms against the landowners, the show got an enthusiastic response from its target audience. But when the peasants offered spare arms to the actors who had sworn liberty or death, the artists demurred, explaining that their work was not to make war but to incite it. The difference between responsible action and reckless representation triggered Boal's reflection on the relationship between art and accountability.

The reflection haunted him during Brazil's military dictatorship while Boal worked in Peru. There he wrote and directed a play based on the problem of a local woman whose deceitful husband would return the next day. Furious at the man, but afraid to be abandoned and more vulnerable, the woman faced a dilemma that the play would try to resolve. At the performance another, physically imposing, woman interrupted from the audience: "You have to be very clear with that man," she bellowed. Each timid adjustment that Boal offered in the script confirmed her scorn for the playwright, until she concluded that he was hopeless, turned her back on the theater, and lumbered toward the door. Exasperated, Boal stopped the woman and urged her to get on the stage and act out what she meant by "being very clear." The smart blow she dealt to the unfortunate actor who played the husband broke the already tired back of traditional theater for Boal.

From that dramatic moment, he has been promoting "Forum Theater," which invites the public to watch with an eye toward intervening at a play's *crisis* points. The one-act tragedies that portray apparently intractable dilemmas (poverty, disease, violence, homelessness) are no longer composed by a playwright but by groups of local subjects, facilitated by a Boal trainee inside *favelas* (shantytowns), marginal schools, and prisons. After the tragedy ends, a second act begins when the facilitator joins the actors on stage and invites volunteers from the audience to identify, replay, and change a particular scene that determined the tragedy but that could have been played otherwise. Through facilitators, Boal multiplies the effect of his art. He no longer trains actors, but teaches enabling agents to assist groups of potential artists to act out, and change, scenes based on their own lives. After several people from the public intervene to adjust the script, participants on and off stage can sense a double dose of magic: Insoluble problems have morphed into artistic challenges that spur competition for creativity, and participants acknowledge new admiration for creative neighbors who can avert tragedy.

When facilitators add a third act, to distribute pieces of paper and pencils for the public to jot down possible laws that would respond to the problems represented on stage, the activity is called "Legislative Theater."[32] Unbelievably, for some skeptics, Augusto Boal was elected councilman for the city of Rio de Janeiro, twice, thanks to the multiplied effects of his interactive theater and also to his public spectacles in defense of democracy (including a funeral procession for that beloved but dead political option).

While he served on the City Council, Boal sponsored legislation collected from audiences and actors in marginal neighborhoods. Thirteen of those laws have passed, and several were adopted at the national level.[33]

Throughout the Americas, creative culture is a vehicle for agency. In the United States, as in Brazil, theater improvisations foster collaboration and find dramatic outlets for frustrations that might otherwise fester or explode into violence. Without the "Teatro campesino," reports a labor organizer for César Chávez, there would be no United Farm Workers' Union. On the flat backs of pickup trucks parked just beyond the limit of a landholder's property, loudspeakers would call campesinos to come watch and join the plays that poked fun at bosses and celebrated workers' solidarity.[34] To mention just one more art of multiplication, photographers are teaching visual literacy and linking the mastery of this skill to related arts and sciences. Photography students learn to read and write in order to add titles and commentary to their pictures; they explore variations through lighting, perspective, composition, adding or subtracting elements. Sometimes coloring in a neighborhood scene, planting a tree, or fixing a roof produces a counterfactual image of imaginable improvement. Nancy McGirr began with a few children living in the city dump of Guatemala City, and now counts one of them as a colleague with a college degree.[35] João Kulcsar trains art students as facilitators who teach photography in the *favelas* of São Paulo.[36] Martín Rosenthal develops artists and entrepreneurs from undervalued teenagers, marginalized in a slum literally called Ciudad Oculta outside of Buenos Aires.[37] Surely readers will think of other cultural agents once they expect to find many more among active citizens.

Humanities in Action: Show and Tell

We humanists can recognize socially responsive agency through at least two standard professional approaches to the arts: We highlight particular creative practices; and we give those practices a theoretical spin.

The first value added by humanists follows from simply noting and commenting on examples of arts that build society. Drawing attention to undervalued creative practices offers them as models to inspire variations and choices for research projects. Young humanists are already discovering agency beyond existing cultural studies.[38] Research begins by locating or formulating a topic; we choose which text, phenomenon, or practice, which perspective or approach, merits extended consideration in a scholarly essay. Allow me to mention my own choice as a case in point. Instead of focusing on popular cultural studies topics such as violence, necrophilia, consumerism, or human rights abuse, I chose to focus a new book and course on "Bilingual Aesthetics."[39]

The invented topic names a common feature of written and performing arts that is underrepresented in scholarship organized by single-language traditions. Bilingual games cross country limits; they evince histories of migration, complicated belonging, and flexible identity, as well as aesthetic (and cognitive, political, philosophical) advantages. My preference for emphasizing these creative compensations for the difficulty of living in two or more languages is meant to renew appreciation for literary specificity in the face of cultural nationalism. It also promotes a new sentimental education that takes seriously the formalist defense of strangeness as art's signature effect. We can learn to enjoy strangeness in both immigrants and native citizens, and thereby to counteract the damaging stigma of speaking home languages in intolerant host countries. The project acknowledges the pleasures and self-respect that code-switchers earn by dint of their virtuosity, despite sometimes making embarrassing mistakes. Mistakes can brighten speech with a *sun-risa*[40] or give the pleasure of a found poem (like the "mistake" of spelling "sunrise" as "sun-risa," giving rise to "risa," laughter). Always, they mark communication with a cut or a tear that comes close to producing an aesthetic effect. The risk and thrill of speaking or writing anything can sting, every time language fails us. Knowing how language can fail makes success feel like a small miracle. In other words, bilingual aesthetics casts the precarious subjects as self-authorizing and original agents, even in the face of monolingual nativists.[41]

The course on "Bilingual Arts" is heavy on theory, partly to demonstrate that theory is practically second nature to bilinguals who normally abstract expression from meaning, and partly to display a range of refinements that follow from the "open sesame" of bilingual re-readings of literary classics from Hemingway and William Carlos Williams, to Kafka and Nabokov. Companion assignments in theory (aesthetics, liberalism, nationalism, language philosophy, deconstruction, formalism, and feminism) underline the advantages of thinking outside of the monolingual box. The course, like the book *Bilingual Aesthetics: A New Sentimental Education*, is about added value, not about remediation. And the addition sets off a chain of enhancements when students engage in the "service learning" component of the course. They teach and translate in local schools, immigration centers, and law offices, where they also learn about the everyday arts of code-switching with a new appreciation.[42]

Cultural agency is an invitation to notice "felicitous" engagements as well as frustrating performances. And since the approach privileges the surprise of ingenious responses to difficult challenges, it can sustain the attention of humanists trained to value art for producing uncommon effects. Alongside the endgame of critique, humanist agents can play the gambit of reflecting on an inexhaustible range of creative moves and on their immediate or delayed effects. The objective for cultural agents is not a partisan victory but the development of "thick" political subjects who participate in democratic life. Democracy depends on sturdy and resourceful citizens able to engage more than one point of view and to wrest rights and resources from limited assets. In other words, nonauthoritarian government counts on creativity to loosen conventional thought and free up the space where conflicts are negotiated, before they reach a brink of either despair or aggression. Aesthetic education, Friedrich Schiller insisted at the beginning of the republican age, is a necessary part of civic development.[43] The sometimes-delayed social effects of an aesthetic education can rush skeptics to conclude that one thing has little to do with another. But hasty conclusions misprise the gradual process of subject formation. In the end, results will be important, as talented administrators like Mockus maintain. He developed innovative, often indirect, measures for changing attitudes of youth and mature citizens, before and after experimenting with particular cultural programs. Among his fans, artists and teachers may be cured of an allergy to numbers.

Self-Authorization

The second contribution that humanists can make to other agents is to distill general observations from a variety of particular events or effects. Theory helps to extract usable lessons for replicating best practices. And theory for humanists today necessarily includes reflections on performance that venture beyond the archives and museums of tangible art into the world of intangible ritual and spectacle as they shape our social lives.[44] A theoretical turn, for example, on the admirable programs in visual literacy might note that the particular medium is photography, but the general message is that art nurtures a knack for decision-making. The process of selection and composition is common to other arts, including literature, music, drama, and painting. Choosing a long shot, a close-up, a profile, or a reflection, a particular adjective or verb in one language or another, harmony or dissonance, a monologue or a chorus, artists know that the material will not determine the product, but that art depends on informed decisions based on skills that can be learned and creativity that can be nurtured.

Making art, therefore, amounts to a kind of creative control over available material. The first ripple effect is a self-authorizing, enabling, sense of engagement with existing material. A second ripple effect of this hands-on training with always-limited resources is the recognition that constraint is a condition of creativity, not a nemesis. Think of a good sonnet inside the prison house of predetermined numbers and order of lines, syllables, and rhymes, or consider the deaf and mute condition of fine silent films, or a jazz riff that stays tethered to one melody. Creative subjects respond to limitation with self-limitation, paradoxically, to enhance aesthetic effects. By a similar and probably related paradox, rational choices in economics and politics limit options in order to promote maximum returns on investments of money and effort.[45] Artists and truly rational citizens know that their own competing values and desires as well as changing conditions make choices subject to change. Related experiments in behavioral economics show an encouraging, even surprising, level of reciprocity and confidence between strangers.[46] Self-interest apparently need not cancel social and moral norms; in fact, as Hannah Arendt reminds us, *"inter-est"* depends on others and on training to imagine their perspectives.[47] Therefore, a third ripple effect of aesthetic education—in the spirit of Schiller's program for modern civility—may well be a generally enhanced faculty for active and democratic citizenship. Training in art and interpretation explores contingencies in ways that do, outdo, and undo human designs. Thanks to this training, citizens can become both self-authorizing and disposed to engage creatively with a variety of perspectives and projects.

Interruption

A different theoretical spin might follow from the pantomime artists who stopped traffic jams in Bogotá. One could note that they have been copied in Lima, Peru, and have also inspired municipal posters in London's underground, urging passengers to go to the end of the cars. But the mimes may not work in other cities. Does that make them useless there? No, not if one extracts the general observation that what makes the mimes work is their interruption of bad habit. Surprise and sudden strangeness of familiar surroundings broke the spell of indifference to rules and refreshed the public's perception of mutual dependence or vulnerability on the streets. The artistic challenge for other cities would be to create other effective interruptions that combine pleasure with a renewed appreciation for public life.

Artful interruptions can unblock procedures mired in habitual abuses or indifference in order to get those practices back on track. Theodor

Adorno explored this function of art when he dismissed art's ultimate autonomy as illusory, but nevertheless valued the magic show for the margin of freedom to offer critique that art makes available.[48] Less supple treatments of the relationship between art and politics suggest a substitution of one term by the other: Either art is a kind of politics and politics a kind of art, or the confusion seems hopelessly misguided. For cultural studies, the overlap acknowledges a mutual dependence of art and politics.[49] But traditional humanism wants art to steer clear of politics, just as conventional social science defends serious research against claims that culture matters much in public life. Cultural agents might take Adorno's lead and reflect on a different relationship between art and politics, beyond both the catachresis of mutually canceling substitutions and the exclusive maps that isolate art criticism from scientific inquiry.

Art can enable politics by interrupting deadlocks, intersecting debates to get past an impasse of breakdown and facilitate a return to procedure. Art need not replace politics, as Walter Benjamin worried it would when Nazis managed to drown deliberation in a rush of enthusiasm.[50] Nor must politics replace art, in mutual metaphors that disappear the difference between thinking and feeling. Instead, art and regulation can name distinct approaches to culture that run interference, one with the other, to keep both in line. Art can disrupt in order to refresh rather than to overwhelm politics. This interruption in order to reframe or reform procedure is the fundamental contribution of cultural agency in the sense I am defending, as opposed to tendentious uses of art in the service of ideology or of nondeliberative politics associated with fascism and Stalinism. To pursue an example from Bogotá, the mimes cut in on the corrupt practice of the traffic police, but when habituation left the public cold, a newly trained police force returned to a city that the mimes had helped to reform. Habit kills art, Viktor Shklovsky might have told Mockus; it kills everything.

The fundamental aesthetic effect of art is to break habit by "defamiliarization," the Russian formalist's name for the surprise that follows from artistic technique. Defamiliarization lifts the pall of unproductive repetition, including the procedure and political arguments that get jammed by corruption or tendentiousness. This makes renewed deliberation a possible aftereffect of art. The formalists did not pursue aftereffects, but cultural agency can suggest some leads. The mimes and participants in other civic games produced the immediately refreshing effect of estrangement. But by the time their performances failed as art, they had succeeded in effecting a secondary delayed result—a renewed respect for law that brought Bogotá a step closer to coordinating law with culture and morality.[51]

NOTES

INTRODUCTION: FUTURE, HETERONOMY, INVENTION
James J. Bono, Tim Dean, and Ewa Plonowska Ziarek

1. For an interesting analysis concerning these two issues, see the collection of essays *The Research University in a Time of Discontent*, eds. Jonathan R. Cole, Elinor G. Barber, and Stephen R. Graubard (Baltimore: The Johns Hopkins University Press, 1994). For an excellent institutional analysis of the three phases of the humanities ranging from the postwar period to the present, see David A. Hollinger, "Introduction," in *The Humanities and the Dynamics of Inclusion*, ed. David A. Hollinger (Baltimore: The Johns Hopkins University Press, 2006), pp. 1–22.

2. For the impact of the inclusion of women and previously excluded social groups on the restructuring of the humanities, see "Social Inclusion," the third part of Hollinger, *The Humanities and the Dynamics of Inclusion*, pp. 189–269.

3. This quotation comes from the statement on Paulson's book jacket. He repeats this sentiment in the opening question of his study: "Do the humanities still have a future?" See William Paulson, *Literary Culture in a World Transformed: A Future for the Humanities* (Ithaca, N.Y.: Cornell University Press, 2005), p. 1.

4. This is for instance Paulson's position.

5. David Marshall, "Introduction," in *The Humanities and its Publics*, ed. David Marshall, Moderator ACLS Occasional Paper, No 61 (New York: ACLS, 2006), p. 1. This publication as a whole addresses the pressing question of the humanities' public accountability.

6. G. W. F. Hegel, *Introductory Lectures on Aesthetics*, trans. Bernard Bosanquet (London: Penguin, 1993), pp. 12–13; Sigmund Freud, *Beyond the Pleasure Principle* (1920), in *The Standard Edition of the Complete Psychological Works of Sigmund Freud*, ed. and trans. James Strachey, vol. 18 (London: Hogarth Press, 1953–1975), pp. 1–64; Ernst Bloch, *The Spirit of Utopia*, trans. Anthony A. Nassar (Stanford, Calif.: Stanford University Press, 2000); Francis Fukuyama, *The End of History and the Last Man* (New York: Free Press, 1992); Lee Edelman, *No Future: Queer Theory and the Death Drive* (Durham, N.C.: Duke University Press, 2004).

7. For example, Tim Lenoir, "Makeover: Writing the Body into the Posthuman Technoscape. Part One: Embracing the Posthuman," *Configurations* 10 (Spring 2002): 203–220; idem, "Makeover: Writing the Body into the Posthuman Technoscape. Part Two: Corporeal Axiomatics," *Configurations* 10 (Fall 2002): 373–385; Donna Haraway, *Modest_Witness@Second_Millenium. FemaleMan©_Meets_OncoMouse™: Feminism and Technoscience* (New York/London: Routledge, 1997); Elizabeth Grosz, *The Nick of Time: Politics, Evolution, and the Untimely* (Durham, N.C.: Duke University Press, 2004); Andy Clark, *Natural-Born Cyborgs: Minds, Technologies, and the Future of Human Intelligence* (Oxford: Oxford University Press, 2003); Mark B. N. Hansen, *New Philosophy for New Media* (Cambridge, Mass.: MIT Press, 2004); Eugene Thacker, *Biomedia* (Minneapolis: University of Minnesota Press, 2004); Richard Doyle, *Wetwares: Experiments in Postvital Living* (Minneapolis: University of Minnesota Press, 2003); and many others.

8. Fredric Jameson, "'End of Art' or 'End of History'?" in his *The Cultural Turn: Selected Writings on the Postmodern, 1983–1998* (London: Verso, 1998), p. 77.

9. Christopher Fynsk, *The Claim of Language: A Case for the Humanities* (Minneapolis: University of Minnesota Press, 2004), p. vii.

10. Jacques-Alain Miller, "*Extimité,*" in *Lacanian Theory of Discourse: Subject, Structure, Society,* ed. Mark Bracher, Marshall W. Alcorn, Jr., Ronald J. Corthell, and Françoise Massardier-Kenney (New York: New York University Press, 1994), pp. 74–87.

11. Jameson, *Cultural Turn,* p. 92.

12. Martin Jay, *Downcast Eyes: The Denigration of Vision in Twentieth-Century French Thought* (Berkeley: University of California Press, 1993).

13. Nancy reinterprets "being in common" as *partage,* that is, as both sharing and division. Jean-Luc Nancy, *The Inoperative Community,* ed. Peter Connor, trans. Peter Connor, Lisa Garbus, Michael Holland, and Simona Sawhney (Minneapolis: University of Minnesota Press, 1991).

14. One notable exception is Donald E. Pease and Robyn Wiegman, "Futures," in *The Futures of American Studies,* ed. Donald E. Pease and Robyn Wiegman (Durham, N.C.: Duke University Press, 2002), pp. 1–42.

LIFE AND EVENT: DELEUZE ON NEWNESS
Paola Marrati

1. Gilles Deleuze, *Cinema 1: The Movement-Image* (1983), trans. Hugh Tomlinson and Barbara Habberjam (Minneapolis: University of Minnesota Press, 1986), p. 11.

2. Gilles Deleuze, "Bergson, 1859–1941," now available in Gilles Deleuze, *Desert Islands and Other Texts: 1953–1974,* ed. David Lapoujade; trans. Michael Taormina (Los Angeles/New York: Semiotext(e), 2004), pp. 22–31; p. 30.

3. Gilles Deleuze, "Bergson's Conception of Difference," in *The New Bergson*, ed. John Mullarkey (Manchester: Manchester University Press, 2000), pp. 42–65; p. 62. This essay is Deleuze's second on Bergson; it, too, now appears in the collection of essays by Deleuze, *Desert Islands*, pp. 32–51.

4. Gilles Deleuze and Félix Guattari, *A Thousand Plateaus: Capitalism and Schizophrenia*, trans. Brian Massumi (Minneapolis: University of Minnesota Press, 1987), p. 412.

5. Henri Bergson, "The Possible and the Real," in *La pensée et le mouvant* (1934), rather unhappily translated as Henri Bergson, *The Creative Mind*, trans. Mabelle L. Andison (New York: Greenwood, 1968), pp. 103–104.

6. Henri Bergson, *The Two Sources of Morality and Religion* (1932), trans. R. Ashley Audra and C. Brereton (Notre Dame: University of Notre Dame Press, 1977).

7. Gilles Deleuze, *Difference and Repetition* (1969), trans. Paul Patton (New York: Columbia University Press, 1994), p. 136.

8. Deleuze, *Cinema* 1, p. 49.

9. Deleuze, *Cinema* 1, pp. 29–33.

10. Ibid.

11. Deleuze, *Cinema* 1, p. 196. Realism thus described distinguishes itself, according to Deleuze, from expressionism and naturalism precisely by virtue of its treatment of places and affects.

12. An example of this is the presence of the community in the films of Ford and Capra; see Deleuze, *Cinema* 1, p. 202.

13. Ibid.

14. It is in this context that the otherwise astonishing remark has to be understood, in which Deleuze affirms that classic cinema, at its best moments, has always been *catholic* and *revolutionary*. Gilles Deleuze, *Cinema 2: The Time-Image* (1985), trans. Hugh Tomlinson and Robert Galeta (Minneapolis: University of Minnesota Press, 1989), p. 222.

15. Deleuze, *Cinema* 1, p. 206.

16. Stanley Cavell, *The World Viewed: Reflections on the Ontology of Film* (New York: Viking, 1971), pp. 62–63.

17. Deleuze, *Cinema* 2, p. 171.

18. Deleuze, *Cinema* 2, pp. 171–173.

19. Gilles Deleuze and Félix Guattari, *What is Philosophy?* (1991), trans. Hugh Tomlinson and Graham Burchell (New York: Columbia University Press, 1994), pp. 74–75.

20. Gilles Deleuze, "Literature and Life," in Gilles Deleuze, *Essays Critical and Clinical*, trans. Daniel W. Smith and Michael A. Greco (Minneapolis: University of Minnesota Press, 1997), p. 4.

21. Bergson, *The Two Sources of Morality and Religion*, p. 41ff.

A PRECURSOR:
LIMITING THE FUTURE, AFFIRMING PARTICULARITY
Andrew Benjamin

1. I have analysed the relationship between the "new" and "repetition" while trying to develop what could best be described as ontology of relations in my *The Plural Event* (London: Routledge, 1993). While it differs in a number of important aspects, the development of a relational ontology is also evident in Jean-Luc Nancy. See, in particular, Jean-Luc Nancy, *Etre singulier pluriel* (Paris: Editions Galilée, 1996).

2. François-René de Chateaubriand, *Itinéraire de Paris à Jerusalem* (Paris: Gallimard, 2005), pp. 275–276. (Author's translation.)

3. All references are to Nathalie Sarraute, *Oeuvres Complètes* (OC) (Paris: Editions Gallimard, 1996).

4. The text in question is "Flaubert le précurseur," in Sarraute, OC, pp. 1624–1640.

5. Flaubert, cited in Sarraute, OC, p. 1624. (Author's translation.)

6. See in this regard the discussion of Mallarmé in Maurice Blanchot, *L'espace littéraire* (Paris: Gallimard, 1955), pp. 33–48.

7. While it has been subjected to a number of different interpretations, the letter written by Bataille to Kojève still remains central to the development of a theory of production that takes a version of negativity as central. (The letter is available in Georges Bataille, *Choix de letters 1917–1962* [Paris: Gallimard, 1997], pp. 131–136.) I have developed this aspect of Bataille's work in the context of architecture in Andrew Benjamin, *Architectural Philosophy* (London: Continuum, 2002). See, in particular, Chapters 1 and 2.

8. Here is the distinction between the nothing as a device for the ordering of a text's presence, and thus the nothing as a stylistic device, and a productive negativity. The latter sense of the nothing will have an important though implicit presence in the treatment of a formulation of Sarraute's in her *L'usage de la parole* (Paris: Gallimard, 1980). The other is also evident in Sarraute's writings. See, for example, her extraordinary reflection on writing for radio: "Le Gant retourné," in Sarraute, OC, pp. 1707–1713, a reflection in which the central element centers on "that which is called 'nothing'" (*ce qui s'appelle 'rien'*), p. 1710.

9. Sarraute, OC, p. 960.

10. While there are a number of the Platonic dialogues through which a concern with the beautiful could be traced, one of the most compelling is Diotima's speech in the *Symposium*. In summing up both her position—a position that functions as a summation of the entire dialogue itself—Diotima argues in the passage 210 e3–211 b5 that a vision of the beautiful is the final object, and thus demands a series of moves whose culmination is that vision. Moreover, once viewed, then it will be clear that the beautiful is not present

in the guise of a face or of hands or any other portion of the body, nor as a particular description nor as a piece of knowledge, nor as existing somewhere in another substance, such as an animal or the earth or the sky or any other thing; but existing ever in singularity of form independent by itself, while all the multitude of beautiful things partake of it in such wise that, though all of them are coming to be and perishing, it grows neither greater or less and is affected by nothing. (Plato, *Lysis, Symposium, Gorgias*, vol. 3, trans. W.R.M. Lamb, Loeb Classical Library [Cambridge, Mass: Harvard University Press, 1953])

11. The most significant interpretation of Dürer's engravings is still Erwin Panofsky's. See Erwin Panofsky, *The Life and Art of Albrecht Dürer* (Princeton, N.J.: Princeton University Press, 1995), pp. 156–171.

12. I have developed a more detailed engagement with this conception of the present in Andrew Benjamin, *Present Hope* (London: Routledge, 1997).

13. It is of course precisely this relation that is captured in the Platonic formulation cited above when it is argued that the "multitude of beautiful things partake" in the independent form of beauty. "Partaking" is the identity-determining relation between universal and particular.

14. While in this context particularity pertains to works of art, the overall position is part of what could be described as metaphysics of particularity. The intention is that this position has a more general extension. I have tried to develop the more general argument in Andrew Benjamin, "Perception, Judgment and Individuation: Towards a Metaphysics of Particularity," *International Journal of Philosophical Studies* Vol. 15, No. 3, 481–501.

VISUAL *PARRHESIA*?
FOUCAULT AND THE TRUTH OF THE GAZE
Martin Jay

1. Michel Foucault, "The Concern for Truth," in *Politics, Philosophy, Culture: Interviews and Other Writings, 1977–1984*, ed. Lawrence D. Kritzman (New York: Routledge, 1990), p. 267.

2. Hubert Damisch, *Huit theses pour (ou contre?) une sémiologie de la peinture* (Paris, 1978), and Jacques Derrida, *The Truth in Painting*, trans. Geoff Bennington and Ian McLeod (Chicago: University of Chicago Press, 1987).

3. Martin Jay, *Downcast Eyes: The Denigration of Vision in Twentieth-Century French Thought* (Berkeley: University of California Press, 1993).

4. John Rajchman, "Foucault's Art of Seeing," *October* 44 (Spring, 1988).

5. David Michael Levin, "Keeping Foucault and Derrida in Sight: Panopticism and the Politics of Subversion," in *Sites of Vision: The Discursive Construction of Sight in the History of Philosophy*, ed. David Michael Levin (Cambridge, Mass.: MIT Press, 1997); Thomas R. Flynn, "The Eclipse of Vision?" in *Sartre, Foucault, and Historical Reason, Volume 2: A Poststructuralist Mapping*

of History (Chicago: University of Chicago Press, 2005); and Gary Shapiro, *Archaeologies of Vision: Foucault and Nietzsche on Seeing and Saying* (Chicago: University of Chicago Press, 2003).

6. Flynn, "The Eclipse of Vision," p. 85.
7. Shapiro, *Archaeologies of Vision*, p. 10.
8. Ibid., p. 294.
9. Jay, *Downcast Eyes*, p. 414.
10. Michel Foucault, "History of Systems of Thought," in *Language, Counter-Memory, Practice: Selected Essays and Interviews*, ed. Donald F. Bouchard, trans. Donald F. Bouchard and Sherry Simon (Ithaca, N.Y.: Cornell University Press, 1977), p. 202.
11. Michel Foucault, "A Preface to Transgression," in *Language, Counter-Memory, Practice*, p. 45.
12. Ibid., p. 41.
13. Michel Foucault, "Truth and Power," in *Power/Knowledge: Selected Interviews and Other Writings, 1972–1977*, ed. Colin Gordon (New York: Pantheon, 1980), p. 118.
14. Michel Foucault, "Afterword" to Hubert L. Dreyfus and Paul Rabinow, *Michel Foucault: Beyond Structuralism and Hermeneutics*, 2nd ed. (Chicago: University of Chicago Press, 1983), p. 252.
15. The motto was based on following lines from Horace: "Nullius addictus iurare in verba magistri, quo me cumque rapit tempestas, deferor hospes." (My words are not owned by any master, where the winds [of reason] lead me, there I find home.) (*Horace, Epistles*, I.i, 14–15) [translator unknown].
16. Michel Foucault, *Fearless Speech*, ed. Joseph Pearson (Los Angeles: Semiotext[e], 2001).
17. Ibid., p. 12.
18. Ibid., p. 19.
19. Foucault, *The Use of Pleasure*, vol. 2 of *The History of Sexuality*, trans. Robert Hurley (New York: Random House, 1985); *The Care of the Self*, vol. 3 of *The History of Sexuality*, trans. Robert Hurley (New York: Vintage, 1988).
20. Foucault, *Fearless Speech*, p. 170.
21. Michel Foucault, "Structuralism and Poststructuralism," in *Aesthetics, Method, and Epistemology*, ed. James D. Faubion, vol. 2 of *Essential Works of Foucault, 1954–1984*, ed. Paul Rabinow (New York: New Press, 1999), p. 444.
22. Didier Eribon, *Michel Foucault*, trans. Betsy Wing (Cambridge, Mass.: Harvard University Press, 1991), p. 254.
23. Foucault, *Fearless Speech*, p. 14.
24. Michel Foucault, *The Birth of the Clinic: An Archaeology of Medical Perception*, trans. A.M. Sheridan (London: Tavistock, 1976), p. xiii.

25. Steven Shapin, *A Social History of Truth: Civility and Science in Seventeenth-Century England* (Chicago: University of Chicago Press, 1994).
26. Foucault, *The Birth of the Clinic*, p. 39.
27. Ibid., p. 120.
28. Gilles Deleuze, *Foucault*, trans. Sean Hand (Minneapolis: University of Minnesota Press, 1988), pp. 49–50.
29. Shapiro, *Archaeologies of Vision*, p. 250.
30. Deleuze, *Foucault*, p. 82.
31. Ibid., p. 121.
32. Michel de Certeau, "Micro-techniques and Panoptic Discourse: A Quid Pro Quo," *Humanities in Society*, 5:3–4 (Summer/Fall, 1982), p. 264.
33. Shapiro, *Archaeologies of Vision*, p. 310.
34. Ibid., p. 312.
35. Martin Jay, "Scopic Regimes of Modernity," in *Force Fields: Between Intellectual History and Cultural Critique* (New York: Routledge, 1993).
36. Michel Foucault, *This Is Not a Pipe*, trans. James Harkness (Berkeley: University of California Press, 1982), p. 20.
37. Ibid., p. 43.
38. Ibid., p. 44.
39. Shapiro, *Archaeologies of Vision*, p. 369.
40. Ibid., p. 247.

ARTICULATION AND THE LIMITS OF METAPHOR
Ernesto Laclau

1. Gérard Genette, "Métonymie chez Proust," in Gérard Genette, *Figures III* (Paris: Editions du Seuil, 1972), pp. 41–63.
2. Stephen Ullmann, *Style in the French Novel* (Cambridge: Cambridge University Press, 1957).
3. All notes and translations in brackets inserted by copyeditor for clarification.
4. Genette, "Métonymie chez Proust," p. 42. (Unless otherwise noted, all translations are by the author.)
5. Ibid., p. 45.
6. Ibid., p. 60.
7. Ibid., p. 56.
8. Ibid.
9. Ibid., p. 63.
10. Marcel Proust, *A la recherche du temps perdu*, vol. 1 (Paris: Gallimard, 1992), p. 804.
11. Translation by Kalliopi Nikolopoulou.
12. Genette, "Métonymie chez Proust," p. 51, n. 5.

13. Ibid., p. 61.
14. Ibid., p. 55.
15. Ibid., p. 58.
16. Roman Jakobson, "Two Aspects of Language and Two Types of Aphasic Disturbances," in Morris Halle and Roman Jakobson, *Fundamentals of Language* ('s-Gravenhage: Mouton, 1956).
17. Ibid., p. 69.
18. Ibid., pp. 90–91.
19. Ibid., p. 91.
20. Ibid., p. 93.
21. Ferdinand de Saussure, *Cours de linguistique générale* (Paris: Payot, 1980), p. 174.
22. Ibid.
23. Ernesto Laclau, "The Politics of Rhetoric," in *Material Events: Paul de Man and the Afterlife of Theory*, ed. Tom Cohen, J. Hillis Miller, Andrzej Warminski, and Barbara Cohen (Minneapolis: University of Minnesota Press, 2001), pp. 229–253.
24. See "Why do Empty Signifiers Matter to Politics?" in *Emancipation(s)* (London: Verso, 1996) and Chapter 4 in *On Populist Reason* (London: Verso, 2005).
25. Joan Copjec, "Sex and the Euthanasia of Reason," in *Read My Desire* (Cambridge, Mass.: MIT Press, 1995), pp. 205–206.
26. Karl Marx, *A Contribution to the Critique of Political Economy* (London, 1971), p. 24.
27. Georges Sorel, *Reflexions sur la violence* (Paris: Seuil, 1990), p. 21.
28. Ibid., p. 25.
29. Ibid., pp. 29–30.

ANSWERING FOR SENSE
Jean-Luc Nancy

1. Emmanuel Loi, *D'Ordinaire* (Romainville: Al Dante, 2000), p. 7. This book is composed of the letters and diaries of a prisoner. [Author's note]
2. Philippe Lacoue-Labarthe, *Phrase* (Paris: Christian Bourgois, 2000).
3. Homer, *The Iliad of Homer*, trans. Richmond Lattimore (Chicago/London: The University of Chicago Press, 1951).
4. The "double-sense" of the French *"entente"* that Nancy refers to is that while the term means "understanding" and "agreement," it is also related to *"entendre,"* the French verb for "to hear." [Translator's note]
5. Nancy writes, *"bouche/oreille,"* which literally means "mouth/ear," but he is here playing with the French expression *"de bouche à oreille,"* which translates in English as "by word of mouth." [Translator's note]

6. Cf. Jean-Luc Nancy, "Sharing Voices," in *Transforming the Hermeneutic Context: From Nietzsche to Nancy*, ed. Gayle L. Ormiston and Alan D. Schrift (Albany: State University of New York Press, 1990), pp. 211–260.

7. Arthur Rimbaud, *A Season in Hell*, in *A Season in Hell and The Drunken Boat*, trans. Louise Varese (New York: New Directions, 1961). [Translator's translation]

"HUMAN" IN THE AGE OF DISPOSABLE PEOPLE: THE AMBIGUOUS
IMPORT OF KINSHIP AND EDUCATION IN *BLIND SHAFT*
Rey Chow

1. Étienne Balibar, *Politics and the Other Scene*, trans. Christine Jones, James Swenson, Chris Turner (New York/London: Verso, 2002), p. 142; emphases in the original.

2. Martin Heidegger, "Letter on Humanism," in *Basic Writings from Being and Time (1927) to The Task of Thinking (1964)*, revised and expanded, ed. and intro. David Farrell Krell (New York: HarperCollins, 1977, 1993), pp. 217–265.

3. Ibid., p. 243.
4. Ibid., p. 225.
5. Ibid., p. 235.
6. Ibid., p. 242.
7. Ibid., p. 234.

8. See Liu Qingbang, "Shen mu," in *Buding jia gei shui* (Changchun: Shidai wenyi chubanshe, 2001), pp. 359–448. In an interview conducted in April 2003, Li Yang mentions that this story was given the Lao She Prize, the highest literary award in China. See Stephen Teo, "'There Is No Sixth Generation!' Director Li Yang on *Blind Shaft* and His Place in Chinese Cinema," *Senses of Cinema* (http://www.sensesofcinema.com/contents/03/27/li_yang.html): 4.

9. See Guan Jingsong, "Jing mang, xin bu mang: zhuanfang dianying *Mang Jing* daoyan Li Yang," *Cream* 14 (November 2003): 114–115. In this interview (conducted at the end of September 2003, when *Blind Shaft* was shown in Hong Kong for the second time that year), Li indicates that because of the film, which was initially banned, he has been prohibited by the Chinese authorities from all film, television, and commercial-making activities. He also mentions his experience of being surrounded and threatened by gun-carrying mine owners and policemen when he visited a coal mine. Reportedly, however, in late 2003 the Chinese Film Bureau "suddenly approved what had previously been labeled an 'illegal film' for release and distribution"—apparently, by removing all explicit sex scenes and the subversive version of the song "Shehuizhuyi hao" ("Socialism Is Good"). For this update, see Michael Berry, *Speaking in Images: Interviews*

with *Contemporary Chinese Filmmakers* (New York: Columbia University Press, 2005), pp. 210, 551; see also the chapter "Li Yang: The Future of Chinese Cinema?," pp. 209–232. Berry's interviews with Li Yang were conducted in May and November 2003.

10. Krell, *Martin Heidegger, Basic Writings*, p. 216; emphasis in the original.

11. This is presented as a fact rather than a suspicion in the original narrative. Li Yang explains the alteration as follows: "In the film I left it a bit hazy. Maybe Fengming is his [the first victim's] son, and maybe he is not. In the novel Liu Qingbang makes it clear that they are indeed father and son, but with a population of 1.3 billion people in China, I thought that was a bit too much of a coincidence. So in the film, I intentionally left this detail open-ended." Berry, *Speaking in Images*, p. 217.

12. *Blind Shaft*, DVD (Hong Kong: Star Treasure Holdings Ltd, 2003), back cover; translation from the Chinese mine.

13. See, for instance, details given in the investigative reports in *Zhonghua tansuo*, November 13, 2004, pp. 2, 4. A report in English sums it up this way: "Two forces driving Chinese industrial development—cheap, poorly protected labor and rapid, some say even reckless, growth—fall especially heavily on China's coal mines. They are often small, poorly equipped and poorly ventilated, but owners have been profiting from China's strong demand for energy ... Work safety officials acknowledge that the hunger for profit and tax revenues among mine owners and local governments often outweighs safety concerns." Chris Buckley, "166 Still Missing from China Mine Blast," *The New York Times*, November 29, 2004, p. A8.

14. These versions, translated from the Chinese, are as they appear in the English subtitles of the film, with my slight modifications. According to Li Yang, he and his crew found the lyrics on the Internet; see Berry, *Speaking in Images*, p. 226. His point is that Tang and Song, like most people in China who received a socialist education, have been left behind by China's new social situation.

15. Ban Wang, "Documentary as Haunting of the Real: The Logic of Capital in *Blind Shaft*," *Asian Cinema* (Spring/Summer 2005): 10.

16. Li Yang's account of his cinematic language is noteworthy: "I intentionally kept the camera at eye level throughout the shoot, so there are hardly any shots above what would be a normal person's perspective. By doing away with all high and low shots, I wanted to strip the film down to the simplest possible cinematic language. I didn't rely on any bird's-eye view shots or experiment with any other shooting angles. The audience is forced to see the film as if they are watching a documentary." The only exceptions, he emphasizes, are the opening scene and the closing shot. Berry, *Speaking in Images*, p. 224.

17. See Liu Qingbang, "Shen mu," pp. 430–431.

18. Heidegger, *The Question Concerning Technology and Other Essays*, trans. and with an intro. William Lovitt (New York: Harper Colophon, 1977), p. 16.

19. There are copious references to kin relations in the original narrative.
20. Teo, "'There Is No Sixth Generation!'" pp. 7–8; emphases mine.
21. Li explains: "When I asked coal miners about what kept them going regardless of the dangers of working in the mines, the response I got over and over was that they needed to send their kids to school. They would often tell me that the only way their situation can change is by making sure their children have a good education. It is this belief that often leads them to risk their lives" (Berry, *Speaking in Images*, p. 222).
22. Teo, "'There Is No Sixth Generation!'", p. 9.
23. Balibar, *Politics and the Other Scene*, p. 144; emphases in the original.

THE FOREIGN, THE UNCANNY, AND THE FOREIGNER: CONCEPTS OF THE SELF
AND THE OTHER IN PSYCHOANALYSIS AND CONTEMPORARY PHILOSOPHY
Rudi Visker

1. Michel Foucault, *The Order of Things: An Archaeology of the Human Sciences* (London: Tavistock, 1977).
2. For more on the role of author and on what I call, with Althusser, the "religious myth of reading," see Rudi Visker, "Philosophy and Pluralism," *Philosophy Today* 48:2 (2004): 115–127.
3. Foucault, *The Order of Things*, pp. 299, 262.
4. Julia Kristeva, *Strangers to Ourselves* (New York: Harvester Wheatsheaf, 1991), p. 192. (Corrected translation.)
5. Ibid.
6. Ibid.
7. Sigmund Freud, "The Uncanny" (1919), in *On Creativity and the Unconscious. Papers on the Psychology of Art, Literature, Love, Religion* (New York: Harper and Row, 1958), pp. 122–161; p. 153.
8. Ibid., p. 129.
9. Ibid., p. 152.
10. Emmanuel Levinas, *Otherwise Than Being: or Beyond Essence*, trans. Alphonso Lingis (Dordrecht: Kluwer, 1991).
11. Ibid., chap. 3, n. 3.
12. Emmanuel Levinas, *Basic Philosophical Writings* (Bloomington: Indiana University Press, 1996), p. 57.
13. For an analysis of the place of these notions in Levinas, see Rudi Visker, "No Privacy? Levinas' Intrigue of the Infinite," in *Truth and Singularity. Taking Foucault into Phenomenology* (Phaenomenologica 155) (Dordrecht: Kluwer, 1999), pp. 235–273.
14. Sigmund Freud, *Civilization and its Discontents* (1930), in *Civilization, Society and Religion (The Pelican Freud Library*, vol. 12*)* (Harmondsworth: Penguin Books, 1985), pp. 243–340, p. 337.
15. Ibid., p. 337.

16. Ibid., p. 302.
17. Ibid., p. 301, n. 1.
18. Ibid., p. 300.
19. Ibid., p. 337.
20. A. Vergote, "Philosophy's Interest in Psychoanalysis," *Philosophy Today* 2 (1958): 253–273, 269.
21. Ibid., p. 266.
22. Freud, *Civilization and its Discontents*, p. 305.
23. Interestingly, Michael Ignatieff's analysis of the Serbo-Croatian case rests on the same moralizing conclusions with regard to Freud's findings as the ones we saw at work in Kristeva: "If intolerance and narcissism are connected, one immediate and practical conclusion might be this: We are likely to be more tolerant toward other identities only if we learn to like our own a little less. . . . The root of intolerance lies in our tendency to overvalue our identities" (Michael Ignatieff, *The Warrior's Honor. Ethnic War and the Modern Conscience* [New York: Henry Holt and Company, 1998], p. 62). Ignatieff's next sentence ("by overvalue, I mean that we insist that we have nothing in common, nothing to share") seems to presuppose that if we would realize what we have in common we would be more tolerant. As we will shortly see, it is on this precise point that Lacan's conception of narcissism becomes critically important.
24. Freud, *Civilization and its Discontents*, p. 305.
25. A similar movement is presupposed whenever (as, for example, in Ignatieff's case) we are called upon to open ourselves for the Other (that is, to give up our initial being closed up in ourselves).
26. Jacques Lacan, "The Mirror Stage as Formative of the Function of the I," in *Écrits. A Selection* (London: Routledge, 1989), pp. 1–7.
27. P. Julien, *Le retour à Freud de Jacques Lacan* (Paris: E.P.E.L., 1990), pp. 43–51.
28. For an analysis of racism along these (Lacanian) lines, see Daniel Sibony, *Le "racisme," ou, la haine identitaire* (Paris: Christian Bourgois, 1997).
29. Bernard Williams, "Relativism and Reflection," in *Ethics and the Limits of Philosophy* (Cambridge, Mass.: Harvard University Press, 1985), pp. 156–173.
30. Sigmund Freud, "Group Psychology and the Analysis of the Ego" (1921), in *Civilization, Society and Religion*, pp. 91–340, p. 131.
31. Sigmund Freud, "The Taboo of Virginity (Contributions to the Psychology of Love)" (1918), in *On Creativity and the Unconscious: Papers on the Psychology of Art, Literature, Love, Religion*, selected with introduction and annotations by Benjamin Nelson (New York: Harper and Row, 1958), pp. 187–205; p. 190.
32. Ibid., p. 187.

33. Sigmund Freud, *Moses and Monotheism: Three Essays* (1939), in *The Origins of Religion* (*The Pelican Freud Library*, vol. 13) (Harmondsworth: Penguin Books, 1985), pp. 237–386, p. 334.

34. Ibid., p. 335.

35. Ibid., p. 336.

36. In *The Inhuman Condition: Looking for Difference After Levinas and Heidegger* (Phaenomenologica 175) (Dordrecht: Kluwer, 2004), I developed systematically the (mè-ontological) view on difference that I am using here.

37. C. Lefort, *Essais sur le politique (XIXe–XXe siècles)* (Paris: Seuil, 1986), p. 256ff.

38. Rudi Visker, *The Inhuman Condition*, pp. 255–299.

39. Bernhard Schlink's wonderful novella, "Die Beschneidung" ("The Circumcision") could be read as one long illustration of the point I am making here. See Bernhard Schlink, *Liebesfluchten* (Zürich: Diogenes Verlag, 2000), translated as *Flights of Love* (London: Phoenix, 2002).

40. Hannah Arendt, *The Human Condition* (Chicago: University of Chicago Press, 1958), p. 50.

AN IMPOSSIBLE EMBRACE: QUEERNESS, FUTURITY, AND THE DEATH DRIVE
Tim Dean

1. Michel Foucault, "Nietzsche, Genealogy, History," in *The Essential Works of Foucault, 1954–1984*, vol. 2: *Aesthetics, Method, and Epistemology*, ed. James D. Faubion (New York: New Press, 1998), pp. 369–391; p. 373.

2. Judith Halberstam, *In a Queer Time and Place: Transgender Bodies, Subcultural Lives* (New York: New York University Press, 2005), p. 2.

3. Leo Bersani, "Is the Rectum a Grave?" in *AIDS: Cultural Analysis/Cultural Activism*, ed. Douglas Crimp (Cambridge, Mass.: MIT Press, 1988), pp. 197–222.

4. Ibid., p. 209.

5. Ibid., p. 212.

6. Bersani launches this argument in Chapter 2 of *The Freudian Body: Psychoanalysis and Art* (New York: Columbia University Press, 1986), and develops it with respect to gay sexuality in "Is the Rectum a Grave?" Pivotal to his argument is Laplanche's original reading of Freud's *Three Essays on the Theory of Sexuality* (in *The Standard Edition of the Complete Psychological Works of Sigmund Freud*, ed. and trans. James Strachey [London: Hogarth, 1953–1974], vol. 7, pp. 123–243), in Jean Laplanche, *Life and Death in Psychoanalysis*, trans. Jeffrey Mehlman (Baltimore: Johns Hopkins University Press, 1976).

7. Laplanche, *Life and Death in Psychoanalysis*, p. 124.

8. Leo Bersani, *Homos* (Cambridge, Mass.: Harvard University Press, 1995), p. 99.

9. Lee Edelman, *No Future: Queer Theory and the Death Drive* (Durham, N.C.: Duke University Press, 2004).

10. Ibid., p. 14.

11. Ibid., p. 16. Edelman's approach mirrors that of right-wing pundit Stanley Kurtz, who argues, in "Zombie Killers," *National Review Online* (www.nationalreview.com), May 25, 2006, that the conservative critique of same-sex marriage should listen to, and even be instructed by, left-wing sociologists and "radical 'queer theorists,'" since these enemies readily acknowledge the extent to which full marriage access undermines traditional marriage. The principal difference between the two sides of the debate, in Kurtz's view, is that while conservatives lament this undermining, "radical 'queer theorists'" celebrate it. Of course, Kurtz's thesis depends on his ignoring those queer theorists who argue contrariwise that, thanks to its normalizing effects, same-sex marriage undermines not traditional marriage but radical queer politics. See Michael Warner, *The Trouble with Normal: Sex, Politics, and the Ethics of Queer Life* (New York: Free Press, 1999).

12. Edelman, *No Future*, p. 22.

13. In Tim Dean, "Art as Symptom: Žižek and the Ethics of Psychoanalytic Criticism," *Diacritics* 32:2 (2002): 21–41, I discuss further this unintended consequence of Žižek's work.

14. Edelman, *No Future*, p. 6.

15. Quoted in Russell Shorto, "Contra-Contraception," *New York Times Magazine*, May 7, 2006, p. 14.

16. Edelman's characterization of queerness or "*sinthom*osexuality" as structurally antisocial replays his earlier account of "homographesis": in his book of that title Edelman aligned homosexuality with writing as understood deconstructively in order to make queer sexuality constitutively disruptive of the order of representation as such. See Lee Edelman, *Homographesis: Essays in Gay Literary and Cultural Theory* (New York: Routledge, 1994). Thus in *No Future* and *Homographesis*, the neologisms *sinthom*osexuality and homographesis perform virtually identical rhetorical tasks.

17. Edelman, *No Future*, p. 11.

18. See Steven Bruhm and Natasha Hurley, eds., *Curiouser: On the Queerness of Children* (Minneapolis: University of Minnesota Press, 2004).

19. Edelman, *No Future*, p. 9.

20. Sigmund Freud, "Instincts and Their Vicissitudes," in *The Standard Edition of the Complete Psychological Works of Sigmund Freud*, ed. and trans. James Strachey (London: Hogarth, 1953–1974), vol. 14, pp. 109–140.

21. Jacques Lacan, "On Freud's 'Trieb' and the Psychoanalyst's Desire," in *Écrits: The First Complete Edition in English*, trans. Bruce Fink (New York: Norton, 2006), pp. 722–725; p. 722.

22. Jacques Lacan, "Position of the Unconscious," in *Écrits*, pp. 703–721; p. 719.

23. Jacques Lacan, *The Other Side of Psychoanalysis (The Seminar of Jacques Lacan: Book XVII)*, ed. Jacques-Alain Miller, trans. Russell Grigg (New York: Norton, 2007), pp. 45–46.

24. Although there is doubtless more to be said about how melodrama—a genre that maximizes heterosexual pathos—is beloved by certain gay men, that discussion falls outside my purview here.

25. Lacan offered his seminar in 1959–60, Laplanche in 1975–77. See Jacques Lacan, *The Ethics of Psychoanalysis: 1959–1960 (The Seminar of Jacques Lacan: Book VII)*, ed. Jacques-Alain Miller, trans. Dennis Porter (New York: Norton, 1992); Jean Laplanche, *Problématiques III: La sublimation* (Paris: Presses Universitaires de France, 1980), and Jean Laplanche, "To Situate Sublimation," trans. Richard Miller, *October* 28 (1984): 7–26.

26. Lacan, *Ethics of Psychoanalysis*, pp. 212–213.

27. In *Imagine There's No Woman: Ethics and Sublimation* (Cambridge, Mass.: MIT Press, 2002), Joan Copjec describes this paradoxical mechanism very nicely:

> Although one of the effects of the death drive may be the free choice of death, this is by no means the drive's only or even assured result. . . . The full paradox of the death drive, then, is this: while the *aim* (*Ziel*) of the drive is death, *the proper and positive activity* of the drive is to inhibit the attainment of its aim; the drive, *as such*, is *zielgehemmt*, that is, it is inhibited as to its aim, or sublimated, "the satisfaction of the drive through the inhibition of its aim" being the very definition of sublimation. Contrary to the vulgar understanding of it, then, sublimation is not something that happens to the drive under special circumstances; it is the proper destiny of the drive. (p. 30; emphasis in original)

28. Freud, "Instincts," pp. 121–122.

29. Sigmund Freud, "The Unconscious," in *Standard Edition*, vol. 14, pp. 159–204; p. 177.

30. Freud, "Instincts," pp. 125–126.

31. In her commentary on Lacan's theory of the drive, Marie-Hélène Brousse explains, "Lacan says that the drive is always partial, meaning that it involves the erogenous zones which are never linked with objects, and are always partial. . . . [T]hese partial objects are not to be considered as a set or totality. You can never construct a whole with these parts" (Marie-Hélène Brousse, "The Drive (II)," in *Reading Seminar XI: Lacan's Four Fundamental Concepts of Psychoanalysis*, ed. Richard Feldstein, Bruce Fink, and Maire Jaanus [Albany: State University of New York Press, 1995], pp. 109–117, p. 113).

32. Lacan, "Position of the Unconscious," p. 720.

33. De Lauretis borrows the term "passionate fiction" from Leo Bersani and Ulysse Dutoit's *The Forms of Violence: Narrative in Assyrian Art and Modern Culture* (New York: Schocken, 1985) and develops it, conceptually and rhetorically, in her reading of Freud in Teresa de Lauretis, *The Practice of Love: Lesbian Sexuality and Perverse Desire* (Bloomington: Indiana University Press, 1994).

34. Bersani, "Is the Rectum a Grave?", p. 222.

35. Gilles Deleuze and Félix Guattari, *Anti-Oedipus: Capitalism and Schizophrenia*, trans. Robert Hurley, Mark Seem, and Helen R. Lane (Minneapolis: University of Minnesota Press, 1983).

36. Deleuze and Guattari discuss creative involution in Gilles Deleuze and Félix Guattari, *A Thousand Plateaus: Capitalism and Schizophrenia*, trans. Brian Massumi (Minneapolis: University of Minnesota Press, 1987), p. 238, though the preoccupation with becoming dates from much earlier works (such as Gilles Deleuze's *Nietzsche and Philosophy*, trans. Hugh Tomlinson [New York: Columbia University Press, 1983]). For recent critical engagement with this idea, see Elizabeth Grosz, ed., *Becomings: Explorations in Time, Memory, and Futures* (Ithaca, N.Y.: Cornell University Press, 1999). On the theme of involution, see Mikko Tuhkanen, "Ontology and Involution," *Diacritics* 35:3 (Fall 2005): 20–45.

37. Paola Marrati, "Life and Event: Deleuze on Newness," in *A Time for the Humanities: Futurity and the Limits of Autonomy*, ed. James J. Bono, Tim Dean, and Ewa Plonowska Ziarek (New York: Fordham University Press, 2008), pp. 17–28, p. 21.

38. See Elizabeth Grosz, *The Nick of Time: Politics, Evolution, and the Untimely* (Durham, N.C.: Duke University Press, 2004) and, idem, *Time Travels: Feminism, Nature, Power* (Durham, N.C.: Duke University Press, 2005); for an insightful discussion of Grosz's project, see Tuhkanen, "Ontology and Involution."

39. Guy Hocquenghem, *Homosexual Desire*, trans. Daniella Dangoor (Durham, N.C.: Duke University Press, 1993).

40. Ibid., p. 150.

41. Ibid., p. 137.

42. Ibid., p. 150.

43. In fact, Bersani equivocates on this issue, arguing in *The Freudian Body* that "masochism serves life" (p. 39), while insisting in *Forms of Being* that, "To approach sex psychoanalytically was to discover sexuality as a massively destructive drive" (Leo Bersani and Ulysse Dutoit, *Forms of Being: Cinema, Aesthetics, Subjectivity*, [London: British Film Institute, 2004], p. 128). It may be a question here of acknowledging the extent to which

sexuality, understood psychoanalytically, serves both life *and* death, yet neither one consistently or exclusively.

44. Edelman, *No Future*, p. 27.

45. I allude here, of course, to the cautionary axiom in Foucault's introductory volume of *The History of Sexuality*: "We must not think that by saying yes to sex, one says no to power" (Michel Foucault, *The History of Sexuality*, vol. 1: *An Introduction*, trans. Robert Hurley [New York: Random House, 1978], p. 157).

46. Edelman, *No Future*, p. 29.

47. For a persuasive critique of Edelman's—and much of queer theory's—emphasis on negativity, see Michael Snediker's very interesting account of queer optimism in his "Queer Optimism," *Postmodern Culture* 16:3 (May 2006), and his book of the same title, forthcoming from University of Minnesota Press.

48. Foucault, *History of Sexuality*, p. 93.

49. See Foucault's comments in Michel Foucault, "The Subject and Power," in *The Essential Works of Foucault, 1954–1984*, vol. 3: *Power*, ed. James D. Faubion (New York: New Press, 2000), pp. 326–348:

> When one defines the exercise of power as a mode of action upon the actions of others . . . one includes an important element: freedom. Power is exercised only over free subjects, and only insofar as they are "free." By this we mean individual or collective subjects who are faced with a field of possibilities in which several kinds of conduct, several ways of reacting and modes of behavior are available. Where the determining factors are exhaustive, there is no relationship of power. . . . Consequently, there is not a face-to-face confrontation of power and freedom as mutually exclusive facts (freedom disappearing everywhere power is exercised) but a much more complicated interplay. (pp. 341–342)

50. Foucault, *History of Sexuality*, pp. 11; 34; 65, respectively. In the original, "*techniques polymorphes du pouvoir*" (p. 20), "*d'une incitation . . . polymorphe aux discours*" (p. 47), and "*d'un pouvoir causal inépuisable et polymorphe*" (p. 88). See Michel Foucault, *Histoire de la sexualité 1: La volonté de savoir* (Paris: Gallimard, 1976).

51. Deleuze, *Nietzsche and Philosophy*, p. 40.

52. Ibid., p. 40.

53. For a powerful account of the unexpected compatibility between Foucault's theory of power and Freud's theory of drive—an account that inspires the present one, though our emphases differ—see Teresa de Lauretis, "The Stubborn Drive," *Critical Inquiry* 24:4 (1998): 851–877.

54. Foucault, "Nietzsche, Genealogy, History," p. 373.

55. Michel Foucault, "Friendship as a Way of Life," in *The Essential Works of Foucault, 1954–1984*, vol. 1: *Ethics: Subjectivity and Truth*, ed. Paul Rabinow (New York: New Press, 1997), pp. 135–140; p. 136. The most enlightening discussion of these and similar comments in Foucault's late work may be found in Bersani's *Homos* and Graham L. Hammill's "Are We Being Homosexual Yet?" *Umbr(a): A Journal of the Unconscious*, Special issue on "Sameness," ed. Mikko Tuhkanen (2002): 71–85.

LUCE IRIGARAY AND THE QUESTION OF CRITIQUE
Elizabeth Weed

1. Joan Copjec, *Read My Desire: Lacan Against the Historicists* (Cambridge, Mass.: MIT Press, 1995).
2. Ibid., p. 6.
3. Ibid., pp. 11–12.
4. See especially Chapter 8, "Sex and the Euthanasia of Reason."
5. Catherine Belsey, *Culture and the Real* (London/New York: Routledge, 2005).
6. Ibid., p. 49.
7. Ibid., p. 156. In their very different modes of reading, Copjec puts poststructuralism and deconstruction more in the camp of the historicists: "So you see, there's no use trying to teach psychoanalysis about undecidability, about the way sexual signifiers refuse to sort themselves out into two separate classes. It's no use preaching deconstruction to psychoanalysis because it already knows all about it" (*Read My Desire*, p. 216). While both Copjec and Belsey engage critically with Judith Butler's work, Copjec finds it too poststructuralist and deconstructive whereas Belsey finds it not poststructuralist enough.
8. Marginalized in France, Irigaray's largest audiences are now Italian and Anglo-American feminist theorists.
9. Jacques Derrida, "Structure, Sign, and Play in the Discourse of the Human Sciences," in *The Structuralist Controversy: The Language of Criticism and the Sciences of Man*, ed. Richard Macksey and Eugenio Donato (Baltimore: The Johns Hopkins University Press, 1972), pp. 247–272; p. 250.
10. Barbara Johnson has shown what a difficult task this is, how even the theoretical texts that seem the smartest can be blind to what she calls their difference from themselves. She quotes from Roland Barthes's *S/Z*, a reading of Balzac's *Sarrasine*, to indicate what it means to speak of a text's difference: "This difference is not, obviously, some complete, irreducible quality . . . it is not what designates the individuality of each text, what names, signs, finishes off each work with a flourish; on the contrary, it is a difference which does not stop and which is articulated upon the infinity of texts, of languages, of systems: a difference of which each text is the return" (Roland Barthes, *S/Z*,

trans. Richard Miller [New York: Hill and Wang, 1974], p. 3). Johnson goes on to show famously how *S/Z* itself is blind to the way it reduces the difference in Balzac's text to identity.

11. Irigaray's earlier works were found by some to promote an essentialist reading of the body. In her more recent works, her essentialism is seen to reside in her heteronormativity.

12. Dylan Evans points out that "sexual difference" is not a theoretical term used by either Freud or Lacan but one given important theoretical resonance by feminist critics. "Freud speaks only of the anatomical *distinction* between the sexes and its psychical consequences. . . . Lacan speaks of sexual *position* and the sexual *relationship*, and occasionally of the *differentiation* of the sexes. . . . However, both Freud and Lacan address the question of sexual difference, and an entry has been included for this term" ("Sexual Difference," in *An Introductory Dictionary of Lacanian Psychoanalysis* [London/New York: Routledge, 1996], p. 178).

13. Irigaray uses the term "sexuation," coined by Lacan, to indicate (psychic) sex division.

14. Irigaray's 1974 book *Speculum of the Other Woman* (trans. Gillian C. Gill [Ithaca, N.Y.: Cornell University Press, 1985]) was her dissertation for a doctorate in philosophy, which followed an earlier doctorate in linguistics in 1968. At the time of publication, she was a practicing analyst, a member of Lacan's École Freudienne, and one of the EFP members who offered courses in the Department of Psychoanalysis at Vincennes. Several months after the publication of the book, Irigaray was suspended from her teaching at Vincennes. Accounts as to why Irigaray was given the cold shoulder by the Lacanian establishment indicate that some considered her book excessively philosophical and inappropriately political. After the expulsion, Irigaray continued to write, to practice psychoanalysis, and to work at the Centre National de la Recherche Scientifique.

15. Luce Irigaray and Sylvère Lotringer, ed., *Why Different? A Culture of Two Subjects: Interviews with Luce Irigaray*, trans. Camille Collins (New York: Semiotext(e), 2000), p. 11.

16. Jacques Lacan, *On Feminine Sexuality, the Limits of Love and Knowledge: 1972–1973 (Encore: The Seminar of Jacques Lacan: Book XX)*, ed. Jacques-Alain Miller, trans. and notes Bruce Fink (New York: Norton, 1999), p. 30.

17. Jacques Lacan, *The Ego in Freud's Theory and in the Technique of Psychoanalysis: 1954–1955 (The Seminar of Jacques Lacan: Book II)*, ed. Jacques-Alain Miller, trans. Sylvana Tamaselli (New York: Norton, 1988).

18. Ibid., p. 5.

19. Bruce Fink, *Lacan to the Letter: Reading Écrits Closely* (Minneapolis: University of Minnesota Press, 2004), pp. 42–43.

20. Lacan, *Seminar XX*, p. 12.

21. Fink, *Lacan*, p. 69.
22. Roland Barthes, *The Pleasure of the Text*, trans. Richard Howard (New York: Hill and Wang, 1975), pp. 18–19. For an exceptional meditation on stupidity, see Avital Ronell, *Stupidity* (Urbana: University of Illinois Press, 2002).
23. Ibid., p. 21.
24. Lacan, *Seminar XX*, p. 131.
25. Ibid.
26. Luce Irigaray, *To Speak Is Never Neutral*, trans. Gail Schwab (New York/London: Routledge, 2002), p. 250.
27. Jacques Derrida, *Positions*, trans. Alan Bass (Chicago: University of Chicago Press, 1981), p. 71.
28. Luce Irigaray, "When Our Lips Speak Together," in *This Sex Which Is Not One*, trans. Catherine Porter with Carolyn Burke (Ithaca, N.Y.: Cornell University Press, 1985), pp. 205–218.
29. Luce Irigaray, *This Sex Which Is Not One*, trans. Catherine Porter (Ithaca, N.Y.: Cornell University Press, 1985), p. 150.
30. Ibid., p. 178.
31. Luce Irigaray, *Marine Lover of Friedrich Nietzsche*, trans. Gillian C. Gill (New York: Columbia University Press, 1991); and idem, "The Envelope: A Reading of Spinoza," in *An Ethics of Sexual Difference*, trans. Carolyn Burke and Gillian C. Gill (Ithaca, N.Y.: Cornell University Press, 1993), pp. 83–94.
32. Barthes, *The Pleasure of the Text*, p. 17.
33. Slavoj Žižek, *The Plague of Fantasies* (London: Verso, 1997), p. 49.
34. Fink, "Knowledge and Jouissance," in *Reading Seminar XX*, ed. Suzanne Bernard and Bruce Fink (Albany: State University of New York Press, 2002), p. 38.
35. Suzanne Bernard, "Tongues of Angels: Feminine Structure and Other Jouissance," in *Reading Seminar XX*, ed. Suzanne Bernard and Bruce Fink (Albany: State University of New York Press, 2002), p. 177.
36. Jacques Lacan, *The Four Fundamental Concepts of Psychoanalysis (The Seminar of Jacques Lacan: Book XI)*, ed. Jacques-Alain Miller, trans. Alan Sheridan (New York: Norton, 1998), p. 205.
37. Ibid., p. 198.
38. Lacan, *Seminar XX*, p. 139.
39. Irigaray, *Sexes and Genealogies*, p. 13.
40. Ibid., pp. 14–15.
41. Luce Irigaray, *Je, Tu, Nous: Toward a Culture of Difference*, trans. Alison Martin (New York: Routledge, 1993), pp. 37–44.
42. Luce Irigaray, "The Forgotten Mystery of Female Ancestry," in *Thinking the Difference: For a Peaceful Revolution*, trans. Karin Montrin (New York: Routledge, 1994).

43. Ibid., p. 108.
44. Ibid., p. 109.
45. Shoshana Felman, *Jacques Lacan and the Adventure of Insight: Psychoanalysis in Contemporary Culture* (Cambridge, Mass.: Harvard University Press, 1987), p. 151.
46. Ibid., p. 144. Felman here cites Lacan, *The Seminar of Jacques Lacan: Book II*, p. 227.
47. Ibid., p. 151.
48. Ibid., p. 121.
49. Ibid., pp. 151–152.

PARAPOETICS AND THE ARCHITECTURAL LEAP
Steve McCaffery

1. Steve McCaffery, "'To Lose One's Way' (for Snails and Nomads): The Radical Labyrinths of Constant and Arakawa and Gins," *Interfaces Image Texte Language* 21/22, vol. 2, pp. 113–144.
2. Gilles Deleuze and Claire Parnet, *Dialogues*, trans. Hugh Tomlinson and Barbara Habberjam (New York: Columbia University Press, 1987), p. 2.
3. David Carroll, *Paraesthetics: Foucault, Lyotard, Derrida* (London: Routledge, 1989), p. xiv.
4. Samuel Johnson, "The Life of Pope," in *The Works of Samuel Johnson, LL.D.*, ed. Sir John Hawkins (London: Buckland, Rivington, Payne et al., 1787), vol. 4, p. 137.
5. *Concise Oxford Dictionary*, 7th ed., s.v. "para-."
6. *Oxford English Dictionary*, Compact ed., 1971, s.v. "para-."
7. Cf. Jacques Derrida, "Pont de Folie—Maintenant L'Architecture," trans. Kate Linker in *Rethinking Architecture: A Reader in Cultural Theory*, ed. Neil Leach (London: Routledge, 1997), p. 324: "The *posts* and *posters* which proliferate today (poststructuralism, postmodernism, etc.) still surrender to the historicist urge. Everything marks an era, even the decentring of the subject: posthumanism. It is as if one again wished to put a linear succession in order, to periodize, to distinguish before and after, to limit the risks of reversibility or repetition, transformation or permutation: an ideology of progress."
8. Ibid., p. 326.
9. A paradisciplinary procedure might take the form Deleuze notes in reflecting on his own use of a biological model. The dangers of mere analogy might be averted "if we restrict ourselves to *extracting from scientific operators a particular conceptualizable character* which itself refers to non-scientific domains, and converges with science without applying it or making it a metaphor." (Gilles Deleuze, *Cinema 2: The Time-Image*, trans. Hugh Tomlinson [Minneapolis: University of Minnesota Press, 1989], p. 129. See also bibliographical details in Gilles Deleuze, *Essays Critical and Clinical*, trans. Daniel W. Smith

and Michael A. Greco [London: Verso, 1998], p. 179.) In other words, vectors should not only be traced and registered as they converge and pass through common values but also tracked as disjunctive syntheses whose governing law is the law of the included middle.

10. Yago Conde, *Architecture of the Indeterminacy*, trans. Paul Hammond (Barcelona: Actar, 2000), p. 251.

11. Ronald Aronson, *After Marxism* (New York: Guilford Press, 1995), p. 227.

12. Bernard Cache, *Earth Moves*, trans. Anne Boyman and Michael Speaks (Cambridge, Mass.: MIT Press, 1995), pp. 108–109.

13. Cf. Gilles Deleuze and Félix Guattari, *What Is Philosophy?* trans. Hugh Tomlinson and Graham Burchell (New York: Columbia University Press, 1994), p. 187.

14. Luis Fernández-Galiano, *Fire and Memory: On Architecture and Energy*, trans. Gina Cariño (Cambridge, Mass.: MIT Press, 2000), p. 114.

15. Ibid.

16. Cited in Fernández-Galiano, *Fire and Memory*, p. 79.

17. Gertrude Stein, *Tender Buttons* (New York: Claire Marie, 1914), p. 63.

18. Jacques Derrida, *Dissemination*, trans. Barbara Johnson (Baltimore: Johns Hopkins University Press, 1981), p. 3.

19. Derrida, "The Double Session," in *Dissemination*, p. 202.

20. Aaron Betsky, *Architecture Must Burn* (Corte Madera, Calif.: Ginko Press, 2000). Like many fashionable architectural publications caught between competing desires of text and image, Betsky's book is irritatingly unpaginated.

21. Derrida, "Pont de Folie," p. 324.

22. The concept of an architectural body has been proposed by the procedural architects Madeline Gins and Arakawa in *Architectural Body* (Tuscaloosa: University of Alabama Press, 2002).

23. Derrida, "Pont de Folie," p. 324.

24. Peter Eisenman and Jacques Derrida, *Chora L Works*, ed. Jeffrey Kipnis and Thomas Leeser (New York: Monacelli Press, 1997), p. 105.

25. B. L. Ullman draws attention to a canny congruity between Gothic architecture and its corresponding scripts. Developing out of the earlier Carolingian form and embracing especially the "picket fence" effect of Merovingian, the main features of Gothic script are angularity and broken lines (*fraktura*); the replacement of circular stress by a polygrammic one; extreme condensation and letter fusions (*textura*); standard heavy shading becomes more decorative with a marked increase in abbreviations and embellishments, for example, hooks, hairlines, and marginal pen flourishes. See B. L. Ullman, *Ancient Writing and Its Influences* (Cambridge, Mass.: MIT Press, 1969), pp. 118–125.

26. John Donne, *Devotions upon Emergent Occasions together with Death's Duel* (Ann Arbor: University of Michigan Press, 1959), p. 165.

27. William Wordsworth, *The Prelude, or Growth of a Poet's Mind* (London: Edward Moxon, 1850), p. vi.

28. Ibid.

29. Ronald Johnson, *ARK* (Albuquerque: Living Batch, 1996), p. 56.

30. Ibid., pp. 50, 56.

31. Mark Scroggins, *Louis Zukofsky and the Poetry of Knowledge* (Tuscaloosa: University of Alabama Press, 1998), p. 295.

32. Quoted in Giorgio Agamben, *Stanzas: Word and Phantasm in Western Culture*, trans. Ronald L. Martinez (Minneapolis: University of Minnesota Press, 1993), p. vii.

33. See Steven Holl's *The Alphabetic City* (New York: Pamphlet Architecture no. 5, 1980) which provides several examples of *E*-, *O*-, *B*-, *L*-, *U*-, *T*-, *X*-, and *H*-shaped buildings and grid blocks. Of particular note are Albert Kahn's 1921 General Motors Building in Detroit, designed as three interlocking and partly superimposed *H* types, and Benjamin Marshall's *X*-shaped Edgewater Beach Apartments in Chicago. Exploration into the analogical possibilities of letterforms and their composition out of a multitude of different beings and objects has a lengthy historical precedent. See, for instance, the rich gatherings contained in Hughes Demeude, *The Animated Alphabet* (London: Thames and Hudson, 1996) and Massin, *Letter and Image*, trans. Caroline Hillier and Vivienne Menkes (New York: Van Nostrand Reinhold, 1970).

34. Cf. Conde, *Architecture of Indeterminacy*, p. 195.

35. Aristotle *Physics* 4.1.208b; cited in Georges Didi-Huberman, *Fra Angelico: Disemblance and Figuration*, trans. Jane Marie Todd (Chicago: University of Chicago Press, 1995), p. 18.

36. Bernard Tscumi, *Architecture and Disjunction* (Cambridge, Mass.: MIT Press, 1996), p. 267, n. 8.

37. Conde, *Architecture of Indeterminacy*, p. 197. See also the important essay "Towards Anarchitecture," in Robin Evans, *Translations from Drawing to Building and Other Essays* (Cambridge, Mass.: MIT Press, 1997), pp. 11–33.

38. Ignasi de Solà-Morales, *Differences: Topographies of Contemporary Architecture*, trans. Graham Thompson (Cambridge, Mass.: MIT Press, 1996), p. 138.

39. Derrida's perdurable challenge to architectural practice is to have introduced the impossible into architectural practice via an insinuant philosopheme: the Platonic *chora*. His architectural collaboration with Peter Eisenman on the Parc de la Villette starts with a lengthy reflection by Derrida on *chora*, an intractable concept found in Plato's *Timaeus*. Although

chora "figures the place of inscription of *all that is marked on the world*," it is a preoriginary "place without space, before space and time" (Derrida and Eisenman, *Chora L Works*, pp. 22, 91). The whole direction of the project moves far beyond the paradoxical origins that Harbison senses in Louis Kahn's Unitarian Church in Rochester, where the architecture gives the sense of "reaching back to early forms which precede anything known to us" (Robert Harbison, *Thirteen Ways: Theoretical Investigations in Architecture* [Cambridge: Mass.: MIT Press, 1997], p. 11). Working to problematize the clear distinction between sensible and intelligible, *chora* is a situational space beyond all normative notions of place and responsible for situating the variant logics of exclusion and inclusion, while remaining beyond the laws it situates. Despite "giving place," *chora* (being neither a donor-subject nor a support or origin) does not give place in the manner of an *es gibt*. Derrida calls *chora* a "paralogical and metalogical superoscillation" (Derrida and Eisenman, *Chora L Works*, p. 15) operating between and above the oscillations of a double exclusion (neither-nor) and of the participational (both this and that). With the sum of its negative features (nonontological, neither a void nor an interval nor a determined place, a something which is not a thing, a reference without a referent, without a self-identity, and incapable of representation other than negatively), it is not surprising that *chora* does not provide the security of architectural ground or a base. It is not that *chora* is absence or the presence of absence, as Eisenman at one point seems to believe, but rather that *chora* remains conceptually intractable and unsayable. Despite Derrida's avowal "that non-representable space could [give?] the receiver, the visitor, the possibility of thinking about architecture" (Derrida and Eisenman, *Chora L Works*, p. 35), one is still prompted to ask: What factor or factors rendered the Parc de la Villette a collaborative failure? The inability to translate deconstruction into architectural thinking and practice? An initially ill-conceived philosophemic contribution on Derrida's part? The patent failure of his collaboration with Eisenman on this project, a project characterized by Derrida's reticence and Eisenman's consistent misprisions, misapplications, and refusals to allow the philosopher's contribution to affect the architect's designs, stands as both a warning and a challenge to paracritical thinking. Both Cache and Solà-Morales demonstrate the impact of Deleuze's thinking on architecture.

40. Evans, *Translations*, pp. 11–33. Inflecting a related sentiment, architect Nigel Coates refers to the "richly stimulating chaos" brought on by the emergent forms of technomedia and communications (Jonathan Glancey, *Nigel Coates: Body Buildings and City Scapes* [New York: Watson Gupthill, 1999], p. 16).

41. Manfredo Tafuri, *Architecture and Utopia: Design and Capitalist Development*, trans. Barbara Luigia La Penta (Cambridge, Mass.: MIT Press, 1976), p. 96.

42. Solà-Morales, *Differences*, pp. 103–104.

43. Cache, *Earth Moves*, p. 15.

44. See for example the design philosophy and projects set forth in Peter Eisenman, *Diagram Diaries* (New York: Universe Publishing, 1999). Lebbeus Woods' visionary engagement with an architecture of cultural memory incorporating reconstructed facades to suggest scar tissue can be found in his *Radical Reconstruction* (New York: Princeton Architectural Press, 1997). Neil Spiller's *Digital Dreams: Architecture and the New Alchemic Technologies* (London: Ellipsis, 1998) raises provocative thinking about the possibilities of cyberspatial architectures. Bernard Tschumi develops the seminal postulate that there can be no architecture without event in his theoretical collection *Architecture and Disjunction* (Cambridge, Mass.: The MIT Press, 1996). *Archigram* chronicles the work of this late 1960s British collective as told by its members. A cross section of Libeskind's theoretical writings and architectural projects, including the Berlin Museum Extension with the Jewish Museum, can be found in his monograph *Countersign* (New York: Rizzoli, 1992). Hejduk's ephemeral, traveling architecture (termed "vagabond" by Antony Vidler) is briefly discussed in Antony Vidler, *The Architectural Uncanny: Essays in the Modern Unhomely* (Cambridge, Mass.: MIT Press, 1992), pp. 207–214. However, the trilogy *Mask of Medusa* (New York: Rizzoli, 1986), *Vladivostok* (New York: Rizzoli, 1989), and *Soundings* (New York: Rizzoli, 1993) offers a chrestomathy of his architectural projects and theories. Hadid's work is readily available in *The Complete Work* (New York: Rizzoli, 1998). Her important architectural statement "Another Beginning" appears in *The End of Architecture? Documents and Manifestos*, ed. Peter Noever (Munich: Prestel-Verlag, 1993), pp. 25–34.

45. Cf. Friedrich Schelling, *The Philosophy of Art*, ed. and trans. Douglas W. Scott (Minneapolis: University of Minnesota Press, 1989), p. 177. As well as his famous proclamation that "architecture is in general frozen music," Schelling also cites the architecturally relevant myth of Amphion, whose music causes stones to inhere and formulate the walls around Thebes. This confluence of the musical and the architectural is echoed in Goethe's later description of architecture as "petrified music" (a description he later modified to "silent music," *verstummte Tonkunst*). See Vidler, *Architectural Uncanny*, p. 231, n. 30.

46. The most cogent critique of Eisenman's approach is Robin Evans, "Not to Be Used for Wrapping Purposes: A Review of the Exhibition of Peter Eisenman's 'Fin d'Ou T Hou S,'" in Evans, *Translations*, pp. 119–151.

47. Peter Eisenman, *Diagram Diaries* (London: Thames and Hudson, 1999), p. 213.

48. Ibid.

49. Cf. Peter Murray, *The Architecture of the Italian Renaissance* (London: Thames and Hudson, 1986), p. 237, n. 5: "An axonometric drawing consists of a plan which is set up truly but turned to a convenient angle. The verticals are then drawn on this and to scale. By these means, all the horizontal and all the vertical elements of the building are represented correctly and so to the same scale. *Anything which is neither truly vertical nor horizontal becomes distorted;* but an axonometric drawing, once one has learnt to disregard the distortions, can teach a very great deal about structure" (emphases added). Axonometric effects, of course, are not novel; they are central to the logic of the paragram and to analytic cubism. Like axonometry, the latter applies a structural logic chiasmatically across the normative rules of figuration and design. Within early-twentieth-century literature the most effective axonometric poetry is Gertrude Stein's *Tender Buttons.* Parapoetics, of course, would investigate the benefits of including distortion within a study of the structural elements.

50. Eisenman, *Diagram Diaries,* pp. 206, 202.

51. See Ron Silliman, "The New Sentence," in *The New Sentence* (New York: Roof Books, 1987), pp. 63–93.

52. Clark Coolidge, "Alien Tatters," *Atelos* 8 (2000): 41.

53. The interpretative analysis here merely laminates a theory onto texts whose disjunctive qualities suggest an analogy to axonometric diagramming. The question of how axonometry can be *consciously* employed as a creative method finds a ready answer in the realm of computer-constructed texts and visual poems, where on-screen deployment and display promise most effective results. The poetic possibilities of axonometric syntax, display, and semantics are not addressed in an otherwise-excellent collection of articles investigating the format and political possibilities of computers and the Internet gathered by Darren Wershler-Henry in *free as in speech and beer. Open Source, Peer-to-Peer and the Economics of the Online Revolution* (Toronto: Prentice Hall, 2002).

54. Derrida and Eisenman, *Chora L Works,* p. 132.

55. Eisenman, *Diagram Diaries,* p. 212.

56. Mark Wigley, *The Architecture of Deconstruction: Derrida's Haunt* (Cambridge, Mass.: MIT Press, 1995), p. 6.

57. Jeffrey Kipnis, "Twisting the Separatrix," in Derrida and Eisenman, *Chora L Works,* pp. 137–160, 138.

58. Greg Lynn, *Architecture for an Embryologic Housing* (Basel: Birkhäuser Verlag, 2002), p. 8.

59. Ludwig Wittgenstein, *Philosophical Investigations,* trans. G. E. M. Anscombe (London: Macmillan, 1953), p. 8e.

60. Sherwood Anderson, introduction to *Geography and Plays,* by Gertrude Stein (New York: Something Else Press, 1968), pp. 7–8.

61. Aldo Rossi, *The Architecture of the City*, trans. Diane Ghirardo and Joan Ockman (Cambridge, Mass.: MIT Press, 1984), p. 29.

62. Lebbeus Woods, *The New City* (New York: Simon and Schuster, 1992), p. 80. See also, for example, Roland Barthes, "Semiology and the Urban," in Leach, *Rethinking Architecture*, pp. 166–172; first presented as a lecture in May 1967 under the sponsorship of the Institut Français and the Institute of the History of Architecture at the University of Naples.

63. Quoted in Glancey, *Nigel Coates*, p. 14.

64. Ibid.

65. As well as Knabb's excellent collection of Situationist texts and reports of specifically architectural interest are Mark Wigley, *Constant's New Babylon: The Hyper-Architecture of Desire* (Rotterdam: 010 Publishers, 1998) and Simon Sadler, *The Sitiationist City* (Cambridge, Mass.: MIT Press, 1998).

66. Richard Rogers, *Architecture: A Modern View* (London: Thames and Hudson, 1990), pp. 7–9.

67. Cited in Liane Lefaivre, *Leon Battista Alberti's Hypnerotomachia Poliphili* (Cambridge, Mass.: MIT Press, 1997), p. 200.

68. Rossi, *Architecture of the City*, p. 10.

69. "It was at Rome, on the fifteenth of October, 1764, as I sat musing midst the ruins of the Capitol while the barefooted fryars were singing Vespers in the Temple of Jupiter, that the idea of writing the decline and fall of the City first started to my mind." Edward Gibbon, *Memoirs of my Life and Writings*, ed. Henry Morley (London: George Routledge and Sons, 1891), p. 151.

70. Rossi, *The Architecture of the City*, p. 21.

71. Pound's own view of the fragment might be deduced from his own Confucian beliefs that structure the relation of parts to whole. "The metaphysic of the Confucian *Chung Yung* or *Unwobbling Pivot*," comments Peter Makin, "is that things are not heaps of contingent dust-drift, but have essential principles, which are durable; which are part of an overarching tendency or Principle in the universe and which, being a shaping and therefore good principle operative in man as in other things, a man may come to understand. This metaphysic is all about the relation between wholes and fragments. The mosaic is not its little glass and gold-leafed fragments; the Virgin shines down from the apse at Torcello when, or if, half of the fragments that make her have fallen" (Peter Makin, *Pound's Cantos* [Baltimore: Johns Hopkins University Press, 1985], pp. 235–236). The architectural pertinence of Makin's observations is obvious.

72. See Georg Simmel, "The Metropolis and Mental Life," in Leach, *Rethinking Architecture*, pp. 69–79.

73. Tafuri, *Architecture and Utopia*, p. 81.

74. It may please Betsky to know that support for his theoretical position is growing. The Italian *Città Lente* (Slow Cities) movement, inaugurated

by Paolo Saturnini, was implemented in 2000 in small towns and cities. An offshoot of Carlo Patrini's Slow Food movement, founded in the early 1990s to counter the proliferation of homogeneous fast-food outlets, *Città Lente* is committed to a preservationist policy of traditional architecture and gastronomy. As reporter Megan Williams explains, Saturnini, the mayor of Greve-in-Chianti, "is carefully constructing barricades to keep at bay the tide of homogeneity that globalization has washed into similar-sized communities around the world. From fast-food chains to cell-phone antennas to car alarms. The Small [sic] Cities people have said 'No thanks' to many of the trappings of modernity." (Meagan Williams, "Ode to Slow," in *The Globe and Mail*, 28 April 2001. Available online at http://www.theglobeandmail.com/servlet/story/LAC.20010428.TRSLOW28/TPStory/special/Travel.)

75. Friedrich Hölderlin, "Reflection," *Sämtliche Werke: Kritische Textausgabe*, ed. D. E. Sattler (Darmstadt: Hermann Luchterhand Verlag, 1979–87), vol. 4., bk.1., pp. 234–235.

76. Marcos Novak, *Trans Terra Form: Liquid Architecture and the Loss of Inscription*, http://www.krcf.org/krcfhome/PRINT/nonlocated/nlonline/non-Marcos.html.

77. Ibid.

78. Ibid.

THE FUTURE OF LITERATURE:
COMPLEX SURFACES OF ELECTRONIC TEXTS AND PRINT BOOKS
N. Katherine Hayles

1. Examples of such machines are Xerox Docutech and Kodak Lionheart. For a summary of the state of the art, see "Seybold Report on Publishing Systems," vol. 24, no. 4, http://www.seyboldreports.com/SRPS/free/ops24/P2404003.htm.

2. John Cayley, "Writing on Complex Surfaces," *dichtung-digital* 35 (Feb., 2005) http://www.dichtung-digital.com/2005/2-Cayley.htm.

3. Noah Wardrip-Fruin, "Surface, Data, and Process," Southern California Digital Culture Group Conference, University of Southern California, January 20, 2006, Los Angeles, Cal.

4. Ibid., p. 1.

5. Loss Glazier makes the point strongly that digital poetics should be placed on a continuum with experimental print literature in *Digital Poetics: Hypertext, Visual-Kinetic Text and Writing in Programmable Media* (Tuscaloosa: University of Alabama Press, 2001).

6. Rita Raley, "Reading Spaces," presentation at the Modern Language Association, December 28, 2005, Washington D.C.

7. Noah Wardrip-Fruin, "Playable Media and Textual Instruments," *dichtung-digital* 34 (January, 2005), http://www.dichtung-digital.com/2005/1/Wardrip-Fruin.

8. Mark B. N. Hansen, *New Philosophy for New Media* (Cambridge, Mass.: MIT Press, 2006).

9. *lens* and *Torus* are described in John Cayley with Dmitri Lemmerman, "Lens: The Practice and Poetics of Writing in Immersive VR (A Case Study with Maquette)," *Leonardo Electronic Almanac*, http://Leoalmanac.org/journal/vol_14_no5–06/cayley.asp.

10. A QuickTime maquette of *lens* is available for download at John Cayley's website, http://www.shadoof.net/in/?lens.html.

11. As Rita Raley reminded me, the effect is reminiscent of Janet Zweig's print artist book *Sheherezade: A Flip Book* (n.l., n. p., 1988), where each successive narrative emerges from zooming into the previous image and finding within it another image and another story.

12. Cayley, "Lens," p. 13.

13. Ibid., p. 6.

14. John Cage, *M Writings '67–'72* (London: Marion Boyars Publishers, 1998); *Mureau* was also performed as a musical composition at the arts program of the 1972 Olympic Games in Munich and elsewhere

15. Jim Rosenberg, *Diagrams Series 4* (1984), http://www.well.com/user/jer/diags.html. Before being ported to the World Wide Web, the *Diagrams* poems were instantiated on sheets of computer paper.

16. The piece is available for download on John Cayley's website, <www.shadoof.net/in>. He describes it in John Cayley, "*overboard*: An Example of Ambient Time-Based Poetics in Digital Art," *dichtung-digital* 32 (2004) http://www.dichtung-digital.com/2004/2-Cayley.htm>.

17. Stanley H. Ambrose, "Paleolithic Technology and Human Evolution," *Science* 291, no. 5509 (March 2, 2001): 1748–1753.

18. This would of course be an environmental effect rather than an evolutionary development. If humans so affected were to have a fitness advantage over others, and if population dynamics translated this fitness advantage into greater numbers of offspring, then over time a co-evolutionary spiral could develop that would result in inherited differences. This is of course a much more speculative hypothesis than assuming environmental effects for children who are exposed to significant computer time at young ages, for which there is already convincing evidence.

19. For a summary of this research, see Wendy Cole, Sonja Steptoe, and Sarah Sturmon, "The Multitasking Generation," *Time*, vol. 167, no. 13 (March 27, 2006): 48–55.

20. Robert Coover, "Literary Hypertext: The Passing of the Golden Age," Keynote Address, Digital Arts and Culture Conference, Atlanta GA, October 29, 1999, available at nickm.com/vox/golden_age.html.

21. Kathleen Fitzpatrik, *The Anxiety of Obsolescence: The American Novel in the Age of Television* (Nashville: Vanderbilt University Press, 2006).

22. Bruce Sterling, *Distraction* (New York: Spectra, 1999).

23. In "Generation M: Media in the Lives of 8–18 Year-olds," a report by the Kaiser Family Foundation, "a nationally representative sample of more than 2,000 3rd through 12th graders who completed questionnaires, including nearly 600 self-selected participants who also maintained seven-day media diaries" were surveyed. The study found that on the average young people spend 3:51 (hours:minutes) a day watching TV and videos, 1:44 listening to music, 1:02 using computers, 0:49 playing video games, and 0:43 reading. A summary and the full report is available at http://www.kff.org/entmedia/entmedia030905nr.cfm.

24. Guillaume Apollonaire, *Calligrammes: poèmes de la paix et la guerre, 1913–1916* (Paris: Mercure de France, 1918).

25. W. J. T. Mitchell, *Picture Theory: Essays on Verbal and Visual Representation* (Chicago: University of Chicago Press, 1995).

26. Cayley, "Lens," p. 6.

27. Stefan Themerson, *Apollonaire's Lyrical Ideograms* (London: Gaberbrocchus Press, 1968), pp. 28–38.

28. Ibid., p. 23.

29. Apparently the 1918 edition used the same frame, as it is identical except for the substitution of a larger *l* in *les* in the fifth type line, apparently a replacement for a type element that was damaged and had to be replaced.

30. N. Katherine Hayles, *Writing Machines* (Cambridge, Mass.: MIT Press, 2002).

31. Quoted in *Apollonaire: Selected Poems*, translated with an introduction by Oliver Bernard (New York: Penguin Books, 1965), p. 7.

32. Raymond Federman, *Double or Nothing: A Real Fictitious Discourse* (New York: Swallow Press, 1971).

33. Jerome McGann, *The Textual Condition* (Princeton: Princeton University Press, 1991) and *Radiant Textuality: Literature After the World Wide Web* (New York: Palgrave Macmillan, 2004); Johanna Drucker, *The Visible Word: Experimental Typography and Modern Art, 1909–1923* (Chicago: University of Chicago Press, 1997) and *Figuring and Word: Essays on Books, Writing, and Visual Poetics* (New York: Granary Books, 1998). Matthew Kirschenbaum has made the point that new media scholars would do well to consult the bibliographic tradition in thinking about the specificities of electronic textuality in "Materiality and Matter and Stuff: What Electronic Texts Are Made Of," *ebr* (October 1, 2001): http://www.electronicbookreview.com/thread/electropoetics/sited.

34. This list can be seen as an adaptation with significant departures from Lev Manovich's well-known "five principles of new media" of numerical representation, modularity, automation, variability, and transcoding (that

is, computerization of culture). My discussion of computer-mediated text includes numerical representation and automation; variability mutates into a recursive dynamic between imitation and intensification; and transcoding is seen here as a dynamic interaction between electronic text and print rather than a one-way movement of the "cultural layer" into the "computer layer." See Lev Manovich, *The Language of New Media* (Cambridge, Mass.: MIT Press, 2002), pp. 27–47.

35. Jonathan Safran Foer, *Extremely Loud and Incredibly Close* (New York: Houghton Mifflin, 2005); Salvador Plascencia, *The People of Paper* (San Francisco: McSweeney's, 2005); Mark Danielewski, *House of Leaves* (New York: Pantheon, 2000).

36. Lev Manovich, *The Language of New Media*, p. 45 and *passim*.

37. Foer, *Extremely Loud*, pp. 269–272.

38. For a discussion of Shannon's information theory, see N. Katherine Hayles, *How We Became Posthuman: Virtual Bodies in Cybernetics, Literature, and Informatics* (Chicago: University of Chicago Press, 1999), chap. 3, pp. 50–83.

39. See Claude Shannon and Warren Weaver, *The Mathematical Theory of Information* (Urbana: University of Illinois Press, 1949), p. 3.

40. Foer, *Extremely Loud*, p. 269.

41. Ibid., p. 281.

42. Ibid., pp. 281–284.

43. Ibid., pp. 327–341.

44. Plascencia, *The People of Paper*, p. 97.

45. Danieleski, *House of Leaves*, pp. 623–628.

46. Larry McCaffrey and Sinda Gregory, "Haunted House: An Interview with Mark Z. Danielewski," *Critique: Studies in Contemporary Fiction* 44, no. 2 (Winter 2003): 99–135.

47. Ibid., p. 117.

48. Ibid., p. 118.

49. Danielewski, *House of Leaves*, p. 139.

50. Mark B. N. Hansen, "The Digital Topography of Mark Z. Danielewski's *House of Leaves*," *Contemporary Literature* 45, no. 4 (2004): 597–636. The sharp break between analog photography and digital technologies that Hansen constructs, working from a quotation by Roland Barthes to the effect that photography requires a body before the camera for its representations, is more complex than his argument allows. Long before digital technologies changed the nature of photography, photographers were manipulating the material to create images of nonexistent phenomena, notoriously, for example, in the "fairy" photographs and similar occult subjects popular in the early years of the twentieth century.

51. Ibid., p. 603.

52. Ibid., p. 609.
53. Ibid., p. 611.
54. For an account of these fields, see N. Katherine Hayles, *How We Became Posthuman*, pp. 222–246.
55. Danielewski, *House of Leaves*, p. 338.
56. Ibid., p. 338.
57. Ibid., p. 165.
58. The process of creating genetic programs that can design circuits is described in John R. Koza, Matthew J. Streeter, William Mydlowec, Jessen Yu, and Guido Lanza, *Genetic Programming IV: Routine Human–Computer Machine Intelligence* (New York: Springer, 2005).
59. Brian Cantwell Smith, *On the Origin of Objects* (Cambridge, Mass.: Bradford Books, 1996), p. 76.
60. N. Katherine Hayles, "Saving the Subject: Remediation in *House of Leaves*," *American Literature* 74 (2002): 779–806.

CRISIS MEANS TURNING POINT:
A MANIFESTO FOR ART AND ACCOUNTABILITY
Doris Sommer

1. Claudio Lomnitz, "Times of Crisis: Historicity, Sacrifice, and the Spectacle of Debacle in Mexico City," *Public Culture* (2003).
2. I am indebted to my colleague Francesco Erspamer for his guidance in re-reading Gramsci.

> **cri·sis:** 1. a. A crucial or decisive point or situation; a turning point. b. An unstable condition, as in political, social, or economic affairs, involving an impending abrupt or decisive change. 2. A sudden change in the course of a disease or fever, toward either improvement or deterioration. 3. An emotionally stressful event or traumatic change in a person's life. 4. A point in a story or drama when a conflict reaches its highest tension and must be resolved. [Middle English, from Latin, *judgment*, from Greek *krisis*, from *krinein*, to separate, judge. See *krei-* in Indo-European Roots.] (www.answers.com/topic/crisis).

3. Antonio Gramsci, "Observations on Certain Aspects of the Structure of Political Parties in Periods of Organic Crisis," from *The Prison Notebooks*. http://www2.cddc.vt.edu/marxists/archive/gramsci/editions/spn/state_civil/cho1.htm.

> When the crisis does not find this organic solution, but that of the charismatic leader, it means that a static equilibrium exists (whose factors may be disparate, but in which the decisive one is the immaturity of the progressive forces); it means that no group, neither the conservatives nor the progressives, has the strength for victory, and that even the conservative group needs a master. [1932–1934: 1st version 1930–1932]

4. Immanuel Kant, *Critique of Judgment*, trans. J. H. Bernard (New York: Hafner Press, Macmillan Publishing Co., Inc., 1951). See also *Essays in Kant's Aesthetics*, ed. Ted Cohen and Paul Guyer (Chicago: University of Chicago Press, 1982).

5. Hannah Arendt, *Lectures on Kant's Political Philosophy*, ed. with an interpretive essay by Ronald Beiner (Chicago: University of Chicago Press, 1982). Before Arendt, Adorno had suggested the ethico-political dimension of Kant's Third Critique. See Theodor W. Adorno, *Aesthetic Theory*, ed. Gretel Adorno and Rolf Tiedemann, ed. and trans. Robert Hullot-Kentor (Minneapolis: University of Minnesota Press, 1997).

6. Richard Florida, *The Rise of the Creative Class: And How It's Transforming Work, Leisure, Community and Everyday Life* (New York: Basic Books, 2002). See also Rob Austin and Lee Devin, *Artful Making: What Managers Need to Know about How Artists Work* (Upper Saddle River, N.J.: Financial Times/Prentice Hall, 2003).

7. Richard J. Deasy, ed., *Critical Links: Learning in the Arts and Student Academic and Social Development* (Washington, D.C.: Council of Chief State School Officers, 2000). See review by Nick Rabkin in *International Journal of Education and the Arts* 3 (October, 2002). Concerning James Catterall's essays, Rabkin notes that:

> Caterall catalogs them and argues that each discipline is connected to significant outcomes. For example, in the visual arts, there are findings about how drawing supports writing skills, and how visualization training supports interpretation of text. In music, researchers found strong connections to spatial reasoning and math, and between instrument instruction and SAT scores. Dance instruction was connected to fluency in creative thinking and to reading skills. Drama, in the form of dramatic enactment, was connected to story comprehension, character understanding, and writing proficiency, and is shown to be a better way for students to process a story than teacher-led discussion. Multi-arts programs had multiple connections: to reading, verbal, and math skills, and to creative thinking. Similar connections are present between art and social and emotional development. Dance is connected to self-confidence and persistence; music to self-efficacy and self-concept; drama to concentration, comprehension, conflict resolution, and self-concept; multi-arts to achievement motivation, cognitive engagement, self-confidence, risk-taking, perseverance, and leadership. Several studies show children become more engaged in their studies when the arts are integrated into their lessons. Others show that at-risk students often find pathways through the arts to broader academic successes.

8. Victor Shklovsky, "Art as Technique," (1917) in *Russian Formalist Criticism, Four Essays*, trans. and intro. Lee T. Lemon and Marion J. Reis (Lincoln: University of Nebraska Press, 1965), pp. 3–24. p. 12.

9. John Beverley, Testimonio: On the Politics of Truth (Minneapolis: University of Minnesota Press, 2004).

10. Bruce A. Kimball, *Orators and Philosophers: A History of the Idea of Liberal Education* (New York: Teachers College Columbia, 1986). He contrasts classical emphasis on forming the good citizen with the Enlightenment emphasis we have inherited, which replaces ethics with reason, responsibility with freedom.

11. George Yúdice, *The Expediency of Culture: Uses of Culture in the Global Era* (Durham, N.C.: Duke University Press, 2003).

12. Cultural studies has been openly political in the sense of resistant to hegemonic power. It has valued oppositional subcultures among workers and then, in the spirit of Herbert Marcuse, among youth. See Tony Jefferson, ed., *Resistance Through Rituals* (London: Hutchinson, 1976), and Dick Hebdige, *Subcultur: The Meaning of Style* (London: Methuen, 1979). Later developments engage audience responses to cultural practices, but not to the practice of interpreting the arts. See Ien Ang, *Watching Dallas* (New York: Metheun 1985), and John Fiske, "British Cultural Studies and Television," in *Channels of Discourse*, ed. R. C. Allen (Chapel Hill: University of North Carolina Press, 1986), pp. 254–289.

13. Jesús Martín Barbero, *De los medios a las mediaciones. Comunicación, cultura y hegemonía* (México: G. Gil, 1987). Also, Néstor García Canclini, *Hybrid Cultures: Strategies for Entering and Leaving Modernity* (Minneapolis: University of Minnesota Press, 1995).

14. Ileana Rodríguez, "'Estudios culturales': quiebres disciplinarios, cambios del oficio crítico y crisis de identidad en la época post-socialista," *Nuevo Texto Crítico* 25–28, ed. Adriana J. Bergero and Jorge Ruffinelli (2000–2001): 169–182, p. 174.

La diferencia fundamental entre los estudios culturales y los subalternos es que los estudios subalternos retienen una noción de agencia que les es central pero que a la vez refuncionalizan. . . . Los estudios subalternos no hacen a un lado la ética, no reducen lo popular a los procesos de mercado y consumo, ni tampoco renuncian al telos. (pp. 174, 176)

15. Alberto Moreiras, "Retirar la cultura," *Nuevo Texto Crítico* 25–28, ed. Adriana J. Bergero and Jorge Ruffinelli (2000–2001), pp. 133–138, pp. 134–135:

¿Si dijéramos que la pregunta misma por la productividad del saber, lejos de constituir el saber como posibilidad política, lo de-constituye hacia una facticidad cómplice con la cotidianidad política que nos vive y que no deja de vivirnos por mucho que intentemos pagarle con

su misma moneda, es decir, interpelar la interpelación misma, rizar el rizo de lo político, afirmar que, en política, todo es cuestión de afirmar más y mejor que el otro, el enemigo?
See also Charles Hale, "El indio permitido."

16. Pierre Macherey, *Pour une théorie de la production littéraire* (Paris: Maspero, 1966).

17. Louis Althusser, "Ideology and Ideological State Apparatuses." The article appeared first in the French journal *La Pensée* in 1970; it was then reprinted in the collection of Althusser's articles translated into English by Ben Brewster and titled *Lenin and Philosophy* (London: New Left Books, 1971), pp. 127–186.

18. J. L. Austin, *How to Do Things With Words* (Cambridge, Mass.: Harvard University Press, 1962).

19. James Clifford, *The Predicament of Culture: Twentieth-Century Ethnography, Literature, and Art* (Cambridge, Mass.: Harvard University Press, 1988); see also various edited volumes by Michael Fischer, George Marcus, and James Clifford. On what one might call the "Heisenberg's Uncertainty Principle" in anthropology—i.e., how our presence in the field either transforms the object of study or how our discipline results from socio-political conditions that also transformed the object of study, see Talal Asad, ed., *Anthropology and the Colonial Encounter*, and also Talal Asad, "The Concept of Cultural Translation in British Cultural Anthropolgy," in *Writing Culture: The Poetics and Politics of Ethnography*, ed. James Clifford and George L. Marcus (Berkeley: University of California Press, 1986), pp. 141–164. My gratitude to J. Lorand Matory for guidance here.

20. Heisenberg's Uncertainty Principle is basically that observation itself affects the outcome. For discussion of Heisenberg's 1927 paper see W.C. Price and S.S. Chissick, ed., *The Uncertainty Principle and the Foundations of Quantum Mechanics* (New York: Wiley, 1977). See also Franz Breuer and Wolff-Michael Roth, "Subjectivity and Reflexivity in the Social Sciences: Epistemic Windows and Methodical Consequences," printed in http://www.qualitative-research.net/fqs-texte/2-03/2-03intro-3-e.htm.

21. Richard Florida, *Rise of the Creative Class*.

22. Eric Slauter, *The State as a Work of Art: The Cultural Origins of the Constitution* (Chicago: University of Chicago Press, 2008). Slauter summarizes in a message of June 5, 2005: "The book will place the U.S. Constitution in the twin contexts: . . . a commitment to an understanding of the state as a work of art (that is, the state as a nonnatural entity); and a debate over the putative primacy of cultural life to political form (Does political form determine cultural life, or is it the other way around?, a question first raised seriously in the Enlightenment and still alive in discussions of proposed constitutions for Iraq and Afghanistan)."

23. See, for example, http://www.culturebase.net/artist.php?229. He discovered Mockus and Boal through the Cultural Agents Initiative at Harvard University. See http://culturalagents.org/.

24. See Kevin F. McCarthy, Elizabeth H. Ondaatje, Laura Zakaras, and Arthur Brooks, *Gifts of the Muse: Reframing the Debate About the Benefits of the Arts* (Rand Corporation: 2005).

25. Shakespeare, *Hamlet*, II:2, 250–251. In *The Complete Works of Shakespeare*, ed. David Bevington, updated 4th ed. (New York: Longman, 1997), p. 1082.

26. See Douglas North, *Institutions, Institutional Change and Economic Performance* (Cambridge, Mass.: Harvard University Press, 1990), and Douglas North, "A Transaction Cost Theory of Politics," *Journal of Theoretical Politics* 2:4 (1990): 355–367.

27. "Wiggle Room" is the title of my introductory essay in *Cultural Agency in the Americas*, ed. Doris Sommer (Durham, N.C.: Duke University Press, 2005).

28. Conversation with Pedro Reyes, June 8, 2005.

29. The celebrated mayor Edi Rama of Tirana, Albania, performed a similar feat by literally painting the town. See Jane Kramer, "Painting the Town," in *The New Yorker*, June 27, 2005, p. 50.

> You hear him everywhere: a gravelly basso exhorting the lazy, seducing the skeptics, booming his way through a hip-hop track about Tirana that half the city seems to own. He is inexhaustible. He spends his days repairing the body and soul of a shattered capital and his nights prowling its streets, seeing that the work got done, and that no one has been stealing street lights or dropping beer bottles or cigarette wrappers—that people are behaving like citizens. Rama is a Balkan original, and maybe the most original thing about him is that he isn't really a politician. He is an artist who, you might say, took Tirana for his canvas.

30. Antanas Mockus, Hedonism and Pragmatism, a course at Harvard University, Fall 2004.

31. See http://www.tonisant.com/aitg/Boal_Techniques/. Thanks to Diana Taylor for pointing out Boal's debt to Jacobo Moreno, disciple of Sigmund Freud, who initiated psychodrama as a therapy technique.

32. Augusto Boal, *Legislative Theater* (New York: Routledge, 1998).

33. Interview with Augusto Boal, Harvard University, December 7, 2003.

34. Marshall Ganz, Presentation in Graduate Student Cultural Agents workshop, November 2003.

35. See http://www.fotokids.org.

36. http://www.aver.org.br/averes/fotocidadaniaprojeto.htm.

37. http://www.arteamundo.com/ph15/.

38. The first Graduate Student Conference on Cultural Agents attracted a great number of proposals, and the excellent papers presented form the core of a forthcoming collection with The Other Press.

39. Doris Sommer, *Bilingual Aesthetics: A New Sentimental Education* (Durham, N.C.: Duke University Press, 2004).

40. Víctor Hernández Cruz, "You Gotta Have Your Tips on Fire," *Mainland; poems* (New York: Random House, 1973), pp. 3–4.

41. By contrast, Samuel Huntington, *Who Are We?: The Challenges to America's National Identity* (New York: Simon and Schuster, 2004) raises concerns about bilingualism.

42. José Luis Falconi, administrator for the course, is also the associate director of the Cultural Agents Initiative at Harvard University.

43. For Schiller's program for modern citizenship see Friedrich Schiller, *The Aesthetic Education of Man in a Series of Letters* (1759), ed. E.M. Wilkinson and L.A. Willoughby (Oxford: Oxford University Press, 1983). He wrote the *Letters* to open dead-ends in politics through art that wrests freedom from contradiction. Sentimental, tormented art like Schiller's, unlike Goethe's naïve genius, can be taught; it thrives in the very distance from nature where poets have freedom to maneuver. Freedom's dependence on self-consciousness, and the promise of a new spontaneity based on reflection, became the themes of Schiller's pedagogy. It turned Kant's lessons about the differences between beauty and the sublime, love and respect, nature and artistic genius, into a progression of before and after aesthetic education. See especially "Ninth Letter," points 1, 2, and 3, p. 55.

44. See Diana Taylor, *The Archive and the Repertoire: Performing Cultural Memory in the Americas* (Durham, N.C.: Duke University Press, 2003). See also Diana Taylor, *Disappearing Acts: Spectacles of Gender and Nationalism in Argentina's Dirty War* (Durham, N.C.: Duke University Press, 1997); and Diana Taylor, *Theatre of Crisis: Drama and Politics in Latin America* (Lexington: University Press of Kentucky, 1991).

45. Jon Elster, *Ulysses Unbound: Studies in Rationality, Precommitment, and Constraints* (Cambridge: Cambridge University Press, 2000), chap. 3. I am grateful to Antanas Mockus for this reference and for so many lessons.

46. Thanks to Antanas Mockus for this point and the following reference: Joseph Henrich, Robert Boyd, Samuel Bowles, Herbert Gintis, Ernst Fehr, Colin Camerer, ed., *Foundations of Human Sociality: Economic Experiments and Ethnographic Evidence from Fifteen Small-Scale Societies* (Oxford: Oxford University Press, 2004).

47. Hannah Arendt, *The Human Condition*, with an introduction by Margaret Canovan, 2nd ed. (Chicago: University of Chicago Press, 1998), p. 182.

48. Theodor Adorno retains Kant's insistence on the formal autonomy of art. But he adds (through Hegel and Marx) that art is embedded in society. The illusion of autonomy helps art achieve its social character. See Theodor Adorno, *Aesthetic Theory* (1970), trans. R. Hullot-Kentor (Minneapolis: University of Minnesota Press, 1997), p. 8.

49. See Douglas Kellner's useful review in his online essay, "Cultural Studies and Ethics." http://www.gseis.ucla.edu/faculty/kellner/kellner.html.

Although members of the school of British cultural studies including Stuart Hall usually omit the Frankfurt school from his narrative, some of the work done by the Birmingham group replicated certain classical positions of the Frankfurt school, in their social theory and methodological models for doing cultural studies, as well as in their political perspectives and strategies.

50. This is a recurring worry for Walter Benjamin. See Walter Benjamin, "Theses on the Philosophy of History," in *Illuminations*, ed. Hannah Arendt, trans. Harry Zohn (New York: Schocken, 1969), pp. 253–264; esp. numbers 2 and 9. In the same volume, see also the Epilogue, "The Work of Art in the Age of Mechanical Reproduction."

> All efforts to render politics aesthetic leads to one thing: war . . . Mankind, which in Homer's time was an object of contemplation for the Olympian Gods, now is one for itself. Its self-alienation has reached such a degree that it can experience its own destruction as an aesthetic pleasure of the first order. This is the situation of politics which Fascism is rendering aesthetic. Communism responds by politicizing art (pp. 241–242).

51. Antanas Mockus, "Anfibios culturales y divorcio entre ley, moral y cultura," *Revista análisis político* no. 21 (Universidad Nacional de Colombia, 1994).

CONTRIBUTORS

ANDREW BENJAMIN is Professor of Critical Theory and Philosophical Aesthetics in the Faculty of Arts at Monash University. His most recent publication is *Style and Time: Essays on the Politics of Appearance* (Northwestern University Press, 2006).

JAMES J. BONO is Associate Professor of History and of Medicine at the University at Buffalo. A past president of the Society for Literature and Science and founding editor of its journal, *Configurations*, he is the author of *The Word of God and the Languages of Man: Interpreting Nature in Early Modern Science and Medicine*, vol. 1: *Ficino to Descartes* (University of Wisconsin Press, 1995), and co-editor of *Ethical Issues in Health Care on the Frontiers of the Twenty-First Century* (Springer, 2000). He spent 2006–07 as an NEH Senior Fellow at the Folger Shakespeare Library completing volume 2 of *The Word of God and the Languages of Man* and working on *Imagining Nature: Technologies of the "Literal," the Scientific Revolution, and Visual Cultures of Early Modern Science.*

REY CHOW is Andrew W. Mellon Professor of the Humanities at Brown University, where she teaches in the Departments of Comparative Literature, English, and Modern Culture and Media. She is the author, most recently, of *The Age of the World Target: Self-Referentiality in War, Theory, and Comparative Work* (Duke University Press, 2006).

TIM DEAN is Professor of English and Comparative Literature and Director of the Humanities Institute at the University at Buffalo (SUNY). He is the author of *Beyond Sexuality* (University of Chicago Press, 2000) and coeditor of *Homosexuality and Psychoanalysis* (University of Chicago Press, 2001). His new book is *Unlimited Intimacy: Reflections on the Subculture of Barebacking* (University of Chicago Press, forthcoming).

N. KATHERINE HAYLES, John Charles Hillis Professor of Literature at the University of California, Los Angeles, teaches and writes on the relations of science, technology, and literature in the twentieth and twenty-first centuries. Her book *How We Became Posthuman: Virtual Bodies in Cybernetics, Literature, and Informatics* (University of Chicago Press, 1999) won the René Wellek Prize for the Best Book in Literary Theory 1998–99, and her book *Writing Machines* (MIT Press, 2002) won the Suzanne Langer Award for Outstanding Scholarship. Her most recent book is *My Mother Was a Computer: Digital Subjects and Literary Texts* (University of Chicago Press, 2005).

MARTIN JAY is Sidney Hellman Ehrman Professor of History at the University of California, Berkeley. Among his works are *The Dialectical Imagination* (University of California Press, 1973 and 1996), *Marxism and Totality* (University of California Press, 1984), *Adorno* (Harvard University Press, 1984), *Permanent Exiles* (Columbia University Press, 1985); *Fin-de-Siècle Socialism* (Routledge, 1989), *Force Fields* (Routledge, 1993), *Downcast Eyes* (University of California Press, 1993), *Cultural Semantics* (University of Massachusetts Press, 1998), *Refractions of Violence* (Routledge, 2003), and *Songs of Experience* (University of California Press, 2004). He is currently working on a book on lying in politics.

ERNESTO LACLAU is Distinguished Professor for Humanities and Rhetorical Studies, Northwestern University, as well as a professor at University of Essex, England. His publications include, among others, *Hegemony and Socialist Strategy: Towards a Radical Democratic Politics*, with Chantal Mouffe (Verso, 1985); *New Reflections on the Revolution of Our Time* (Verso, 1990); *Emancipation(s)* (Verso, 1996); *Contingency, Hegemony, Universality*, with Judith Butler and Slavoj Žižek (Verso, 2000); and *On Populist Reason* (Verso, 2005).

STEVE MCCAFFERY is the author of over 23 books of poetry and criticism, most recently *Slightly Left of Thinking* (Chax Press, 2008). He was a founding member of both the Toronto Research Group and the sound poetry ensemble "Four Horsemen." He has presented his performance, sound, and video art with Fluxus and at both national and international venues. He teaches in the English Department at the University at Buffalo, where he is The David Gray Professor of Poetry and Letters.

PAOLA MARRATI is Professor of Humanities and Philosophy in the Humanities Center and the Department of Philosophy at The Johns Hopkins University, Baltimore. She directs the Steering Committee of the Program for the Study of Women, Gender, and Sexuality at the School of Arts and Sciences of the same university and was Directrice de Programme de Recherche at the Collège International de Philosophie, in Paris. She is the author of *Genesis and Trace: Derrida Reading Husserl and Heidegger* (Kluwer, 1998; Stanford University Press, 2005) and of *Gilles Deleuze: Cinema and Philosophy* (Johns Hopkins University Press, 2008). She is currently completing a book project on *The Event and the Ordinary: On the Philosophy of Stanley Cavell and Gilles Deleuze*.

JEAN-LUC NANCY is Professor of Philosophy at the Université de Strasbourg. He is the author of more than 30 books, including *The Inoperative Community* (University of Minnesota Press, 1991), *The Birth to Presence* (Stanford University Press, 1993), *The Experience of Freedom* (Stanford University Press, 1993), *The Muses* (Stanford University Press, 1996), *The Sense of the World* (University of Minnesota Press, 1997), *Being Singular Plural* (Stanford University Press, 2000), *The Speculative Remark* (Stanford University Press, 2001), and *Hegel: The Restlessness of the Negative* (University of Minnesota Press, 2002). He is the co-author, with Philipe Lacoue-Labarthe, of *The Literary Absolute* (SUNY Press, 1988) and *The Title of the Letter* (SUNY Press, 1992).

DORIS SOMMER is Director of the Cultural Agents Initiative at Harvard University, where she holds the Ira and Jewell Williams Chair in Romance Languages and Literatures. She has studied with and written about exemplary agents of change who harness the power of arts in order to build civil society. Among her publications are *Foundational Fictions: The National Romances of Latin America* (University of California Press, 1991), *Proceed with Caution, When Engaged by Minority Writing in the Americas* (Harvard University Press, 1999), *Bilingual Aesthetics: A New Sentimental Education* (Duke University Press, 2004), and *Cultural Agents in the Americas* (editor, Duke University Press, 2005).

RUDI VISKER is Professor of Philosophy in the Institute of Philosophy of the Katholieke Universiteit Leuven, Belgium. He is the author of numerous articles and books, including *Truth and Singularity* (Kluwer, 1999) and, most recently, *The Inhuman Condition* (Kluwer, 2004).

ELIZABETH WEED is Director of the Pembroke Center at Brown University. Her fields are literary criticism and psychoanalytic and feminist theory, and she teaches in the Department of Modern Culture and Media. She is founding editor, with the late Naomi Schor, of *differences: A Journal of*

Feminist Cultural Studies, and is the editor of several books on feminist theory. She is currently working on a book entitled *Reading for Consolation: Psychoanalysis, Feminism, the Waning of Critique*.

EWA PLONOWSKA ZIAREK is Julian Park Professor of Comparative Literature and founding director of the Humanities Institute at the University at Buffalo (SUNY). She is the author of *The Rhetoric of Failure: Deconstruction of Skepticism, Reinvention of Modernism* (State University of New York Press, 1995), *An Ethics of Dissensus: Feminism, Postmodernity, and the Politics of Radical Democracy* (Stanford University Press, 2001), the editor of *Gombrowicz's Grimaces: Modernism, Gender, Nationality* (State University of New York Press, 1998), and the co-editor, with Tina Chanter, of *Revolt, Affect, Collectivity: The Unstable Boundaries of Kristeva's Polis* (State University of New York Press, 2005) and *Intermedialities: Philosophy, Art, Politics* (forthcoming).

INDEX

Adami, Valerio, 46
Adorno, Theodor, 225, 259n5, 263n48
affirmation of the particular, 6–8, 18–19, 33–34, 38–44
agency, 1–14, 27, 139, 184–85, 188, 204–8, 213–18, 221; cultural, 222–225; human, 3–5, 7, 9, 13, 22–23, 26, 207; of time, 3–5, 7, 19
Althusser, Louis, 155, 214, 247n2
Ambrose, Stanley, 187
Anderson, Sherwood, 175
Apollonaire, Guillaume, 191–93
architecture, 6, 12–13, 47, 161, 163–79; and poetry, 6, 161–79
Arendt, Hannah, 121, 211, 224, 259n5; *The Human Condition*, 121
Aristotle, 48, 53, 169
Aronson, Ronald, 164
Augustine, 90, 115, 118, 169
Austin, J. L., 215
autonomy: of art, 9, 45, 217, 263n48; of the drive, 132, 136; of the humanities, 2; of politics, 9; of the subject, 1–3, 12, 125, 177, 207; of the visible, 54. *See also* agency; difference; heterology; heteronomy; otherness; the Other

Bachelard, Gaston, 167
Balibar, Etienne, 94, 95, 105
Barthes, Roland, 147–48, 150–51, 155, 176, 244n10, 257n50; *The Pleasure of the Text*, 147; *S/Z*, 244n10
Bataille, Georges, 33, 48–49, 166, 230n7
becoming, 50; and Deleuze, 5, 6, 7, 12, 14, 17, 22, 26–27, 135–36, 139–40; and Foucault, 122, 139
Belsey, Catherine, 142, 244n7
Benjamin, Andrew, 6, 7–8, 265
Benjamin, Walter, 225, 264n50
Bentham, Jeremy, 47, 54

Bergson, Henri, 17–21; and Deleuze, 17–22, 26, 28; time, difference, and life, 18–20; *The Two Sources of Morality and Religion*, 21, 28
Bernard, Suzanne, 151–54
Bersani, Leo, 123–25, 134–37, 239n6, 242n43
biopower, 139
Blanchot, Maurice, 33, 163
Boal, Augusto, 14, 217, 219–21, 262n31
Bogotá, 24, 218–19, 224–25

Cache, Bernard, 164, 169–71, 249n39
Cage, John, 173, 186
Carroll, David, 162
Cartesian, 51, 55–56. *See also* Descartes, René
Cavell, Stanley, 26
Cayley, John, 181, 184–85, 187, 189, 191
Celan, Paul, 162
Certeau, Michel de, 54
Cezanne, Paul, 45–46, 55, 57
Chaplin, Charlie, 67
Chateaubriand, François-René de, 29
China, 6, 10, 94, 97–105
Chow, Rey, 5, 6, 7, 10, 11, 265
Coates, Nigel, 176
Colet, Louise, 31
Coolidge, Clark, 173
Coover, Robert, 182, 188
Copjec, Joan, 71–72, 142, 241n27, 244n7
cosmopolitanism, 6, 11, 110, 113, 115. *See also* Freud, Sigmund: anti-cosmopolitanism
criticism, 5, 7–8, 30, 33, 44, 51, 56, 118, 150–51, 171, 210, 213, 225
critique, 5–14, 18, 21, 48, 55, 94–95

Damisch, Hubert, 45
Danielewski, Mark, 169, 197, 203–9

Dante, 168–69
data flows, 12, 13, 183, 188–89, 202
Dean, Tim, 11, 265
Debord, Guy, 46
Deleuze, Gilles, 6, 7, 11, 12, 13, 14, 47, 53–54, 132–37, 139, 161–163, 165, 169, 174, 229n3, 229n11, 229n14, 242n36, 247n9, 250n39; and agency, 22–23, 25–27; *Anti-Oedipus*, 23, 135, 136; and becoming, 5, 6, 7, 12, 14, 17, 22, 26–27, 135–136, 139–140; and Bergson, 17–22, 26, 28; *Cinema 1: The Movement-Image*, 17, 18, 23, 229n11, n12; *Cinema 2: The Time-Image*, 23, 27, 229n14, 247n9; *Difference and Repetition*, 18–19, 21; and emancipatory politics, 22–23; and film, 23–25; and modernity, 21, 22, 26, 27, 28; *A Thousand Plateaus*, 22, 27; *What Is Philosophy?*, 27
Derrida, Jacques, 13, 45–46, 55, 57, 142–43, 148, 155, 179, 204, 247n7; and architecture, 172, 174, 249n39; and the frame, 163–65; *Glas*, 46; *La verité en peinture* (The Truth in Painting), 45, 55, 164; and writing, 166–68
Descartes, René, 47, 50–52, 148. *See also* Cartesian
difference, 4, 5, 14, 37, 38, 42, 74, 87, 110, 143–44, 173, 178, 199; constitutive, 18–22; cultural, 115, 120; psychoanalytic effect of, 112–15, 117–20; sexual, 11–12, 144–157, 245n12; textual, 173–74, 178, 207, 244n10. *See also* heterology; heteronomy; the Other; otherness
digitality, 13, 180–81, 190, 197, 205, 209; digital environments, 181–186, 203; digital literature, 6, 180–91, 193–209, 254n5; digital technologies, 3, 4, 6, 189–209, 257n50. *See also* digital technologies; media: new; media: electronic
digital technologies, 3, 6, 12. *See also* digitality; media: new; media: electronic
Donne, John, 168
drive, the, 11, 114, 123, 129–34, 136, 139, 242n43, 243n53; death drive, 2–4, 6, 10–12, 123–131, 134–39, 241n27, 242n43; vs. instinct, 114–15, 129–34, 152, 157. *See also* Freud, Sigmund; Lacan, Jacques
Drucker, Joanna, 193

Duncan, Robert, 165
Dürer, Albrecht, 35–36, 231n11

ébranlement. See shattering
Edelman, Lee, 3, 11, 122–38, 240n11, 240n16, 243n47; *No Future*, 3, 11, 123
education, 2, 102–5, 189, 211–12, 222–25, 236n14, 237n21, 263n43
Eisenman, Peter, 171–74, 249n39, 251n44
Eisenstein, Sergei, 23–25, 77
emancipatory politics, 6, 8, 10, 14, 22. *See also* Deleuze, Gilles
Enlightenment, 4, 20, 260n10
Eribon, Didier, 51
experimentation, interdisciplinary, 12

Federman, Raymond, 193
Felman, Shoshana, 157–58
fiction, contemporary, 180–209
Fink, Bruce, 147, 151
Fitzpatrick, Kathleen, 190
Flaubert, Gustave, 31–32, 34, 62
Flynn, Thomas, 47
Foer, Jonathan Safran, 197–200
foreign, the, 10–11, 119–21
Foucault, Michel, 8, 46–57, 110, 136–39, 142, 161–63, 243n45, 243n49, n53; *The Birth of the Clinic*, 51; *The Care of the Self*, 51; *Discipline and Punish*, 54–55; *Fearless Speech*, 50–51; and Freud, 139, 243; *The History of Sexuality*, 51; *The Order of Things*, 57, 110; *The Use of Pleasure*, 51. *See also parrhesia*; scopic regimes
Freud, Sigmund, 2, 65, 68, 128, 242n33, 262n31; and anti-cosmopolitanism, 113–16, 238n23; *Beyond the Pleasure Principle*, 129; *Civilization and Its Discontents*, 113; and ego, 111, 114, 116, 124, 132, 134; and Foucault 139, 243; *Group Psychology and the Analysis of the Ego*, 118; "Instincts and Their Vicissitudes," 114, 129, 132, 133, 134; and Irigaray, 155–58, 245n14; and Kristeva, 112–17; and Lacan, 4, 11, 117, 129–34, 145–48, 155–58, 245n12; *Moses and Monotheism*, 119; "The Taboo of Virginity," 119; and uncanny, 112–14, 119–20. *See also* drive, the; narcissism; Oedipus complex; pleasure principle; polymorphous perversion; sexuality; sublimation; unconscious

Fromanger, Gerard, 47, 56
Fukuyama, Francis, 2
futurity, 12–14, 20–27, 29–30, 35–36, 102–4, 141; and crisis, 210–11; and critique, 141; and literature, 180–209; and queerness, 122–40. *See also* reproductive futurism
Fynsk, Christopher, 4

Gasché, Rodolphe, 174
Genette, Gérard, 9, 61–65, 67, 69, 79, 83
globalization, 1, 6, 7, 98–99, 104, 176–77, 253*n*74
Gramsci, Antonio, 75, 82, 210–11, 258*n*3
Griffith, D. W., 23–25, 67
Guattari, Félix. *See* Deleuze, Gilles

Hansen, Mark, 183, 204–8, 257*n*50
Hayles, N. Katherine, 3, 12, 13
Hegel, Georg Wilhelm Friedrich, 2, 33, 87, 148, 162, 263
Hegelianism, 20, 32, 33, 75, 95
hegemony, 1, 9, 69, 74, 80, 82; of the eye, 46, 47, 53
Heidegger, Martin, 45–46, 94–96, 100, 104–5, 120, 144, 148, 167
Heideggerianism, 10, 26
Heine, Heinrich, 113–14
Herbert, George, 168, 191
hermeneutical, 13
heterology, 40–43, 167. *See also* agency; autonomy; difference; heteronomy; the Other; otherness
heteronomy, of art, 6, 9–10, 12–13; of the future, 6–8, 13–14; of the human, 9–10; of politics, 5–6, 8–9, 10–11, 73, 82; of the subject, 1, 4, 6, 10–11. *See also* agency; autonomy; difference; heterology; the Other; otherness
heteronormativity, 11, 122–23, 137–38, 135–37, 245*n*11. *See also* reproductive futurism; sexuality
Hobbes, Thomas, 113
Hoffman, E. T. A., 120
Homer, 84, 87, 88, 90, 264*n*50
humanism, 94–99, 99, 225, 247*n*7
humanities, 110; crisis in, 1–6, 189–190, 210–25; future of, 5, 12–14, 214–225
Husserl, Edmund, 20
hyperattention, 12, 13, 188–89, 203, 208

imaginary, the. *See* Freud, Sigmund; Lacan, Jacques
invention, 5, 8, 10–11, 18–19, 28–29, 134–35, 140
Irigaray, Luce, 11–12, 142–58; and Lacan, 142–56, 244*n*8, 245*n*11, 245*n*13, 245*n*14; *Marine Lover*, 150

Jakobson, Roman, 9, 64–67
Jameson, Fredric, 3, 6
Jay, Martin, 6, 8
Jodorowsky, Alejandro, 217
Johnson, Ronald, 168, 173
Johnson, Samuel, 162
jouissance, 6, 11, 135, 138, 151, 156; and the text, 146–51
Joyce, James, 32, 90

Kant, Immanuel, 19, 45, 87, 163, 211–13, 263*n*43, 263*n*48; *Critique of Practical Reason*, 5
Kantianism, 47, 54, 163, 178
kinship, 3, 4, 6, 8, 10, 11, 101–5
Kittler, Friedrich, 189
Kojève, Alexandre, 33, 230*n*7
Krell, David Farrell, 96
Kristeva, Julia, 109–14, 117, 120, 238*n*23; and Freud, 112–17; *Strangers to Ourselves*, 110

Lacan, Jacques, 48, 72, 119, 126, 129–30, 133, 143, 170, 238*n*23, 241*n*31, 245*n*12; and ego, 115, 116, 117; and Freud, 4, 11, 117, 129–34, 145–48, 155–58, 245*n*12; and imaginary, symbolic, and real registers, 4, 127, 142, 144, 148; and Irigaray, 142–56; *The Mirror Stage*, 11; *Seminar II*, 145; *Seminar VII*, 130; *Seminar XI*, 151, 152; *Seminar XVII*, 130; *Seminar XX* (*Encore*), 145, 147, 148, 151–55. *See also* drive, the; narcissism; Oedipus complex; pleasure principle; polymorphous perversion; sexuality; sublimation; unconscious
Laclau, Ernesto, 9
Lammerman, Dmitri, 184
Leibniz, Gottfried, 19
Lenin, 9, 81–82
Leninism, 73, 80–82
Levin, David Michael, 47
Levinas, Emmanuel, 113, 120, 237*n*13

Li Yang, 10, 95–106, 235n9, 236n11, 236n16, 237n21
Lyotard, Jean-François, 17–18, 48; *The Postmodern Condition*, 18

Magritte, René, 47, 55–56
Mallarmé, Stéphane, 33, 230n6
Manet, Edouard, 47, 55–57
Manovic, Lev, 195, 197, 256n34
Marrati, Paola, 3–4, 6–8, 11, 135, 137
Marx, Karl, 22, 75, 77. *See also* Marxism
Marxism, 9, 20, 75–82, 95, 145, 162. *See also* Marx, Karl
masochism, 124–25, 242n43
McCaffery, Steve, 6, 12–13
McGann, Jerome, 193
media: electronic, 13; new, 2, 4, 6, 12–13, 181, 183, 190, 256n33, 256n34. *See also* digitality; digital technologies
Menchú, Rigoberta, 223–24
metaphor and metonymy, 9, 61–83
Michals, Duane, 47
migrant workers, 95–99
Mitchell, W. J. T., 191
Mockus, Antanas, 14, 210, 217–19, 223, 225
modernity, 7, 21–22, 26–28, 30–32, 167, 253n74

Nancy, Jean-Luc, 6, 9–10, 228n13, 230n1; *The Inoperative Community*, 9
narcissism, 4, 114–18, 248n23; of minor differences, 114–18, 119, 238n23. *See also* Freud, Sigmund; Lacan, Jacques
new, the, 4, 7–14, 140, 143; and Deleuze, 17–22, 28, 135–37; and novelty, 17–20, 29–30; and precursors, 29–44. *See also* novelty
Nietzsche, Friedrich, 21, 26, 47, 48, 111, 122, 135, 148, 150
Nietzschean, 26, 139
Novak, Marcos, 178
novelty, 5, 8, 17, 20, 29. *See also* new, the

Oedipus complex, 11, 114, 133–36, 144, 154. *See also* Deleuze, Gilles: *Anti-Oedipus*; Freud, Sigmund; Lacan, Jacques
Other, the, 7, 11, 19, 24, 34, 85–86, 88–93, 109–21, 144–45, 151, 152–58, 179, 230n8, 238n25. *See also* difference; heterology; heteronomy; otherness

otherness, 4, 173; of self, 10, 112–13, 115–16, 119. *See also* difference; heterology; heteronomy; the Other

Panopticon, 8, 47, 55
parapoetics, 12–13, 161–79
parrhesia, 8, 50–57
particularity, 7–8, 36–44, 71, 72, 73, 231n14
Pascal, Blaise, 27
Paulson, William, 2
Persephone, 156–58
Plascencia, Salvador, 197, 200–202
Plato, 35–36, 73, 86, 90, 230n10, 231n13, 249n39; *Symposium*, 35, 230–231
Plautus, 113
pleasure principle, 124, 130. *See also* Freud, Sigmund; Lacan, Jacques
poetics, contemporary, 12–13, 161–79
poetry, 6, 30, 41–43, 66–67, 162–79, 91–93, 181, 215, 217, 252n49; and architecture, 6, 161–79. *See also* poetics, contemporary; *poiesis*
poiesis, 12–14, 96, 100, 104, 167, 170
polymorphous perversion, 128. *See also* Freud, Sigmund; Lacan, Jacques
praxis, 1, 3–4, 9, 13–14
precursor, 7, 29–44
printing: digital, 193–197, 200–207; predigital, 191–93
Proust, Marcel, 9, 61–65, 67–69, 74, 79, 83, 184
public sphere, 14

queer theory, 6, 11, 122–40, 240n11, 240n16, 243n47

Rajchman, John, 47–48
real, the. *See* Freud, Sigmund; Lacan, Jacques
repetition, 29–30, 32, 43–44, 79, 86, 131, 205, 230n1, 247n7
reproductive futurism, 124, 128, 133–39
Reyes, Pedro, 216–18
Ricardou, Jean, 62
Rimbaud, Arthur, 91
Rogers, Richard, 176
Rosenberg, Jim, 186
Rossi, Aldo, 175, 177
Rouch, Hélène, 155
Rousseau, Jean-Jacques, 22, 114

Sarraute, Nathalie, 30–37, 40, 230n8
Sartre, Jean-Paul, 95, 111
Saussure, Ferdinand de, 66, 68, 69, 71
Schapiro, Meyer, 45–46
Schelling, Friedrich, 112, 251n45
Schiller, Friedrich, 224, 273n43
Schlegel, Friedrich, 162
scopic regimes, 7, 8, 47–48, 55–56
sexual difference, 11–12
sexuality, 3–6, 124, 127, 242n43; heterosexuality, 122–24, 241n24; homosexuality, 123–27, 136, 138, 139, 249n6, 240n16; infantile, 128–29. *See also* Freud, Sigmund; heteronormativity; Lacan, Jacques
Shannon, Claude, 198–99, 207
Shapin, Steven, 52–53
Shapiro, Gary, 47–48, 54–57
shattering, 124, 126–28, 136–37
Shklovsky, Victor, 169, 212–13, 225
Situationist, 161, 176
Socrates, 145, 149
Solà-Morales, Ignasi de, 13, 171, 249–59
Sommer, Doris, 6, 12–13
Sorel, Georges, 9, 73, 77–79, 82; *Reflections on Violence*, 77
Spiller, Neil, 171, 252n44
Stein, Gertrude, 165, 175, 252n49
Sterling, Bruce, 190
sublimation, 130–31, 132, 137, 241. *See also* Freud, Sigmund; Lacan, Jacques

symbolic, the. *See* Freud, Sigmund; Lacan, Jacques

technē, 96, 100, 104
Thoreau, Henry David, 173, 186
Tschumi, Bernard, 170–71

Ullman, B. L., 248n25
Ullmann, Stephen, 61
unconscious, the, 3, 10, 48, 72, 110–14, 129–31, 133–34, 146–48, 153, 156. *See also* Freud, Sigmund; Lacan, Jacques

Van Gogh, Vincent, 45
Velazquez, Diego, 57
Vergote, A., 114
Virgil, 90
Visker, Rudi, 10–11
visuality, 46, 49, 50, 53, 54, 57

Wardrip-Fruin, Noah, 181–83
Warhol, Andy, 47, 56
Weed, Elizabeth, 11–12
Williams, Bernard, 118
Wittgenstein, Ludwig, 19, 71, 175
Woods, Lebbeus, 171, 176, 152n44
Wordsworth, William, 168
writing, 6, 9–10, 13, 30–31, 46, 62, 64, 71, 84–93, 147–48, 166–68, 172–73, 181, 240n16; committed, 9, 86

Žižek, Slavoj, 126, 151